Journal of the
Critical Ethnic Studies Association

VOLUME 2 · ISSUE 1
SPRING 2016

Coeditors' Introduction

The Educational Thing: Intellectual Labor
and the Stakes of Struggle

JOHN D. MÁRQUEZ AND JUNAID RANA

This introduction represents our final intervention as the founding co-editors of this journal, an intellectual project designed as a tool for the educational component of the Critical Ethnic Studies Association (CESA). As both of us were involved in establishing this organization through our participation in the initial CESA working group, our solidarity and friendship grew out of a persistence and consideration for the essential intellectual labor needed within CESA as a formal organization. Within the working group, it became immediately clear that collective members would have to constantly foster a generative and working relationship to both tackle the large number of emergent projects as well as function as an institution that would continue with relative ease as active members rotated off.

From the outset both of us were concerned that there was a presumed solidarity among those of us invited to help inaugurate the critical ethnic studies project and that the ties that bound us together might be weaker, or more artificial, than they were imagined to be. In sum, it seemed that our collective came together in an urgency to build an alternative to a historically colonial and imperial institution—namely, the university—and to the neoliberal conjuncture that the academic industrial complex was situated within. The imperative, it seemed, was to build an organization outside of the appropriating logics of neoliberal multiculturalism and the corresponding role that ethnic studies units in academic institutions often seem to play within this colonial project. The irony, of course, was that it was our positions within universities, as ethnic studies faculty members and as professional academics, that brought us together.

With this concern came the presumption that those of us who had committed ourselves to this institutional and organizational work were on the same page and that our politics and allegiances were proportionate to the task at hand. And like so many other endeavors of the academic or activist world, the visibility of work and labor were often obscured by an uneven distribution—not only as observable differences that typically emanate in terms of the gendered divisions of labor that we must always work against but through the perceptions and consciousness of work that goes unrecognized. Editorial work is a labor of intellectual guidance and mentorship, and for the most part it involves the unglamorous and time-consuming work of copyediting and drafting. Hidden within our work as coeditors is the outstanding, patient, and generous work of the managing editor, Kelly Chung, and the anonymous reviewers who aided in the task of making the scholarship of our authors stand out. Their time and vision has helped create an intellectual foundation for this emergent field of critique, analysis, and theory. For us, this is another aspect of collective work that we only imagine as expanding and intensifying in the process of finding new protocols and forms of expression from which this journal will continue to function.

Yet what we do and how we do it is often still obscured in the academy. CESA has often been regarded as a group of like-minded scholars and activists who are carving out a distinct niche within the crowded halls of academe. What's more is that we are creating this intellectual space alongside activist and social movement organizers with an explicit critique and theorization of the world we live in. As editors, we depend on the knowledge and vast experience of the networks of scholars who we turn to for their expertise in the areas and themes that help us move forward the essays from which this journal is based. Likewise, we hope to create a conversation that is not exclusively the terrain of academics but is involved in the work of documenting, historicizing, and theorizing activist work and social movements, the literal making of other worlds within often underresourced, criminalized, and violently imperiled spaces, some of which we call home, make our home, or think otherwise.

In our attempts to create otherwise, there remains much work to be done. This journal emerges out of the paradoxical space of education and the neoliberal/imperial university. As a known entity in the hierarchies of knowledge production, academic journals are housed in the digital realms of the university that control access to information through paywalls and specialized membership as students, staff, and faculty. This contradiction of the academic industrial complex is one that we seek to overturn, proliferating insurrectionary possibilities through what Fred Moten and Stefano Harney call study and organization,[1] albeit in the structured capacity of the academy. As such, these ideas percolated from the basement to the walls of the library, which serve a number of purposes that maintain and are constitutive of the logics of the academy, the state, and global capitalism, as Rod Ferguson reminds us.[2] Yet, in this space of contradictory alignments, critical intellectual work is also a preparation, a readying for things to come.

THE STAKES

In our introductory essay from the inaugural issue of the journal, we described the intellectual initiatives and organizing principles that led to the fruition of the journal and CESA. Here we wish to account for the lessons in what we see as the cost of intellectual labor and the stakes of struggle. As we launched this journal, two phenomena occurred nearly at the same time that framed the urgency of our thinking in the context of numerous other struggles. These two phenomena, moreover, have structured much of our thinking about the future and the limits of the critical ethnic studies project, as we transition out of it.

In early August 2014, Steven Salaita was unhired by the University of Illinois at Urbana-Champaign for criticizing the violence of Israeli settler colonialism.[3] A week later, the August 9 police killing of Mike Brown in Ferguson, Missouri, incited a new era of militant protest among black and other youth of color. That they also occurred relatively near to us and with personal consequences only heightened the attention to a conjunctural analysis. The Salaita case unraveled on a college campus and in relationship to the proliferation of academic organizing to the social movement of Boycott, Divestment, and Sanctions (BDS). The Brown case helped to create a new kind of organizing—largely outside of the academy—that draws on histories of black freedom and black liberation. In both examples, ethnic studies, as an academic field that offers an analytic and frames intervention, demonstrates itself not only as an interdisciplinary component of the status quo of the university but also as a site of challenge and innovation.

The Salaita scandal drew national attention to the reckless administration of university power, the debasement of widely assumed standards of academic freedom, and the general vulnerability of ethnic studies scholars who raise critical questions about liberal reform in ways that unsettle the truth-sanctioning protocols of traditional disciplines. At the heart of the Salaita case, however, was always the Palestinian exception in the U.S. public and the challenge the academic boycott to Israeli academic institutions has created as a point of debate in the U.S. public. We point out both Edward

Said's famous claim that Palestine is the last taboo in the United States[4] and the dramatic rise in the increasingly public exposure of Israeli settler colonialism and occupation of Palestine created through academic boycott. A number of academic associations, CESA included, have led the movement for solidarity with the call of Palestinian civil society and the BDS movement. The growing conversation of Palestinian liberation in the context of Israeli settler colonialism signals not only an important shift in the awareness of global politics but also the expansion of connections that reflect critiques of liberal modernity, settler colonialism, native dispossession, genocide, white supremacy, and global capitalism that are central to the critical ethnic studies project. And yet while the fear of speaking out against Israeli violations and atrocities against Palestinians and their lands has been lifted, there remains a long list of victims of the Zionist assertion of infallibility to which Steven Salaita must now be added. Even further, the example of Israeli settler colonialism speaks to the failure of the modernist project that has had widespread stakes and implications for indigenous peoples in a global sense. The framing of a critique of Israel requires a sobering account of the possibilities of a decolonial future.

The Black Lives Matter movement emerged in response to the heightened visibility of black expendability, antiblackness, and the rampant and often state-sanctioned destruction of black lives by police and/or vigilantes. The organizing model of Black Lives Matter was unique for its leaderless and antihierarchical approach mobilized by social media and digital technology,[5] an experiment and the culmination of a number of radical social critiques that, in large part, have a related source within critical ethnic studies[6] and the challenges that feminist, queer, and scholars of color have provided. As many have argued, this represents a shift in ideological goals, a strategy that is not strictly based in any one approach (such as a civil rights or invisibility-to-visibility frame), or for that matter, within the trajectories of revolutionary nationalism. Instead, Black Lives Matter is unique for how and what it facilitates, for how it imagines and organizes collectives in anticipation of a future justice in society. Much like our approach within CESA, the tools and means of our collective injustice can be refashioned in ways to create a possible justice: contingent, ephemeral, but nonetheless real and worth struggling for. The danger for Black Lives Matter and related movements, of course, is to fall into the liberal trap of recognition and rights without continuing to build a transformative challenge to white supremacy. The refashioning of social-movement approaches into people building for the digital age opens up a space for critical intellectual inquiry or exchange for us to consider the more recent interventions of political theorists like Joanne Barker, Glen Coulthard, Audra Simpson, Sylvia Wynter, and others, who have raised serious questions about political recognition within the confines and protocols of colonial/liberal governance and instead develop decolonial models that eschew liberalism.[7] These theorists challenge the liberal humanist frame of rights and recognition that would have justice imagined as a deferral of possibility and instead force us to think of our politics anew in the terms of tactics and strategies that intervene, disrupt, and destabilize, such that radical epistemological breaks become apparent and immanent.

These overlaps between strategies of resistance within the academy and those that transpire outside of it are not new. There is, to be sure, an extensive genealogy of ethnic studies that precedes the naming and forming of the field in the late twentieth century, as Aldon Morris has clarified in his recent study of the life and often-neglected work of W. E. B. Du Bois.[8] The scandal of the occupation of Palestine and the escalation in the visibility of black death provide examples that are unique for the stakes involved: the intimacy between our intellectual work as scholars and the devaluing of racialized lives that continues to transpire despite rhetorics of reform or reconciliation.

These examples also highlight what we perceive as sites of inquiry and analysis that deserve more attention within the critical ethnic studies movement. As this movement has opened up new sites and methods for theorizing rightlessness and expendability, the combined force of recent critical work by black studies scholars and the new surge in black youth protests, we believe, represents a challenge to the critical ethnic studies movement. It forces the movement to innovate in a more cautious fashion, to not gloss over the foundational nature of antiblack racism within its emphasis on including and linking together the epistemologies of multiple groups, and to include more black thinkers and organizers in its planning.

Bearing this in mind, we feel that critical ethnic studies could also be better linked to the U.S.–Mexico borderlands, the Caribbean, Mexico, and Latin America, as well as to the decolonial and intellectual imperatives of Latin@ studies and Chican@ studies. This seems especially true of Chican@ feminists, such as Gloria Anzaldúa, Emma Pérez, Cherríe Moraga, and Chela Sandoval, whose work has been central to debates regarding decolonization for decades. The historic and ongoing criminalization, scapegoating, targeted incarceration, and police killings of Latin@s enhances this priority as well as the need for us to organize against and theorize conditions, such as antiblackness and (as with the case of Palestine) settler colonialism, beyond the United States' geopolitical borders. And as critical ethnic studies as a field continues to globalize its object of analysis, the repercussions of the Global War on Terror and U.S. empire will continue to challenge scholars and activists alike to formulate research agendas, organize tactics and strategies, and confront the methodological challenges of scholarly inquiry that is actively discouraged and often penalized.[9] Despite the recent growth in the studies on Palestine, scholars often do so at risk to their careers and personal lives, as the Salaita case and so many others testify. With the rise in academic solidarity with Palestinian liberation, such blatant intimidation and curtailing of academic freedom have become even more transparent, as others begin to join in the struggle for the right to public dissent.

Beyond these examples of future research is the intellectual work that we can remark on as labor *and* solidarity. We do what we do not because of some immediate gain or monetary future but because this work has meaning toward a future that imagines life otherwise. These are high stakes that imagine a decolonized, anticapitalist, antiracist, nonhomophobic, nonsexist horizon of sociality while existing and partaking in the earthly possibilities of the present. This is a metaphysic of intellectual labor and political solidarity. Academic inquiry is inherently political. To align with social movements is not to the detriment of professional values but is instead a valuable ethical model and research methodology.[10] Increasingly, activist research as part of organized movements has become specialized labor with the adoption of social-movement work in a nonprofit framework and the reliance on empirical sociology and traditional archival research about the resilience of the oppressed and the richness of their culture rather than on critical theorizations of oppression and its pervasiveness. These remain vital connections for academic scholars to make with organized and activist spaces in developing mutual relationships that work against the interests of the neoliberal university in developing and practicing decolonizing methodologies.

THE CONJUNCTURAL MOMENT

In meditating over this current predicament that places us in the heart of a paradoxical relationship to intellectual work and commitments, we offer an example of critical thinking from the revolutionary intellectual and organizer Fred Hampton. As a practitioner of decolonial study and organizing, Hampton (whose work took place in Chicago, where our editorial work for this journal has transpired and where we each make a home) offers an instructive case. During a scene in the documentary film *The Murder of Fred Hampton*,[11] Hampton, the chairman of the Chicago chapter of the Black Panther Party, is approached by two activists about their plans to form independent black institutions in Chicago's South Side and West Side neighborhoods, a step beyond the Black Panther Party's free breakfasts and free health clinics. The group proposed, among other things, a "credit union," or what they described to Hampton as "a bank run by the people and for the people." Though sympathetic, Hampton responds with a concern regarding the proliferation of black institutions or programs. He explains, "The thing for me, you dig, is I need to know some more about, I wish you had some literature about the educational thing here. Because, as far as we're concerned, the way we look at the struggle, this all depends on the educational thing." He then chronicles the genealogy and pitfalls of anticolonial struggles across the African diaspora (in Haiti and Cuba) and Kenya to complicate a conventional wisdom regarding self-determination. In crafting his analysis in relationship to those sites, Hampton frames those examples to explain that despite the urgency or revolutionary spirit of the moment, rushing to construct separate institutions, alternatives to the colonial regime's infrastructure, carries the risk of repeating or reproducing colonial relations of power, albeit in a way that is disguised by revolutionary rhetoric.

Vibrant and difficult intellectual exchange, or what Hampton called the "educational thing," was at least as important as institution building not only within the cause of Black Power but also within his broader goal of unsettling racial capitalism. As Hampton explained to those Black Power activists, "Education is important to ensure that people are able to control themselves. With no education, people will take this local foundation and start stealing money because they won't be really educated as to why it's a people thing anyways. Without education, you can have neocolonialism instead of colonialism." He goes on to demonstrate how even the more critical expressions of resistance and self-determination are often at risk of being undermined by capitalist logics and/or imperatives. Solidarity, in Hampton's view, was thus not a finite goal but a practice, more verb than noun, an attribute established via what he dubbed "the educational thing."

This is not the 1960s, and we remain wary of the nostalgia of that era in addition to, as Erica Edwards has effectively demonstrated,[12] the discursively masculine and heteronormative traits of how revolutionary leaders have been glorified and martyred. As two cisgendered, heterosexual, brown men, we have also valued the ways that our own positions within this critical collective (CESA) have been scrutinized. And we would argue that as

part of our collective work, such self-scrutiny and vigilance is always necessary. Hampton, to be sure, was speaking within the particular conjuncture
of the Cold War; the racial power movements of the 1960s and 1970s; the
tense anticolonial struggles in Asia, Latin America, the Middle East, and
Africa; and the dramatic rise of the U.S. military hegemony across the globe.
The intellectual or educational work that Hampton prioritized was a task
that would occur in what Harney and Moten might describe as "the surround": the spaces outside of and against which modern and liberal institutions such as banks or universities are constructed. Hampton, like other
racial power leaders of his day, was thus interested in organizing outside of
the colonial system—in building within the surround, the domain of those
whom liberal modernity produced as savage, unincludable, and deemed
worthy of either quarantine or elimination.

Some things have changed. Today there exists a difference between how
Black Power is spoken of in the university and in black communities, where
it exists as a common sense practice of everyday approaches and positional-
ities. At the second major critical ethnic studies conference in Chicago, for
example, Beth Ritchie, during her plenary presentation on this tradition and
transition, explained that she first encountered and interacted with black
studies within circles of black women studying tactics for survival and liberation in salons, private homes, and other communal spaces.

The shift from this generally community-oriented approach to the creation of ethnic studies classrooms and professionals within the university
marks what Stuart Hall might describe as the kind of rupture that char-
acterizes the postcolonial condition or conundrum.[13] It is a conjunctural
shift that structures how the political economy functions but does not alter
its racial/colonial architecture and logic. As Moten and Harney, Ferguson,
Sara Ahmed,[14] and others have noted, the university, by its defining logics,
is a colonial institution, fundamental to settler colonial societies like the
United States—a correctional institution that accompanies the prison and
the mission as pillars of the "civil" sector of society and that is produced in
opposition to the surround. Our belated inclusion as indigenous or racially
subaltern subjects into the university has been enlivened by liberation struggles of the past, and yet we face unique challenges to how we can enliven or
further them in the present. The threat of appropriation looms large, especially for how ethnic studies can correspond with the imperatives of racial/
global capitalism and U.S. nation building. Granted, Hampton and other
leaders of his era were wary of appropriation. The educational thing that
Hampton prioritized, for example, conveyed an implicit decolonial ethic,

a commitment toward the fashioning of an alternative set of relations to self, land, and community outside of the framework or conventions of what generally constitutes an anticolonial struggle. He seemed to suggest that the creation of black capitalism, the belated inclusion of black peoples into the world of finance, might offer a temporary sense of refuge, and yet it would do little to unsettle the dispossessing and alienating logics of racial/colonial capitalism. This remains true. The schema and sites through which the struggle occurs are the difference in these strategies of transformation.

As the state criminalized and attempted to crush those liberation struggles, and as persons like Hampton were either assassinated or incarcerated due to their prophetic visions, their capacity at galvanizing solidarity, or their decolonial imagining, colonial authority mutated, marking the advent of this neoliberal conjuncture. Core colonial institutions deployed a strategy to absorb and manage dissent and to remix the meaning of "difference" as part of the remaking of, for example, the university's veneer and its symbolic transformation into a liberally reformed or presently race-conscious institution. Ethnic studies, as an academic field, developed as a component of this conjunctural shift, envisioned as an apparatus through which multiculturalism could be celebrated as part of the professionalization of a new class of consumers and management, persons who had mastered the art of lamenting the oppressed. CESA and other similar organizations have thus emerged as attempts to flee this appropriating logic.

THE UNDERCOMMONS AND THE GOOD COMRADE

While Hampton and others advocated for the importance of intellectual exchange prior to and concurrent with institution building in the surround, the current conjuncture requires much of our critical work to take place within what Moten and Harney describe as the undercommons, a space where we can be, think, and act in fugitive ways and yet also exist as a part of a colonial institution: the university. Hampton's hesitancy to sanction the building of new institutions because they are described via rhetorics of black power and self-determination and his insistence on difficult conversations and study about race, colonialism, and capitalism (and that there is an educational component to resistance) speaks to the work that we've envisioned for this journal. The conjuncture is different. The risks and tasks are similar.

As we mentioned in the inaugural introduction, this work has not been easy or without contention. To this end, our experience within CESA and as coordinators of its educational/intellectual component has reminded us that there are similar and distinct dynamics to each type of work. Organizing and intellectual work are always intimately connected, yet each also represents a distinct set of challenges and/or imperatives. Organizing requires a strong sense of, or an investment in, a culture of solidarity. Organizing resistance at the grassroots level brings distinct risks as indicated in the fate of those such as Hampton and so many other leaders. It was thus important to him and other visionaries to value being a good comrade. In other words, comradeship ensured that organizers were dedicated first and foremost to not only supporting one another when they faced pushback from colonial authorities but also dignifying and expressing gratitude toward each other's work as a method to sustain resistance and maintain the bonds of what constitutes a political collective. Whether in the community or in the university, this ethic of solidarity, this surrender of selfhood in prioritizing the collective, remains a priority. Waging resistance or building collectives among academics by using the spaces and resources afforded to us by academic institutions and the profession within which we are employed brings with it another set of challenges or protocols, ones that seem to strain our capacity to be good comrades. The primary danger is what Moten and Harney describe as the ethics of professionalization.

At the grassroots level, there are heightened risks of not being a good comrade; of not dignifying the work and sacrifices of struggle; of not being transparent; or of not communicating about procedure, about foundational work that has been done for the collective, and about the collective's future. The risks, generally speaking, are not the same in the academy or among professional intellectuals such as ourselves as they were for organizers like Hampton. Our lives, by contrast, are partially structured by a set of protocols that both breeds and depends on individualism and/or competition—a system of rewards, notoriety, and celebrity that reinforces colonial authority and its protocols of recognition even in moments when we are actively critiquing those same protocols. Professionalization thus presents a true challenge to practicing solidarity with one another. It strains our capacity to engage in decolonial imagining and organizing within the university's undercommons.

These represent important dynamics that, we believe, can often be ignored by ethnic studies scholars and even those who have distinguished themselves as members of critical collectives. Fugitive acts within the neoliberal university can be isolating, unnerving, and risky. Without good comrades to sustain us, to dignify and value our time and effort, and to support us when we've taken on personal risks on behalf of a collective, there remains less incentive to do this kind of work.

How then do we engage in the insurrectionary work of intellectuals and activists of not only critiquing the world but also participating in its re-making? This question, we believe, is at the heart of our labor, which pivots on the notion of being "critical." Critique is not just interpretation, it is a position from which to find oneself in the world. Indeed, as critical ethnic studies seeks to set itself apart, there are the first principles of how we resist the rationales and logics of corporate professionalization that dominate the academy. We nonetheless inhabit academic professionalization as we work within the structures of the university and outside of the academy in spaces of decolonial study and organizing. For us, in this individuating and individualizing space of the university and the academy, it is the collective and the idea of collaboration that has brought us together. The practice of nonhierarchy, consensus-building, and an anticapitalist politics informed the CESA approach. The success of this work, at once, depends on ideas of transparency and constant communication. The peril is that our politics, or more accurately our points of dissent, become a process of normalizing positions rather than growth, expansion, and the building of possible futures.

As coeditors of this journal, the two of us did not know one another when we joined the CESA working group, and we were still just getting to know one another when we agreed to take on the task of launching the journal and editing the first issues. We were comrades based solely on some similarities in our scholarship and teaching. We have, however, become good comrades as a result of doing this work together, by practicing solidarity, by working through an assortment of inherited obstacles and dilemmas to help secure a space for the "educational thing" within CESA's larger organizing imperatives by dignifying one another's time and sacrifices along the way, by challenging one another in generative ways, by caring for one another's families and other obligations, and by clarifying the essential work that remains possible within the university and its undercommons.

It was a leap that we gladly took despite not really knowing what we were getting into. No part of this process, often encumbered by the burdens of multiple projects and tasks and conversations we were not privy to, has been easy. We were constantly presented specific challenges along the way. But what we did learn, in addition to the importance of being a good comrade, is that as nascent as this project is, it is well on its way. The authors in this volume attest to this in the set of issues and approaches that they undertake as part of critical ethnic studies scholarship. As we shut down our shop and turn over our keys to the new coeditors, we do it with comradely appreciation for the task ahead and in solidarity. Toward our decolonial future . . .

JOHN D. MÁRQUEZ is assistant professor of African American studies and Latino/a studies at Northwestern University and the author of *Black-Brown Solidarity: Racial Politics in the New Gulf South* (2013).

JUNAID RANA is associate professor of Asian American studies at the University of Illinois at Urbana-Champaign, with appointments in the Department of Anthropology, the Center for South Asian and Middle Eastern Studies, and the Unit for Criticism and Interpretive Theory. He is the author of *Terrifying Muslims: Race and Labor in the South Asian Diaspora* (2011).

NOTES

1. Stefano Harney and Fred Moten, *The Undercommons: Fugitive Planning and Black Study* (New York: Minor Compositions, 2013).

2. Roderick A. Ferguson, *The Reorder of Things: The University and Its Pedagogies of Minority Difference* (Minneapolis: University of Minnesota Press, 2012).

3. For an elaboration, see Steven Salaita, *Uncivil Rites: Palestine and the Limits of Academic Freedom* (Chicago: Haymarket Books, 2015).

4. Edward Said, "America's Last Taboo," *New Left Review* 6 (November–December 2000).

5. Barbara Ransby, "Ella Taught Me: Shattering the Myth of the Leaderless Movement," *Colorlines,* June 12, 2015, http://www.colorlines.com/articles/ella-taught -me-shattering-myth-leaderless-movement.

6. For example, see Cathy Cohen, "Deviance as Resistance: A New Research Agenda for the Study of Black Politics," *Du Bois Review* 1, no. 1 (2004).

7. Joanne Barker, *Native Acts: Law, Recognition and Cultural Authenticity* (Durham: Duke University Press, 2011); Glen Coulthard, *Red Skin, White Masks: Rejecting the Colonial Politics of Recognition* (Minneapolis: University of Minnesota Press, 2014); Audra Simpson, *Mohawk Interruptus: Political Life across Borders of Settler States* (Durham: Duke University Press, 2014); Katherine McKittrick, ed., *Sylvia Wynter: On Being Human as Praxis* (Durham: Duke University Press, 2015.)

8. Aldon Morris, *The Scholar Denied: W. E. B. Du Bois and the Birth of Modern Sociology* (Berkeley: University of California Press, 2015).

9. Lara Deeb and Jessica Winegar, *Anthropology's Politics: Disciplining the Middle East* (Stanford: Stanford University Press, 2016).

10. For example, see Ruth Wilson Gilmore, *Golden Gulag: Prisons, Surplus, Crisis, and Opposition in Globalizing California* (Berkeley: University of California Press, 2007). In the discipline of anthropology, activist approaches have received considerable methodological attention. See, for example, Charles R. Hale, ed., *Engaging*

Contradictions: Theory, Politics, and Methods of Activist Scholarship (Berkeley: University of California Press, 2008); Faye V. Harrison, *Outsider Within: Reworking Anthropology in the Global Age* (Urbana: University of Illinois Press, 2008); Victoria Sanford and Asale Angel-Ajani, eds., *Engaged Observer: Anthropology, Advocacy, and Activism* (New Brunswick: Rutgers University Press, 2006).

11. Howard Alk, dir., *The Murder of Fred Hampton,* Chicago Film Group, MGA Inc., 1971.

12. Erica R. Edwards, *Charisma and the Fictions of Black Leadership* (Minneapolis: University of Minnesota Press, 2012).

13. Stuart Hall and Doreen Massey, "Interpreting the Crisis," *Soundings* 44 (Spring 2010): 57–71, 15.

14. Sara Ahmed, *On Being Included: Racism and Diversity in Institutional Life* (Durham: Duke University Press, 2012).

ESSAYS

Vanishing Palestine

LILA SHARIF

On March 20, 2013, U.S. president Barack Obama boarded Air Force One with a magnolia sapling by his side. He and his maximum-security unit were bound for Shimon Peres's presidential quarters in the Israeli state's segregated capital. The magnolia, reportedly a "direct descendant" of an original magnolia tree from the White House's very own grounds, was to symbolize the intimate relationship between the United States and the state of Israel: "It's an incredible honor to be able to offer this tree to this beautiful garden with so much history with somebody who is a champion on behalf of the Israeli people and a champion on behalf of peace. And we're very good gardeners. I'm sure this tree is going to do great," Obama announced during the tree-planting ceremony.[1]

A photo from the ceremony features the Israeli president watching with pleasure as Obama plants the sapling in his perfectly tailored suit. Encircled by yellow, purple, and white pansies, Obama is jovial, slightly bent with his hands gripping a shovel, a show of determination and focus. As he tends to the magnolia tree that will now be part of the Israeli state's landscape, Peres watches a short distance away, bowing his face slightly at Obama, his veiny hands clasped by his sides. The sun illuminates Obama's cheerful face and the luscious green that surrounds him. The symbolic and material transfer of the sapling literally connects the U.S. soil to Israel. That Obama is "honored" to plant in Peres's "beautiful garden" indicates that the tree is a site of joy, honor, and friendship. (Ironically, shortly after Obama planted the tree, Israeli officials began digging it up reportedly to inspect and quarantine it for security reasons.)

The statements that both Obama and Peres are "very good gardeners" are haunting. They reveal the ongoing transformation of indigenous landscapes due to the persistent structures of settler colonialism in the United States and Israel. In both the United States and Israel, the Europeanization of the landscape continues to be an intrinsic part of ongoing settler-colonialism;

since the colonial encounter, Zionist and European colonizers interpreted the indigenous landscapes as physical manifestations of the abject native that had to be vanished and replaced. In *Ecological Imperialism*,[2] Alfred Crosby argues that North America was transformed into a physical landscape of remarkable similarity to Europe through the introduction of European crops, weeds, livestock, commensal species, and diseases into the New World. Similarly, in his article "Social and Physical Landscapes of Contact," Stephen W. Silliman argues that Indian country experienced material transformation ranging from "the expansion of European plants and animals into North American habitats to European over-harvesting of indigenous species, and from the deadly spread of pathogens and epidemics to the substantial impacts of colonialism on the health and diet of the indigenous population, issues involving the physical and biological landscape."[3]

In Palestine, "good gardening" practices by Israeli and Zionist organizations have contributed to a process I call "eco-occupation"—through the planting of nonnative trees to resemble European landscapes and the appropriation of the natural habitat to expand colonial settlement, Israeli settler colonialism is produced through an intricate, systematic process of environmental transformation, replacement, and disappearance. Here, "eco" refers to the social, political, ideological, and material landscapes that fix Palestinian life to land; "occupation" refers to the militarized, settler-colonial presence of Israel in the occupied Palestinian territory of the West Bank as well as the mundane and seemingly benign practices of settler colonialism, including "good gardening" practices that promise to make a feminized wilderness more aptly penetrable for colonial development and expansion.

Indeed, the image of Obama and Peres as "good gardeners" invokes the origin story of a barren landscape that was made fertile by the productive external forces of European Zionists. In effect, this narrative epistemologically disappears native peoples from the land. There is no mention that, for example, the very site of the presidential complex where Obama planted his friendship seed once housed a thriving Christian Palestinian community where Palestinian postcolonial theorist Edward Said—among others—once called home.

These omissions point to the various cultural, epistemological, and material forms of disappearing native peoples. Indigenous bodies, memories, and lands are but a blip in a colonial history imagined as complete, coherent, and natural. In my work, I introduce "vanishment" as a poetic and epistemological concept that is broadly situated within postcolonial feminist theory. Vanishment refers to the processes of erasure that rely on the appropriation of the earth's elements, the removal and replacement of native landscapes, and the erasure of indigenous culture through a system of conditional inclusion. Palestinian lands, particularly the olive tree, figure into the process of eliminating what was deemed to be a characteristically Palestinian landscape—that is, a racially abject and soiled environment in need of colonial modernity's raking and raping. In this paper, I link vanishment to what Gary Fields has defined as *landscape*—a social product that represents the outcome of power relations that mediate human interaction with material sites: "Both product and process, landscapes are representations of the societies anchored to them and the relations of power that govern them."[4] Taking my cue from Fields, I examine the Israeli settler-colonial replacement of Palestine, particularly as it relates to the transformation of and vanishing of Palestine's landscape. Rather than reproducing the narrative of vanishment or romanticizing an authentic, premodern past, I look to Palestinian literature to formulate more complex narratives for environmental justice practice and theory. I argue that in the context of settler colonialism, new sites of knowledge necessarily emerge from the realm of the imagination where disappearances haunt through the most seemingly benign sites. I draw from the autoethnographic novel *Palestinian Walks: Forays into a Vanishing Landscape,* by Palestinian writer Raja Shehadeh, in order to contribute to environmental justice studies. My purpose is twofold: (1) to center native writing as an alternative epistemological practice that allows us to contend with the violence of eco-occupation, and (2) to bring Palestine into critical ethnic studies and cultural studies to offer up new trajectories in native environmental justice.

"MAKING THE DESERT BLOOM": GREEN-WASHING, TREES, AND ECOLOGICAL DISAPPEARANCES

Many studies in environmental injustice in Palestine are framed as a combination of infrastructural failures and corruption within Palestinian political factionalism. Kimberley Kelly and Thomas Homer-Dixon explain the environmental degradation in the Gaza Strip as follows:

> The interaction between severe supply, demand, and structural scarcities has constrained development and has contributed to the impoverishment of Gaza's population. Deteriorating economic and social conditions have produced collective grievance and violence against Israel. . . . Solutions to water crises in Gaza will not in themselves resolve conflict. Nonetheless,

steps toward conservation and rehabilitation of the aquifer and the more equitable apportionment of the water that is available will be essential elements to a stable peace.[5]

In this passage, the authors emphasize Gaza's inability to cope with the severe supply and demand, coupled with its violence against Israel and unequally distributed potable water sources. These and other factors, the authors suggest, are the reason for Palestinians' inability to develop. In this way, Kelly and Homer-Dixon bolster the rhetoric of subaltern failures; instead, ecological ruin is represented as a result of "population growth, an agriculturally intensive economy, a fragile water ecosystem, and a highly inequitable distribution of resources."[6] Through an elaborate catalog of figures and charts, Kelly and Homer-Dixon imply that Palestine is committing ecological suicide—even quoting a Palestinian making such claims—through their poorly managed reproduction practices, destructive lifestyles, and uncivilized practices.

Indeed, because of the rapid decline in both the quantity and quality of its water supply, Gaza has been the poster child for ecological crises: regular outbreaks of diseases resulting from contaminated water, increased alkalinity and salinity in the soil, and the absence of proper sewage facilities have led Gaza to its slow death. However, while the case studies featured in the book (Gaza, Chiapas, South Africa, Pakistan, and Rwanda) are subsumed within the title "eco-violence," here "violence" is reduced to a list of explanatory variables, rather than the structures of elimination that inform them. Discriminatory acts committed by Israel are equated with those perpetrated by Palestinian authoritarian regimes, suggesting that Israel and Palestine are equal players in the ecological devastation of Gaza. What is missing, then, is a serious analysis of the context of an ongoing settler-colonial occupation in Palestine.

Popular media reinforce the notion that Palestine's ecological disasters are a result of its own failures to modernize; and, where critique of settler colonialism has been part of the dialogue, it has been limited to spectacular moments of violence rather than everyday acts of vanishment. In March 2007, when a river of raw sewage and debris overflowed in the Gazan village of Umm Naser from a collapsed earth embankment into a refugee camp, major U.S. media outlets including the *New York Times* and the *Washington Post* blamed Gaza's inability to provide adequately for its population. The *Daily Alert* (the organ of the Presidents of the Major American Jewish Organizations) blamed the Palestinians who they claimed were removing sand to sell to construction contractors, thus undermining the earth embankment.[7] Sociologist James Petras conversely argues that the "shoddy infrastructure" is, in actuality, a result of "Israel's massive sustained bombing attack on Gaza in the summer of 2006: demolished roads, bridges, sewage treatment facilities, water purification and electrical power plants".[8] His online publications reveal the cross-generational effects of Israel's mass killings on Palestinian bodies and land. While his reports counter the hegemonic representations of the self-destructive native, the culprit he names in this particular incident is Israel's assault on Gaza in the summer of 2006.[9] In this way, he privileges a spectacular moment of death and elides the violence of the mundane forms of settler-colonial violence.

Patrick Wolfe has argued that settler colonialism is premised on the "logic of elimination."[10] As Gary Fields and Rana Sharif have documented, these structures can manifest in the most unspectacular forms—extending from racist legal measures to lack of access to health care concealed as mere features of Israeli bureaucratic processes. Analyzing the deliberate placement of Israeli settlements in ways that contribute to Palestinian "enclosure," Fields states:

> Embedded in the seemingly ubiquitous buildings with red roofs is a process of land confiscation in which Palestinian land is transferred into a new status as Israeli land. At the same time the settlement, as a gated community, functions as impassible space, off limits to its former owners. In a similar vein, the wall, and its accompanying element, the guard tower, embodies land taken from Palestinian owners, but its primary function is to establish and reinforce a system of impassible partitions on the landscape.[11]

In this way, Palestine's landscape becomes the exclusive property of Israeli state bureaucracy and Jewish settlement. Through legal measures, genocide is embedded in the very architecture of Israeli settler-colonial occupation in ways that make impossible Palestinian claims to land. The "off limits" status of Palestinian lands also manifests within architectures of surveillance and confinement, as biopolitical forms of genocide. Reflecting on the works of Achille Mbembe, transnational feminist scholar Rana Sharif describes the ways in which Israel also regulates immaterial capital, such as time, space, and health care access, through the imposition of racist permit regimes:

> The difficulty of accessing care for sick bodies in Palestine is exacerbated by the material consequences of occupation. As Member has suggested, the necropolitical state is invested in contouring not only the parameters of life

(biopower) but also, and perhaps more aptly for the actual life of Palestinians, of death. It is as though life is lived on threads. Buying time, navigating space, accessing units, filing forms, waiting in lines, waiting at checkpoints are all manifestations of the lived reality of Palestinian everyday life that are occluded when one considers only the "legal formalities" Israel has put in place, formalities which seem to allow for access to certain spaces for sick bodies, but in fact hinder or deny every attempt to do so.[12]

The eco-occupation of Palestine thus extends beyond spectacular massacres to mundane forms of genocide vis-à-vis the regulation and monitoring of Palestinian land and biopolitics. As a result of these measures, "life is lived on threads" in such a way that is obscured by the regimes of legality where the management of bodies masquerade as due processes that render Palestinian lifeways and landways "off limits."

These seemingly benign structures of elimination call for analyses of the eco-occupation of Palestine particularly as landscapes become a contested site of settler colonialism through the imposition of European-style landscapes. Irus Braverman has cogently argued that apparently innocuous acts such as planting, cultivating, and uprooting trees become "acts of war"[13] that bifurcate the natural landscapes of Israel–Palestine: the pine tree is associated with the Zionist project of afforesting the Promised Land into a Western European landscape aesthetic; the olive tree is the material and symbolic signification of the abject native that must be eliminated in both land and body. In addition to the racial abjection of the Palestinian body vis-à-vis the land, Braverman's work also illustrates Zionism's gendered logics of barrenness and fertility to promote settler-colonial projects disguised as progressive and developmental.

The clearest example of the colonial move to develop a barren swamp comes from the Jewish National Fund (JNF). Branded as an environmentally friendly charity, the JNF has been a central agent in the expulsion and replacement of Palestinian ecologies since its establishment in 1901. The organization's primary objective was to "purchase land for a Jewish State in Ottoman-controlled Palestine."[14] The creation of the State of Israel in 1948 meant the expulsion of two-thirds of the Palestinian population from historic Palestine. During that time, the new Israeli government "transferred" lands from 372 of the 522 depopulated Palestinian villages over to the JNF, achieving a Jewish majority in historic Palestine. However, the JNF's gardening practices in historic Palestine precede the 1948 establishment of the Jewish state on indigenous Palestinian lands. Since the early 1900s, trees were planted in Palestine and then in Israel to honor births of Jewish babies worldwide as part of bar and bat mitzvahs, and offered in place of party favors for Jewish marriages worldwide. The blue JNF collection boxes were distributed as early as 1904 and became one of the most familiar symbols of Zionism, "taken to be the symbol of world Jewry's support for Israel."[15]

These measures naturalize the Zionist colonization of Palestine by literally obscuring the evidence of previous Palestinian landscapes. Palestinian lands are at once the site of Palestinian death (extermination of Palestinian villages) and the aggressive penetration of Israeli life, bearing the Zionist-imposed pine sapling. In response to the JNF's ongoing campaign to make use of neglected "swamps," Sara Kershnar, Mich Levy, and Jesse Benjamin state: "Contrary to the deception propagated by the JNF, Israel and Zionist mythology, the trees are not planted in a barren desert empty of inhabitants that Jewish people have come to populate and make flourish. . . . As the Palestinian refusal to succumb to colonial rule and expulsion perseveres, decade after decade, intifada after intifada, it sheds unavoidable light on the dark underbelly of 'making a desert bloom' in a place that is fully inhabited."[16] The JNF projects were thus attempts to "greenwash" the ongoing history and legacies of colonial settlement in Palestine. According to Max Blumenthal:

> The pine trees themselves were instruments of concealment, strategically planted by the Jewish National Fund (JNF) on the sites of the hundreds of Palestinian villages the Zionist militias evacuated and destroyed in 1948. With forests sprouting up where towns once stood, those who had been expelled would have nothing to come back to. Meanwhile, to outsiders beholding the strangely Alpine landscape of northern Israel for the first time, it seemed as though the Palestinians had never existed. And that was exactly the impression the JNF intended to create. The practice that David Ben Gurion and other prominent Zionists referred to as "redeeming the land" was in fact the ultimate form of greenwashing.[17]

By burying Palestinian history within pine, the JNF managed to turn the tree—the universal symbol of virtue and abundance—into a weapon of vanishment. In addition to pine, the eucalyptus tree, which is found all over the state of Israel, became part of this eco-occupation scheme. According to "The Hebrew Podcasts," which offers descriptive information about Israeli topography: "The Eucalyptus is an Australian tree. It was brought to Israel at the end of the nineteenth century to dry the swamps because it grows so quickly."[18]

The image of an unloved, chaotic swamp that needs to be tempered and broken are colonial ideologies that reinforce a raced and gendered logic of elimination. Theodor Herzl, the celebrated founder of political Zionism, observed: "If I wish to substitute a new building for an old one, I must demolish before I construct."[19] In his memoirs, David Ben Gurion, the first Israeli prime minister, stated, "When I look out my window today and see a tree standing there, that tree gives me a greater sense of beauty and personal delight than all the vast forests I have seen in Switzerland or Scandinavia. Because every tree here was planted by us."[20] It is in these gendered and racial ways that eco-occupation emerges to provide a sense of naturalness to colonial penetration—what Lorenzo Vericini calls "the indigenisation of settlers,"[21] which he states "is driven by the crucial need to transform a historical tie ('we came here') into a natural one ('the land made us')."[22]

NATIVE STUDIES AND ENVIRONMENTAL JUSTICE

Recent works that link the structures of settler colonialism and environmental justice have offered generative analyses of the ways in which indigenous peoples' experience of environmental injustices links land vanishment with cultural survival. According to Winona La Duke, a leading Native American activist and writer, native scholars understand environmental justice through "a genocidal analysis rooted in the Native American cultural identification, the experience of colonialism, and the imminent endangerment of their culture."[23] Similarly Devon Peña argues that to "the extent that we construct our identities in place, whenever the biophysical conditions of a place are threatened, undermined, or radically transformed, we also see these changes as attacks on our identity and personal integrity."[24] As these authors suggest, land destruction and environmental degradation is part and parcel of settler colonialism. As Lance Hughes, director of Native Americans for a Clean Environment, asserts: "We are not an environmental organization, and this is not an environmental issue. This is about our survival."[25]

At the same time, the dominant discourse in the field of environmental justice tends to privilege a sociological analysis through its promulgation of statistical data, case studies, and empiricist methods of inquiry, thus obscuring other forms of knowledge, such as cultural and textual analyses, produced by subaltern peoples.[26] These methodological tools in sociological and community-based studies on environmental justice use demographic data and statistics "stemming from the movement's political need to quantify, measure, and prove that environmental racism exists by public policy standards."[27] Heeding Julie Sze's cue to move "from environmental justice literature to the literature of environmental justice,"[28] I highlight a moment of eco-occupation by centering native literature. I argue that native literature offers an "alternative strategy to analyzing the roots of environmental racism";[29] in particular, Palestinian literature offers a new way of conceiving environmental justice within the context of settler-colonial vanishment. As Sze suggests, this new way of looking references the "real" problems of communities struggling against environmental disappearance and is simultaneously liberated from providing a strictly documentary account of the contemporary world and the ways in which colonized peoples experience the world.

Indeed, the costs of the eco-occupation of Palestine cannot be encapsulated in numbers and figures; as described above, settler colonialism has been buried into the very landscape of Palestine in ways that cannot be observed, patterned, or policed, particularly as the "legal" language of the Israeli state has been a primary technology of Palestinian vanishment. Moreover, the notion that we need to quantify Palestinian settler-colonial environmental injustices suggests that public policy is the primary site for redeeming these injustices, and that settler-colonial violence can be rectified once the proper actors, agencies, politicians, or organizations are made aware of their impacts. The recurring fact here is that the very laws, architectures, and landscape have been central players in the process of Palestinian vanishment.

Using "haunting" as a productive tool to make visible that which has been slated for vanishment, I turn to the autobiographical novel *Palestinian Walks: Forays into a Vanishing Landscape,*[30] by Palestinian author and lawyer Raja Shehadeh. The stakes of such an analysis are to contend with the violence of eco-occupation in such a way that does not reduce Palestinian life to the empirical, legal, and positivist renderings of "facts"—particularly these lay buried between a "bloom" of pine and eucalyptus. However, I also want to center the role of Palestinian literature as a way to bring the daily experiences and impacts of Palestine into native studies, postcolonial theory, and critical ethnic studies. Following Gordon's critique of the sociological imagination, one where *ghostly matters* of settler colonialism are disappeared, I analyze Palestinian literature as a site that evidences the ongoingness of settler colonialism. Rather than reproducing the trends and patterns of disappeared Palestinian landscapes, which ontologically render Palestine as always already disappeared, an analysis of this novel suggests that Palestine has not ceded to the condition of disappearance but is submerged within an ongoing process of vanishment—at the interstices of being spoken for and speaking. I center native literature as an epistemologically generative tool for the field of environmental justice. As Avery Gordon eruditely asserts in *Ghostly Matters,*[31] literature offers the "evidence" of residual and ongoing systems of violence, particularly when they are said to be over or cannot be encapsulated in observable statistics. As such, I look to Palestinian literature as a way of return and pause—a moment to contend with and make rhetorically palpable the processes of vanishment.

PALESTINIAN WALKS, ECO-OCCUPATION, AND NARRATIVES OF VANISHMENT

Palestinian Walks is a first-person nonfictional novel written by Palestinian author and human rights lawyer Raja Shehadeh, residing in the city of Ramallah in the occupied Palestinian territories of the West Bank since his birth in 1951. The novel won Shehadeh the Orwell book prize—Britain's most prestigious award for political writing—in 2008. Shehadeh is considered one of the most prominent diarists of modern Palestinian life. As such, for Shehadeh, writing became a part of his own survival amid the process of Palestinian vanishment surrounding him, and though he knew that time and space were quickly disappearing, he desired to capture the fragments and faces he found in the surrounding hills.

> Ever since I learned of the plans to transform our hills being prepared by successive Israeli governments, which supported the policy of establishing settlements in the Occupied Territories [of the West Bank and Gaza Strip], I have felt like one who is told that he has contracted a terminal disease. Now when I walk in the hills I cannot but be conscious that the time when I will be able to do so is running out.

The notion that time is "running out" once again points to the notion that vanishment is always pending. For decades, Shehadeh sought comfort in walking through the shield of the olive groves, vineyards, stone buildings, rolling hills, wadis (valleys), and cliffs of Palestine. However, as his novel makes clear, the landscapes that once offered him comfort were quickly vanishing. The first words of the memoir encapsulate the daunting effect of pending Palestinian annihilation: "When I began hillwalking in Palestine a quarter of a century ago, I was not aware that I was traveling through a vanishing landscape." As such, while Shehadeh invites his reader to roll through the hills around Ramallah, ascend through the wilderness of the wadis in Jerusalem, and flirt with the gorgeous ravines by the Dead Sea, this is not a touristic novel. As we walk alongside with Shehadeh, the reader witnesses the mundane violence of everyday life under occupation, including harassment by Israeli soldiers and settlers as well as the bulldozers ripping up landscapes, and its psychological and emotional toll on his hopes for a better future for his Palestine. We hear his tone become increasingly more devastated and his footsteps heavier and more calculated. The novel is both beautiful and tragic, encapsulating the stakes of environmental disappearance and settler colonialism—in these ways, it is a tale of eco-occupation.

> As our Palestinian world shrinks, that of the Israelis expands, with more settlements being built, destroying forever the wadis and cliffs, flattening the hills, and transforming the precious land that many Palestinians will never know.

At the same time, Shehadeh's narrative unsettles the Zionist origin story of a barren landscape in need of a "good gardener"—one that claims intimate and exclusive knowledge of the landscape through a patrimonial lineage dating back three thousand years. "Palestinians built their villages to embrace the hills not to ride them. [This] gave them protection from strong winds." In this quote, the relationship between Palestinians and the land is evident in their respect for the surrounding landscape. Unlike Israeli structures that are modeled after suburban U.S. and European landscapes, Palestinian dwellings "embrace" the hills. Their intimate knowledge of the land has allowed them to build in such a way that protects their dwellings from the wind but without disrupting the coherence of the natural landscape. Israel, as I noted above, planted various nonnative trees brought from Australia and elsewhere to "break up" the landscape, fragmenting the natural ecologies in the name of modernity.

Moreover, *Palestinian Walks* can also be read as writing against a post-9/11 Orientalist current that depicts Palestine as unbeautiful, unloved, and wretched. His is an alternative account of Palestine, one that departs from the commonplace observations of nineteenth-century Western travelers in search of the biblical "Holy Land." He writes, "They came, saw and recorded their fantasy and their disappointment, and bound them together into a beautiful canon of half-truths and outright lies that first helped shape popular perception and finally were used to help justify the colonization of Palestine." Writing against this grain, Shehadeh repositions Palestinians as the original "gardeners" by detailing Palestinian attachment to the land: "In

Palestine, every wadi, spring, hillock, escarpment and cliff has a name." Moreover, Shehadeh's narration of Palestine is one centered on love and appreciation of land—which included making love in the open spaces by the hills, knowing the edible herbs from the wild, naming every natural formation, accidental or natural, and cultivating the land with hands for days on end. Unlike the accounts of Orientalist travelers, Shehadeh's hills are full of people, not only the ghosts of his ancestors but also the plaintiffs he represents in court who sought his help to protect their land from settler appropriation. His journeys through the hills highlight the love and pleasure in exploring the Palestinian landscape—a multisensory experience that sits awkwardly against the Orientalist depictions of a degenerate native. Shehadeh recalls William Thackeray's vivid depiction of Palestine as "parched mountains, with a grey bleak olive tree trembling here and there; savage ravines and valleys paved with tombstones—a landscape unspeakably ghastly and desolate" and Herman Melville's description of "whitish mildew pervading whole tracts of landscape—bleached-leprosy-encrustations of curses-old cheese-bones of rocks—crunched, gnawed, and mumbled—mere refuse and rubbish of creation . . . all Judea seems to have been accumulations of this rubbish." Writing against this current, Shehadeh states: "The accounts I have read do not describe a land familiar to me but rather a land of these travelers' imaginations. Palestine has been constantly reinvented, with devastating consequences to its original inhabitants."

Because feminist literary criticism cannot be isolated from the structure of settler-colonialism, *Palestinian Walks* is a form of narrating the processes of vanishment. The "evidence" lays in the hills and valleys, which offer up memories of Shehadeh's great-uncle and great-aunt, whom he finds amid the silhouette of the hills, whispering an irrecoverable past of a simpler life of cultivating and tilling the land. *Palestinian Walks* shows how Shehadeh's life and the fate of the disappearing landscape of Palestine are utterly intertwined. While he finds solace in the majestic hills that sit like a tiered cake in the West Bank, each tier its own color and texture, his narration laments the irreversible losses caused by the encroachment of Israeli settlements and the erection of the apartheid wall, the irrecoverable hills and pathways of his grandfather's time, and the vanishing landscapes that impede the ancient Palestinian tradition of the *sarha*:

> To go on a *sarha* was to roam freely—at will—without restraint. . . . A man
> going on a *sarha* wanders aimlessly, not restricted by time and place, going
> where his spirit takes him to nourish his soul and rejuvenate himself. But

not any excursion would qualify as a *sarha*. Going on a *sarha* implies letting go. It is a drug-free high, Palestinian-style.

Shehadeh describes the curtains formed of vineyards, the nurturing branches of olive groves and the succulent sustenance provided by fruit trees; he encounters gazelles, goats, cattle, mules, and birds that inhabit the ecological terrain of Palestine along with the layered rock formations amid the hills that used to shield his ancestors from rain and jackals. And he narrates the continuous evanescence and ghostly traces—the vanishment and the irrecoverable loss brought by Israeli settler-colonial occupation. As one West Bank hilltop after another is claimed by Israeli settlers, all that remains is the Palestinian contours of the hills, causing his *sarha* journeys to become increasingly suffocating. He walks and his tone becomes more desperate, attempting to relocate what has been vanished. By his sixth walk, Shehadah is no longer sulking in the mystery of the material landscapes around him but is forlornly witnessing what has faded away—not only a testimony of Palestine's disintegration but also his own feelings of failure in not being able to stall time, freeze Palestinian annihilation, or protect himself from the bleak embitterment that consumes him. "The biography of these hills is in many ways my own, the victories and failures of the struggle to save this land also mine." Through his first-person autoethnographic account of six meditative walks—or *sarhat* (singular: *sarha*)—across different regions of Palestine over the span of twenty-six years, beginning in 1978 and ending in 2006, Shehadeh produces a poetics of vanishment that underscores the relationship between environmental injustice and eco-occupation in Palestine. His descriptions of these increasingly vanishing pathways offer an alternative historiography of the settler-colonial occupation of Palestine.

Shehadeh's novel opens with him walking to the hilly countryside of the surrounding mountains of Ramallah attempting to locate the *qasr*—a stone structure that had once sheltered his great-uncle Abu Ameen. The scenery in the surrounding hills is wild and freeing as though a cool zephyr is breathed into each reflective line:

Before visiting the *qasr*, I took a moment to look around. It was as though the earth was exploding with beauty and color and had thrown from its bosom wonderful gifts without any human intervention. I wanted to cry out in celebration of its splendor. As I shouted "S-A-R-H-A!" I felt I was breaking the silence of the past, a silence that had enveloped this place for a long time. My cry of greeting echoed against one hill then another and another, returning to me fainter and fainter until I felt I had touched the entire landscape.

On his first *sarha* in 1978, Shehadeh finds his great-uncle Abu Ameen's abandoned stone *qasr*: "It was as though in this *qasr* time was petrified into an eternal present, making it possible for me to reconnect with my dead ancestor through this architectural wonder." Abu Ameen rejected the family's city-dwelling life and worked amid the stones as a builder. This memory plugs in the internal tensions that consumed Palestinian social relations as the Israeli occupation produced new notions of productivity that meant finding resources elsewhere through Western models of progress, modernity, and city life.

> My family was judgmental, arrogant, and proud of their education and status. They looked down on Abu Ameen and his family. "What has he made of himself?" they would ask accusingly. "Nothing, nothing at all. He was but a stonemason who sat under a rough canopy day in and day out, pecking at stone."

And yet, Shehadeh is deeply nostalgic about the man who was "but a stonemason," constantly seeing his image caked in the landscape as he conducts his first walk—"the pale god of the mountains." Shehadeh recounts a story of Abu Ameen who on his honeymoon builds a *qasr*—a fortified sanctuary—with his new bride Zariefeh. The beautiful story of Abu Ameen and his wife Zariefeh building shelter amid the mountains is one of love, labor, and land. Abu Ameen, whose first name is Ayoub, was Shehadeh's maternal great-uncle. As a child, Ayoub and his cousin Saleem attended Christian schools run by English missionaries. Unlike Saleem, who was the perfect student who even challenged their teachers, Ayoub saw school as a prison and waited for any opportunity to work with his hands in the land. Ayoub found his cousin Saleem annoying, unable to understand why Saleem took his education so seriously. Neither men owned any land, and Ayoub's goal was to acquire a plot to build on. After leaving school, Ayoub found satisfaction and endless work as a stonemason. He worked long days and saved his money. Saleem was disturbed by what he saw as his cousin's lack of ambition: "A stonemason? Is that all you aspire to make of yourself?" Saleem found his way to the United States where he studied law; later, he returned to Jaffa to work as a judge in the British courts (at the time, Palestine was a

British mandate). In 1948, when the air strikes rained over Palestine, Saleem escaped to Ramallah but found the conditions unbearable. He sought refuge in Beirut by the sea, a scene that replicates Jaffa, and died alone.

Ayoub, on the other hand, stayed in Ramallah. In between the First World War, the end of Ottoman rule, and the British takeover, he succeeded in buying land, though it was far from the city and covered in stones. But Abu Ameen knew how to clear the stones and cultivate the land. He soon married. Originally he had wanted to make a *qasr* on the land before he was married. Instead, he brought his new bride to the rough plot that would one day be their shelter and together they cleared the land and built a shelter from the earth. Shehadeh recounts the narrative about Abu Ameen's honeymoon that had impressed him each time he heard it:

> On the first day they thought they would return to Ramallah at dusk but they lost themselves in work and when they stopped the sun had already gone down. If they started back now they would have to walk in the dark and this was not safe because of the possibility of being attacked by jackals. So they decided to stay on their land and sleep overnight. Ayoub went and fetched water from the spring. In her *zewadeh* Zariefeh had brought bread, white goat cheese, onions, dried figs, and raisins. . . . They worked like this for six consecutive days. It was only because Zariefeh knew what was edible in the wild that they were able to survive in the hills on the provisions they had brought with them. . . . They rationed the bread and found wild asparagus, watercress, and thyme. In the evenings she prepared chamomile tea from the fresh herbs she found growing in the side of the hill. They ate and drank what they could collect and managed to keep hunger away, working continuously, stopping to rest only for brief intervals. He was too shy at first to touch her in the open, it felt so exposed. But on the third day his desire was so strong it could not be contained.

The story of Abu Ameen and Zariefeh offers a beautiful narrative of Palestinian attachment to land. In this scene, Palestine becomes a site of love, food, and lovemaking embedded in the very landscape. Abu Ameen shields his wife from jackals by building a fire by where she slept. Though they were far from home, Zariefeh portioned the herbs, bread, and dried fruit to sustain them and used her earthly knowledge to brew teas of herbs and water Abu Ameen fetched from a nearby spring. In this tale, Abu Ameen is a humble, hardworking, and determined man who finds paradise in the hills of Palestine with his love, Zariefeh. Zariefeh is described as a pretty woman who always wore a turban decorated with coins. On the sixth day, the young couple celebrates the completion of their new home. Zariefeh "removed her turban, pulled up her *thob* (traditional Palestinian embroidered dress), took her husband's hand, and together they danced around their new home until they fell to the ground with exhaustion." Through the story of Zariefeh and Abu Ameen, Palestine is momentarily suspended from tragic disappearance and is redeemed through Shehadeh's memory. The image of the young couple eating and drinking from the earth and making love beneath the sky by Palestine's hills is a counternarrative of Palestine that is imagined to be a loveless place.

However, as Shehadeh returns to the present of groaning bulldozers, pouring concrete, and infested hilltops, his tone is once again tragic and fragile. Reflecting on the slow erosion of these lands under settlement construction, Shehadeh wonders how his great-uncle Abu Ameen would react to the ruins of his *qasr*: "Would his spirit be brimming with anger at all of us for allowing it to be destroyed and usurped, or would he just be enjoying one extended *sarha* as his spirit roamed freely over the land, without borders as it had once been?"

The subsequent *sarhat* occur as two decades go by. During this time, Shehadeh witnesses the hills transform into a swarm of racially exclusive settlements with accompanying roads that are dangerous and illegal for Palestinians to traverse. In one scene, he and a colleague encounter two Palestinian youths along a path adjacent to a newly developed Jewish-only road that leads into the settlement of Talmon:

We soon realized that we had walked into the open sewers of the Jewish settlement of Talmon to the north. This settlement might have had a rubbish collection system but it did not have one for treating sewage, which was just disposed of down the valley into land owned by Palestinian farmers. We tried to step lightly so as not to drown our shoes in the settlers' shit. As we trudged through the soggy ground we met two boys who showed us the way out of the bog. We noticed they were taking us away from the paved road and told them that was where we were headed.

"It's too dangerous," they said.

We asked them why.

"The settlers," they said. "If you're walking and they drive by they swerve and hit you. They ran over Mazen. And if an army jeep comes they shoot. No one uses the road."

This scene conjures the environmental justice issue of dumping material waste on Palestinian lands. However, taking this a step further, the scene also captures the mundane violences of everyday life that are central components of Israeli settler colonialism—the image of two Palestinian men avoiding a sewer reflects the devaluation of native life in which Palestinian farmlands are equated with sites where human waste can be dumped without legal recourse. That Shehadeh "trudged through the soggy ground" is as symbolic as it is literal: Palestine life has become equated with the swamp that the Zionist origin story is based on. This "trudging" also symbolizes the ways in which native bodies are not only made to disappear through corporeal death but to some extent are already equated to human waste, suggesting that they have disappeared through their devaluation. Furthermore, the children's insistence that violence is imminent through the almost passing statement that "they ran over Mazen" reinforces the precarious condition of Palestinian life—particularly through the notion that the settlers (bolstered by "the tanks"—the Israeli military) are prepared to kill Palestinians should they attempt to trespass exclusively Jewish property erected just years before. Elsewhere, Shehadeh recounts a time when, attempting to return home from work, Israel had imposed a curfew and he is confronted by an armed member of the Israeli military who refuses to let him go home.

> I had to implore the Israeli soldier. I told him that I really did not know a curfew had been imposed on Ramallah. I was away all day and hadn't listened to the news. "I'm tired," I said, "please let me through." Oh the humiliation. . . . Why should I endure all these hardships? Why should I spend so much of my time thinking of the dismal future? Living as a hunted, haunted human with a terrible sense of doom pervading my life? . . . But I knew why. If I and people like me were to leave rather than stay and resist the occupation, we would wake up in a few years with a new reality, our land taken from under our feet. We had no alternative but to struggle against our predicament.

Old dirt roads that once ran along the contours of the land where Palestinian communities resided are now paved highways that penetrate straight through, disfiguring the landscapes and fragmenting Palestinian communities. The open spaces where Palestinians once picnicked in the summertime, nurtured by the trees, are now cemented over with tanks of liquid concrete to accommodate the new inhabitants. Still, Shehadeh continues to pursue pilgrimages of solace and serenity in the wild hills. As the natural landscape changes, Palestinian–Israeli relations evolve as well, and Shehadeh records this evolution too. Initially an idealistic lawyer battling for Palestinian claims to land in Israeli courthouses, he becomes increasingly disenchanted, even bitter, as case after case is decided against the indigenous inhabitants. The law was set in motion for Palestinian disappearance, he realized very quickly.

Anxiously negotiating the rapidly transforming landscape—isolated Palestinian enclaves, obstructed roads, curfews and closures, Israeli checkpoints, an ever-expanding network of settler-only bypass roads, and the apartheid wall—Shehadeh describes the ways in which he felt as settlers began to swarm the hilltops: "The Palestine I knew, the land I thought of as mine, was quickly being transformed before my eyes." Observing the shrinking environmental landscapes surrounding Ramallah, Shehadeh dwells on the "cruel paradox" in the Zionist image of "Judea and Samaria" (the Hebrew names for the West Bank) that at once rely on a landscape that is characteristically Palestinian, only to settle, colonize, and disappear the very native inhabitants that crafted the terrain:

> The very thing that renders the landscape "biblical," its traditional habitation and cultivation in terraces, olive orchards, stone building and the presence of livestock, is produced by the Palestinians, whom the Jewish settlers came to replace. And yet the people who . . . render the landscape biblical are themselves excluded from the panorama. The Palestinians are there to produce the scenery and then disappear.

The eco-occupation of Palestine thus requires a contradictory production of the native, the subject of settler colonialism, through which notions of authenticity become reinscribed into settler-colonial narratives of attachment. The very landscape developed by indigenous peoples becomes the site of identity of the settler colonizer, yet the settler colony's existence becomes contingent on their disappearance.

Through each *sarha*, the reader walks and witnesses the multifaceted processes of eco-occupation: the draining of the Dead Sea to irrigate settlement lands, the concrete "poured over these hills" to support Israel's expanding industrial zones, and to the wall that not only isolates Palestinian communities from one another but also destroys their land and livelihood. Shehadah continuously navigates the interstices of life and death in Palestine's vanishment, taking us through a suffocating circular and contradictory journey.

Where love and simplicity inspired his *sarha,* the journeys become increasingly more desperate and obsessive—attempting to trace backward to a Palestine landscape evacuated and decimated and to freeze in time that which remains. Over time, the hills become robbed of their simplicity and begin to contradict themselves, evoking both solace and grief, freedom and imprisonment, and sustenance and danger. Finally, we return to the hills that once provided Shehadeh with an escape from the choking grip of occupation. But, they, too, have vanished. The delicious hills, where lovers once feasted on bread, goat cheese, and herbs, and drank from spring water, have been transformed into the very landscape that Thackeray's and Melville's wretched descriptions had inspired. These hills that only several walks before had promised a counternarrative of Palestine as a place of love and pleasure—the hills whose silhouette had contained the contours of Abu Ameen's face—had become a bleached, suburban settlement with dwellings situated like identical lego squares, red-roofed and beige.

It is the gentle and unpredictable tone that makes vanishment particularly unbearable. Of the most tragic consequences of vanishment is the inability to recover what is lost. Shehadeh's eagerness for some sort of reparation finds itself to be an unfulfilled promise that only itches away at the invisible wound of disappearance. Indeed, Shehadeh's memoir is also a story of the failure of law to contend with settler-colonial vanishment.

> My first encounter with the language of the hills was at the law courts, when as a young man I used to accompany my father, who was a recognized expert in land law. He took on many cases of disputes between landowners who possessed kawasheen (certificates of ownership) for unregistered land where the boundaries of the plot were described in terms of the physical features, in the language of hill farmers. . . . In later years, when the Israeli occupation forces became interested in claiming Palestinian land for Jewish settlements and I appealed against land acquisition orders to Israel courts, the ambiguity in these documents was used against the farmers to dispute their ownership.

As the policies of registration made legible an Israeli statehood on Palestinian lands, Palestinians became subject to a new kind of erasure. The very notion of "rights" has become the hegemonic way by which subaltern groups are allowed to make their unlivable conditions legible. Since Palestine is not a sovereign state, Shehadeh and others must make appeals in Israeli courts of law for Palestine to not vanish, for Palestinians to maintain their lands and identity. However, as a settler-colonial power, Israel's implementation of direct and indirect structures of genocide ranges from outlawing the word *nakbah* in historical textbooks and colloquial discourse, to providing a Palestinian homeowner one week to demolish their own home or be imprisoned and fined, to eliminating any trace of Palestinian life in areas like Jabal Abu-Ghneim. For Shehadeh, Israeli "law" meant that members of his family legally did not exist:

> Under Israeli law, Fareed and those members of my family who were not residing in the West Bank when Israel occupied it in June 1967 and carried out that first crucial consensus are considered absentees and their property outside the town has been taken from them. It was vested in the Israeli state for the exclusive use of Israeli Jews. I had read the law making this possible many times but its full import never struck me as it did now. A Palestinian only has the right to the property he resides in. Once he leaves it for whatever reason it ceases to be his, it "reverts back" to those whom the Israeli system considers the original, rightful owners of "Judea and Samaria," the Jewish people, wherever they might be.

The story of vanishment, then, is one that cannot be encapsulated only by statistics, archives, and observations. In the context of ongoing settler-colonial vanishment and the accompanying transformation (disappearance, replacement) of the Palestinian landscapes, we need to heed the ghostly traces—the buried "social facts" that lay beneath the surface.

CONCLUSION:
WRITING AGAINST VANISHMENT

In this article I have argued for the importance of Palestinian narrative to contend with the violence of eco-occupation in ways that cannot be addressed by legal, empirical, and positivist renderings of "facts," particularly in a context that is slated for vanishment. Heeding the calls by Avery Gordon and Julie Sze, I center Palestinian literature as generative sites that reveal the insidious and painful manifestations of vanishment in Palestine. On the surface, the critical acclaim of *Palestinian Walks* might reveal a certain fixation on and fascination with vanishment. Indeed, both mainstream and avant-garde media outlets have hailed the novel as a humanitarian portrayal of a devastating condition of rapid environmental peril. Lora Gordon's review, featured in the Electronic Intifada, observes:

Honest, haunting and heartbreaking, this travelogue hits close to home while transporting us not only into Palestine's telling geography, but also into our own daily paths, making us question how they, too, shape our lives.[32]

These reviews, while empathetic and evocative of humanity, hinge on a sort of retreat to disappearance as both linear and inevitable. In my reading, however, the novel's articulation of Palestinian vanishment is not a surrender but a form of evidence of (and against) the myth of the disappearing native. I read the novel as a form of political writing that archives various forms of eco-occupation that are made invisible by Israeli greenwashing and landscaping practices. I am inspired here by the words of Rajini Srikanth, who addresses the novel in a paper entitled "Step by Step, Frame by Frame: A Palestinian Record of Presence":

> Shehadeh's walking does not have the visibility of a protest march or rally and does not seek to draw attention to him. He would prefer if the walk were to be unobserved, because that would indicate to him that he could traverse the landscape without being surveilled and without having to explain his presence.[33]

Like Srikanth, I see *Palestinian Walks* not only as a descriptive account of loss and irrecoverability, but also as a political statement against vanishment. Indeed, Shehadeh's treks allow for a moment to reconcile with the violence and pain of eco-occupation and mark the processes of vanishment. Upon further excavation, however, the novel allows for a "record of presence"—an active labor of refusal through the articulation of loss. Such a reading points to the ways in which a transnational ethnic studies can contend with the structures of erasure deployed through epistemological, cultural, and legal manifestations. It also allows for critical ethnic studies to take up new modes of knowledge formation from native communities as a way to center the voices of people who are perpetually spoken for and, therefore, symbolically disappeared in most academic conventions concerned with visible and traceable social patterning. With this in mind, I argue for native writing as a site of recovering memory, particularly that which has been slated for *vanishment*.

LILA SHARIF is a Palestinian-native feminist scholar. She earned dual PhDs in sociology and ethnic studies from the University of California, San Diego in 2014. She is the first Palestinian to receive a PhD in ethnic studies.

NOTES

1. See http://www.theblaze.com/stories/2013/03/20/no-joke-israels-agriculture-ministry-digs-up-obamas-gift-tree-hours-after-he-plants-it/.

2. Alfred Crosby, *Ecological Imperialism: The Biological Expansion of Europe, 900–1900* (Cambridge: Cambridge University Press, 1993 [2nd. ed., 2004]).

3. Stephen W. Silliman, "Social and Physical Landscapes of Contact," in *North American Archaeology,* ed. Timothy R. Pauketat and Diana DiPaolo Loren (Malden, Mass.: Blackwell, 2005), 274.

4. Gary Fields, "Landscaping Palestine: Reflections of Enclosure in a Historical Mirror," *International Journal of Middle East Studies* 42, no. 1 (2010): 64.

5. Thomas Homer-Dixon and Kimberly Kelly, *Ecoviolence: Links among Environment, Population, and Security* (Lanham, Md.: Rowman and Littlefield, 1998), 99.

6. Ibid., 73.

7. See http://www.counterpunch.org/2007/04/02/the-political-economy-of-a-disaster/.

8. Ibid.

9. On June 28, 2006, Israel conducted a two-month military operation in the Gaza Strip that exacted a heavy toll on the 1.4 million Palestinians living in the Gaza Strip. Two hundred and two Palestinians, including 44 children, were killed when "Operation Summer Rains" (the Israel Defense Forces name for the offensive) began; thousands of Palestinians were forced to flee their homes due to repeated ground incursions and intensive shelling by the IDF. Israel launched at least 267 air strike attacks on the Gaza Strip. Only a limited amount of humanitarian aid reached the Gaza Strip during that time.

10. Patrick Wolfe, "Settler Colonialism and the Elimination of the Native," *Journal of Genocide Research* 8, no. 4 (2006): 387–409.

11. Fields, "Landscaping Palestine," 70. See also Gary Fields, "Ex-communicated: Historical Reflections on Enclosure Landscapes in Palestine," *Radical History Review* 108 (2010): 139–53.

12. Rana Sharif, "Bodies, Buses, and Permits: Palestinians Navigating Care," *Critical Legal Thinking* 4, no. 1 (2014).

13. Irus Braverman, *Planted Flags: Trees, Land, and Law in Israel/Palestine* (Cambridge: Cambridge University Press, 2014).

14. See http://www.jnf.org/.

15. Ibid.

16. Sara Kershnar, Mich Levy, and Jesse Benjamin, "Introduction," in *Greenwashing Apartheid: The Jewish National Fund's Environmental Cover Up,* ed. Jesse Benjamin, M. B. Levy, Sara Kershnar, and Mortaza Sahibzada (n.p.: IJAN, 2011).

17. Max Blumenthal, "The Carmel Wildfire Is Burning All Illusions in Israel," in Benjamin et al., *Greenwashing Apartheid,* 43–47.

18. See https://www.hebrewpodcasts.com/treesofisrael.html.

19. Quoted in Wolfe, "Settler Colonialism," 388.

20. Quoted in Blumenthal, "The Carmel Wildfire," 43–47.

21. Lorenzo Veracini, *Settler Colonialism: A Theoretical Overview* (New York: Palgrave Macmillan, 2010).

22. Ibid., 17.

23. Quoted in Celene Krauss, "Women of Color on the Front Line," in *Unequal Protection: Environmental Justice and Communities of Color,* ed. Robert D. Bullard (San Francisco: Sierra Club Books, 1994), 267.

24. Devon Peña, "Nos Encercaron: A Theoretical Exegesis on the Politics of Place in the Intermountain West" (paper presented at the New West Conference, Flagstaff, Ariz., 1999). Quoted in David Schlosberg, "Reconceiving Environmental Justice: Global Movements and Political Theories," *Journal for Environmental Politics* 13, no. 3 (2004): 525.

25. Quoted in David Schlosberg, "The Justice of Environmental Justice: Reconciling Equity, Recognition, and Participation in a Political Movement," in *Moral and Political Reasoning in Environmental Practice,* ed. Andrew Light and Avner de Shalit (Cambridge, Mass.: MIT Press, 2003), 91.

26. The foundational environmental justice texts are largely associated with the work of sociologist Robert Bullard, who is referred to as the "father of environmental justice" and served as an environmental correspondent for former U.S. president Bill Clinton.

27. Julie Sze, "From Environmental Justice Literature to the Literature of Environmental Justice," in *The Environmental Justice Reader: Politics, Poetics, & Pedagogy,* ed. Joni Adamson, Mei Mei Evans, and Rachel Stein (Tuscon: University of Arizona Press, 2002), 165.

28. Ibid., 163.

29. Ibid., 165.

30. Raja Shehadeh, *Palestinian Walks: Forays into a Vanishing Landscape* (New York: Simon and Schuster, 2008).

31. Avery F. Gordon, *Ghostly Matters: Haunting and the Sociological Imagination* (Minneapolis: University of Minnesota Press, 2008).

32. Lora Gordon, "Taking You Home: Palestinian Walks," July 21, 2008, www.electronicintifada.net.

33. Rajini Srikanth, "Step by Step, Frame by Frame: A Palestinian Record of Presence" (paper presented at the MLA Conference, January 2015). Cited with the author's permission.

Troubling Ecology

Wangechi Mutu, Octavia Butler, and Black Feminist Interventions in Environmentalism

CHELSEA M. FRAZIER

The prevailing disciplinary and theoretical frameworks for comprehending black feminist subjectivity and its integral relationship to world/land/territory/earth ethics are impoverished. One way to address this impoverishment is by turning to black women cultural producers like author Octavia Butler and visual artist Wangechi Mutu to configure a heteromorphic understanding of the social, political, and physical worlds we currently inhabit. Through narrative and visual culture, Wangechi Mutu and Octavia Butler articulate social and political ecologies that move beyond the limited correctives made available through the standards and conventions of Western formal politics. Moreover, I argue that Octavia Butler and Wangechi Mutu disrupt environmental studies frameworks informed by colonial European notions of "the political." These disruptions allow both Butler and Mutu to aesthetically reconstitute the (un)limits of humanity and construct alternative conceptions of ecological ethics within our present world and beyond it.

Octavia Butler's *Parable of the Sower* is emblematic of the ways in which cultural critiques of racist, sexist, and classist practices are interwoven into and exceed central tenets within environmental studies. The pessimistic *Parable* transports us to a not-so-distant future in which the world has slowly but steadily descended into social, environmental, and economic chaos. Octavia Butler's harrowing and seemingly apocalyptic depiction of the future centers the instability of the racial, spatial, and gendered organization of our present world. Along a similar vein, visual artist Wangechi Mutu's boldly colored and richly textured collages featured in her touring 2013 exhibition, *Wangechi Mutu: A Fantastic Journey,* detail far-off worlds and seemingly foreign protagonists that defy, challenge, and critique nearly all our racial, spatial, and gender assumptions. Characterizations of black public figures in the mainstream—and sometimes within formal academic research—often reinforce the erroneous notion that black people do not care about or are indifferent to issues pertaining to the natural environment.[1] This conventional wisdom might explain, in part, why Mutu as an artist and public figure and Butler as a social theorist and author offer alternative perspectives that often go overlooked in feminist and environmentalist circles.

The logic behind linking these two black women cultural producers, who occupy very different *and* intersecting ethnic, cultural, and geographical social positions, emerges from my utilization of a black diasporic framework. The late Octavia Butler, despite her refusal to adhere to the color-blind or whitewashed conventions of science fiction writing, has occupied an exalted place within the genre since her first published novel, *Patternmaster,* in 1976. Across her extensive catalog of novels and short stories she has centered black female subjects and characterized them as "evolved human[s], the next evolutionary step."[2] A focus on female subjectivity is one of the most obvious connectors between the two artists. As Mutu herself has clearly articulated, "The power for me is to keep the story of the female in the center, to keep discussing and talking about women as protagonists."[3]

Despite their similarities, their differences are notable, especially as Butler is a writer hailing from (and often writing about) California and Mutu is a visual artist born and raised in Nairobi, Kenya. But I dwell on their shared preoccupations and creative commitments because their work lends itself so generously to understandings of black feminist critical culture across time, place, and genre within African diasporic formations.[4] I also highlight their differences in nationalities and invoke the term "diaspora" to confront and critique comparative frameworks that abound in diaspora and critical ethnic studies. As Alexander Weheliye signals for us,

> The particularities of national diasporic groupings occupy central positions in current diaspora discourse, and they do so through the lens of the comparative method. As a result, the empirical existence of national boundaries, or linguistic differences that often help define the national ones, become the ultimate indicators of differentiation and are in danger of entering the discourse record as transcendental truths, rather than as structures and institutions that have served repeatedly to relegate black subjects to the status of western modernity's nonhuman other.[5]

Though I am investigating Mutu and Butler within and through conceptions of diaspora, a central intervention this essay aims to make in critical ethnic studies and diaspora discourse is a commitment to resisting the comparative frameworks that presently flourish in the field(s). I would be remiss if I did not acknowledge that Mutu and Butler's nationalities and cultural and geographic locations inform their visions and work. My investigation into their visual and literary contributions, however, refuses an analytic that focuses on the ways in which their national and cultural differences/particularities justify their connected exploration. Instead, this article focuses on the through-lines that bridge Mutu and Butler: centered black female subjectivity, attention to place and displacement, land connectivity, scrutinized notions of citizenship, and the reconfiguration of the human subject. These through-lines ultimately work to reorder rather than reify the "structures and institutions that have served repeatedly to relegate black subjects to the status of western modernity's nonhuman other."[6]

Furthermore, I make fundamental use of Richard Iton's critical notions of diaspora. As he explains,

> Approaching diaspora as anaformative impulse, in other words, that which resists hierarchy, hegemony, and administration, suggests a different orientation toward this category of politics. From this perspective, which might be thought of as a temporally distinct stage from that characterized by the denial and desiring of "Africa," the primary focus is on deconstructing colonial sites and narratives and rearticulating them in ways that delink geography and power. This would require a politics not reducible to the language of citizenship and governance, and accordingly, allergic to the sensibilities underlying the national (and, to some extent, the international and transnational to the degree that they depend on or reinscribe the nation-state). Moreover, it would mean being suspicious of homeland narratives and indeed any authenticating geographies that demand fixity, hierarchy, and hegemony. Conceiving of diaspora as anaform, we are encouraged, then, to put (all) space into play.[7]

Octavia Butler's *Parable of the Sower* and Wangechi Mutu's A *Fantastic Journey,* read through the lens of "diaspora as anaformative impulse," perform the aesthetic work of "deconstructing colonial sites and narratives and rearticulating them in ways that delink geography and power." Additionally, in the worlds Butler and Mutu create, their protagonists are illegible within the confines of anything resembling a nation-state. Thusly, the politics—often explicitly stated by Butler's characters or embedded within Mutu's visual fields—are irreducible to the language of citizenship, cultural particularity, and national governance as we currently conceive of it. Butler's *Parable of the Sower* and Mutu's A *Fantastic Journey* both bespeak "the denial and desiring" of their respective homelands (in ways that are legible and reducible to the language of citizenship, cultural particularity, and national governance) but often do so to signal the necessary transformation of these geographies. Through narrative and visual culture, Butler and Mutu delink geography and power and put all space into play in order to keep critical attention on black female subjectivity and resistive notions of ecological relationality.

Delinking geography and power is a significant step toward reconfiguring our earth ethics, particularly as environmental studies frameworks have traditionally been informed by colonial European notions of "the political."[8] More specifically, I mean that environmental studies and activism has traditionally been aligned with mainstream political discourse in its emphasis on liberal reform as an ideal strategy for addressing its concerns. Sylvia Wynter reveals a key flaw in this line of reasoning. In her essay "Unsettling Coloniality," Wynter opens by asserting:

> [My] argument proposes that the struggle of our new millennium will be one between the ongoing imperative of securing the well-being of our present ethnoclass (i.e., Western bourgeois) conceptions of the human, Man, which overrepresents itself as if it were the human itself, and that of securing the well-being, and therefore the full cognitive and behavioral autonomy, of the human species itself/ourselves.[9]

Wynter argues that Western philosophy has constructed and continually reinforced the idea of Western Man as the measure of humanity. She also emphasizes that the securing of Western Man as an ethnoclass is fundamentally at odds with the securing of "the human species itself/ourselves." Elsewhere, Wynter has argued that

> our present master discipline of economics discursively functions as a *secular priesthood* of the U.S. nation-state's economic system. As well as, therefore, of the overall globally incorporated world-systemic capitalist economic order in its now neoliberal and neo-imperial, homo-oeconomicus bourgeois ruling-class configuration at a world-systemic level—of which the United States is still its superpower hegemon.[10]

Here, Wynter explains that the United States and its role as global superpower facilitates the existence of a "world systemic capitalist economic order" based on neoliberal and neoimperial ethics. These ethics are rooted in and inextricably linked to the notion of Western Man as human. The kind of environmental studies or activism that tethers itself to a neoliberal, neoimperial ethics that sustains our present "world systemic capitalist economic order" can never retard or alleviate our struggles rooted in environmental degradation. If anything, by uncritically relying on traditional approaches to environmental rehabilitation and conservation via legislative reform, for example, many environmentalist activists and scholars reinforce the very system they claim to be fighting. Wynter outlines this conflict quite clearly as she argues:

> The correlated hypothesis here is that all our present struggles with respect to race, class, gender, sexual orientation, ethnicity, struggles over the environment, global warming, severe climate change, the sharply unequal distribution of the earth's resources (20 percent of the world's peoples own 80 percent of its resources, consume two-thirds of its food, and are responsible for 75 percent of its ongoing pollution, with this leading to two billion of earth's peoples living relatively affluent lives while four billion still on the edge of hunger and immiseration, to the dynamic of overconsumption on the part of the rich techno-industrial North paralleled by that overpopulation on the part of the dispossessed poor, still partly agrarian worlds of the South)—these are all differing facets of the central ethnoclass Man vs. Human struggle.[11]

Following Wynter, I insist that "the West" itself—its divisions of space and its rigid notions of the human subject—are insufficient frameworks through which "global warming, severe climate change, and the sharply unequal distribution of the earth's resources" can be effectively addressed. We must consider these issues while concurrently addressing a central conflict from which these issues emerge: a fraught and delimited understanding of human subjectivity.

In her effort to connect environmental struggles with a delimited understanding of human subjectivity, Jane Bennett questions the very necessity of an "environmentalist" stance entirely. In her book *Vibrant Matter: A Political Ecology of Things*, Bennett ponders "whether environmentalism remains the best way to frame the problems, whether it is the most persuasive rubric for challenging the American equation of prosperity with wanton consumption, or for inducing more generally, the political will to create more sustainable political economies in or adjacent to global capitalism."[12] Bennett's questions about the persuasiveness of environmentalism, coupled with Wynter's critiques, implore me to consider Bennett's alternative for framing these problems: vital materialism. According to Bennett, traditional environmental ethics are reliant on an abstraction of human bodies from their "passive environments" and leave little room for "animals, vegetables, or minerals" to be considered fully acknowledged political subjects. Furthermore, according to Bennett, a vital materialist stance is more useful than an environmental one because it (1) makes human and nonhuman relationality horizontal as opposed to vertical/hierarchical, and (2) insists on the vitality or aliveness of all matter—drawing out the ways in which humanity in its bacterial and mineral makeup is not as distinct from "everything else" as we would like to believe. Bennett's vital materialism not only includes a far more nuanced understanding of our relationships to other forms of materiality but also aims at drawing out horizontalized connections to others—human and nonhuman. Given the history of racialized exclusion in mainstream environmental discourse, a horizontalized vital materialism seems to speak back to those inherent hierarchies that not only abstract human bodies from their "passive environments" but also agitate political structures and hierarchies "that have served repeatedly to relegate black subjects to the status of western modernity's nonhuman other."[13]

While Bennett's interventions are incredibly useful, at second glance, her proposition does have problems that she herself anticipates. There are dangers in an approach that seeks to lessen the distinctness between "humanity" and "the rest of matter." Despite her attempt to democratize all forms of materiality, Bennett's vital materialist stance retains the potential of opening the floodgates for even more ruthless forms of instrumentalizing human beings. Bennett tries to address these dangers, emphasizing the idea that "if matter itself is lively, then not only is the difference between subjects and objects minimized, but the status of the shared materiality of all things is elevated."[14] Additionally, Bennett aims to demonstrate that vital materialism relies on an understanding that "all bodies become more than mere object, as the thing-powers of resistance and protean agency are brought into sharper relief."[15] Given the extensive colonial and Middle Passage histories of the violent instrumentalization of black subjects who have struggled for centuries to be recognized as "human," a restructuring of ecological ethics that retains the readied potential for *further* objectification is worrying at best and preposterous at worst. At the same time, given the messy (non) distinctions between so many different forms of materiality that Bennett highlights, it becomes difficult to completely dismiss her logic.

Both Wynter and Bennett signal that a "new" environmental politics cannot come as a result of liberal reform or black inclusivity within extant mainstream political discourse but only after understandings of relational human subjectivity are deeply scrutinized and restructured. Moreover, because of the roots of all the "isms" that Wynter coherently reports for us, a truly "new" environmental politics would render our present world unrecognizable. This article is concerned with the work of imagining this other world and other relationalities between material forms. In the pages that follow, I examine the ways Octavia Butler and Wangechi Mutu effectively *trouble ecology* as they lead us away from the limitations of traditional environmental studies while offering transgressive visions that center black female subjectivity, challenge the (dis)connections between human and non-human entities, and initiate alternative notions of environmental/ecological ethics.

BUTLER'S *PARABLES*

In this section I argue that in Octavia Butler's *Parable of the Sower* her protagonist Lauren Olamina troubles conceptions of environmentalism and offers a radical model of ecological ethics that exceeds and critiques assumptions outlined in ecology, political theory, and black feminist discourses. As Sylvia Mayer highlights, "Octavia Butler uses the genre of speculative fiction to delineate a plausible scenario of a future ecological and socioeconomic catastrophe and to tell stories of diverse attempts to come to terms with it."[16] I wholly agree with this assessment but pause when Mayer asserts that "the novel belongs to the tradition of apocalyptic ecologism that was started in the United States by Rachel Carson's publication of *Silent Spring* in 1962."[17] Though Mayer is interested in situating *Parable of the Sower* within a tradition of environmental literature, she is careful to distinguish Butler's work by pointing out that "like Carson's text, it focuses on the effects of largely anthropogenic ecological damage, but even more than Carson, Butler foregrounds issues of environmental justice."[18] Finally, Mayer reinforces her insistence on Butler's inclusion in a tradition of mainstream environmentalism by emphasizing that by "using a narrator from a socially marginalized group, the young, female, black Lauren Oya Olamina, and by focusing on the experiences of low income, multiethnic, largely though not exclusively, non-white communities [Butler] puts emphasis on the nexus of social justice and environmental degradation."[19] Mayer's characterizations of Butler's novel are convincing, but the conceptual framing under which she builds her argument enables some limiting implications. The tradition of U.S. environmentalism has been very white and very wed to the notions of liberal reform that inevitably support a "world systemic capitalist economic order." Mayer claims that Octavia Butler "belongs to the tradition" of U.S. environmentalism started by Rachel Carson but that "belonging" or inclusion in that tradition, according to Mayer's logic, is predicated on the idea that environmental justice must be foregrounded. In the United States, the canon of environmental literature has historically been dominated by transcendentalist figures, such as Henry David Thoreau and Ralph Waldo Emerson, and thus predominated with constructions of nature that emanate from a perspective of white male subjectivity. On the one hand, Mayer's rhetorical move can be read as a necessary move that seeks to include a more diverse set of voices in environmental literary studies. On the other hand, the price of including a dynamic voice like Butler's becomes the relegation of her literary and theoretical contributions to the proverbial "environmental justice corner." This flattens the usefulness of her work and does little to acknowledge the ways in which *Parable of the Sower* gestures toward an abolishment of the larger white supremacist, capitalist-driven structure of American society and thus mainstream environmentalism with it. That said, my argument moves against the well-meaning intentions behind Mayer's intervention and instead regards Butler's novel as an articulation of strategic divestment (not improvement) of the gendered, spatialized, and racialized, structure of "the West." Butler's engagement with environmentalism troubles it, disallowing its seamless inclusion into a genre predicated on rigid racial and anthropocentric hierarchy.

The scorched and decayed landscape of a future California—the central setting in *Parable of the Sower* and its sequel, *Parable of the Talents*—serves as a physical representation of the terrifying world that Lauren Olamina struggles against both physically and emotionally. Lauren lives in the United States during and following the year 2024. Food and water are scarce, extremely severe natural disasters are commonplace, and the government infrastructure tasked to address these circumstances has completely collapsed. As Adam Johns points out, "Butler's dystopia is created by continuing current trends, such as global warming or radicalizing Christian fundamentalism, to their logical extremes, without sudden transitions as no definitive cataclysm is ever experienced."[20] Lauren's world looks postapocalyptic, but is probably a world that Rob Nixon would say has fallen victim to "slow violence"—which is environmental and social violence that moves gradually and often invisibly while enabling hellish conditions for poor, marginalized groups.[21] The gap between the wealthy and the poor has widened beyond any kind of conceivable balance, and the only pockets of somewhat stable life are within small walled-in communities throughout the States. Lauren lives in one of these communities in Robledo, California. She narrates,

> And we're in Robledo—20 miles from Los Angeles, and according to Dad, a once rich, green, unwalled little city that he had been eager to abandon when he was a young man. . . . Crazy to live without a wall to protect you. Even in Robledo, most of the street poor—squatters, winos, junkies, and homeless people in general—are dangerous. They're desperate or crazy or both. That's enough to make anyone dangerous. . . . Worse for me, they have things wrong with them. They cut off each other's ears, arms, and legs . . . they carry untreated diseases and festering wounds. They have no money to spend on water to wash with so even the unwounded have sores. They don't get enough to eat so they're malnourished—or they eat bad food and poison themselves. As I rode, I tried not to look around at them, but I couldn't help seeing—collecting—some of their general misery.[22]

Misery, disease, and starvation run rampant, and services provided by firemen or police officers—services that are viewed in the modern West as basic human necessities—have become unaffordable to anyone who is not grossly wealthy. The most jarring element of Butler's future California is its similarities in aesthetics and patterns to the world we inhabit presently. The descriptions sound like the aforementioned pronouncements by Wynter as she details the "sharply unequal distribution of the earth's resources."[23] Wynter's analysis reminds us that right now there are communities in the United States and globally in desperate conditions—conditions that propagate the kind of violent and disturbing behavior Lauren describes. The affective dimension of these conditions are intensified within the aesthetics of Butler's novels, where she narrates what Lance Newman[24] might identify as the material processes of exploitation that "prop-up" the untreated diseases and festering wounds of the poor—and with them white supremacy and patriarchy.

The obvious connection to present-day conditions has left many critics challenged by the myriad symbols that populate Butler's work. Slavery, across her novels, is a prominent component. As Madhu Dubey incisively points out,

The last of Butler's novels to contain direct and extended allusions to the fugitive-slave narrative, *Parable* marks a departure from *Kindred* and *Wild Seed* in its orientation toward the future rather than the past: the novel depicts a twenty-first-century dystopian society marked by widespread debt bondage to multinational corporations. Inserting repeated references to antebellum slavery into this futurist dystopia, Butler exploits the distinctive temporality of extrapolative science fiction in order to capture the novel forms of inequality spawned by global capitalism.[25]

Dubey's argument connects directly to environmental justice themes elucidated through an engagement with slavery. The "novel forms of inequality spawned by global capitalism" in *Parable* of which Dubey speaks is a recurrent theme in radical minority discourse as well as in environmental discourse. The connections here are also conversant with the theoretical underpinnings of black feminist theorist Hortense Spillers. In her seminal essay "Mama's Baby, Papa's Maybe," Spillers provides a synopsis of the reconfiguration(s) of black female subjectivity within and after the Middle Passage. She notes that

> in the historic outline of dominance, the respective subject-positions of "female" and "male" adhere to no symbolic integrity. At a time when current critical discourses appear to compel us more and more decidedly toward gender "undecidability," it would appear reactionary, if not dumb, to insist on the integrity of female/male gender. But undressing these conflations of meaning, as they appear under the rule of dominance, would restore, as figurative possibility, not only Power to the Female (for Maternity), but also Power to the Male (for Paternity). We would gain, in short, the potential for gender differentiation as it might express itself along a range of stress points, including human biology in its intersection with the project of culture.[26]

Essentially, Spillers explains how "the historic outline of dominance"—in another context possibly understood as global capitalism, or even modernity—male and female are emptied of their highly contingent symbolic meaning. For Spillers, acknowledging this point allows her to theorize the possibility of subjects to name and position their subjectivities outside of traditional gender-binaried expectations and "along a range of stress points, including biology in its intersection with the project of culture." When Spillers historicizes the unmaking of gender as we conceptualize it generally, her theoretical framing encourages a potential for dismissing the impulse to "insist on the integrity of female/male gender"—especially for black subjects.[27] The theoretical contributions of Butler and Spillers are conversant with one another. Butler insists on unmaking the gender of her protagonist, Lauren Olamina, throughout the narrative. This not only becomes crucial to Lauren's survival but also vital to her development of a critical ecological ethics and to her envisioning of a truly "new" ordering of the world.

Lauren is unique for many reasons; central among them are her disruptive gender identity and performance, her hyperempathy syndrome (a psychic delusion that allows her to feel/share the pain and pleasure of those around her), and her self-authored religion, Earthseed. All these deeply correlative elements are critical to the construction of the character and Butler's imagining of a "new" black female subject.

Butler describes Lauren's considerable height and intelligence as standout characteristics among her peers. Lauren's differences, even as they are sometimes viewed as undesirable, prove fruitful for her in many respects. The ways in which Lauren responds to and uses both her biologically determined attributes and her subject position within the larger capitalist-driven, patriarchal, ecologically imbalanced, and Christian fundamentalist culture are emblematic of what Spillers calls for when she acknowledges "the potential for gender differentiation as it might express itself along a range of stress points, including human biology in its intersection with the project of culture."[28]

In Lauren's world, the "project of culture" includes a dizzying and disappointing array of conservative dynamics that frustrate and annoy her. As she narrates, "Not many girls in the neighborhood have babies before they drag some boy to my father and have him unite them in holy matrimony."[29] In another explication of the gender dynamics in her Robledo community, Lauren accounts,

> The Mosses don't come to church. Richard Moss has put together his own religion—a combination of the Old Testament and historical West African practices. He claims that God wants men to be patriarchs, rulers, and protectors of women, and fathers of as many children as possible. He's an engineer for one of the big commercial water companies, so he can afford to pick up beautiful, young, homeless women and live with them in polygamous relationships. He could pick up twenty women like that if he could afford to feed them. I hear there's a lot of that kind of thing going on in other neighborhoods. Some middle class men prove they're men by having a lot

of wives and temporary or permanent relationships. Some upper class men prove they're men by having one wife and a lot of beautiful, disposable young servant girls. Nasty. When the girls get pregnant, if their rich employers won't protect them, the employer's wives throw them out to starve.[30]

In her indictment of the horribly unequal gender relations that crowd her time-space, Lauren continues the work of casting aside the symbolic integrity of male/female gender. The "manhood" of the subjects Lauren mentions is reduced to their behavior and the ways in which they "prove they're men" at the expense of not only the young, poor (though not necessarily black) women at their disposal, but their displeased wives. Butler exposes the inadequacies of these dynamics as she writes,

> The Moss girls were both bullied and sheltered. They were almost never allowed to leave the walls of the neighborhood. They were educated at home by their mothers according to the religion their father assembled and they were warned away from the sin and contamination of the rest of the world. I'm surprised that Aura was allowed to come to us for gun handling instruction and target practice. I hope it will be good for her—and I hope the rest of us will survive.[31]

For some women, like the wives and children of Richard Moss, participation in the Robledo community-organized target practice falls outside of what is expected of women. Presumably, they do not need to learn to protect themselves because they have husbands and fathers to protect them. Lauren articulates these beliefs as silly and dangerous. Furthermore, Lauren's rejection of conservative gender roles and her recognition of the necessity of target practice allows her to gain a better understanding of how her hyperempathy syndrome works when she is forced to take a nonhuman life. As she explains,

> I didn't like it, but it wasn't painful. It felt like a big soft, strange ghost blow, like getting hit with a huge ball of air, but with no coolness, no feeling of wind. The blow, though still soft, was a little harder with squirrels and sometimes rats than with birds. All three had to be killed, though. They ate our food or ruined it. Tree-crops were their special victims: Peaches, plums, figs, persimmons, nuts . . . and crops like strawberries, blackberries [and] grapes. . . . Whatever we planted, if they could get at it, they would.[32]

Most importantly, her expanded knowledge of her hyperempathy syndrome is what shapes her understanding of her place in relationship to not only other human beings but other forms of nonhuman life as well. When describing the sensation/experience of shooting small animals like birds or squirrels, she explains that though shooting animals triggers her hyperempathy syndrome, it does so in a way that differs from her experiences that are triggered by humans. Her (over)attention to the feelings of others as a result of her hyperempathy syndrome (arguably her biology) as well as her attention to her subject position as a young, black woman result in the discrete moments where her ethical relationship to other forms of nonhuman life are most pronounced. In a later scene at target practice, Lauren explains:

> I did some shooting today, and I was leaning against a boulder watching others shoot, when I realized there was a dog nearby watching me. Just one dog—male, yellow-brown, sharp-eared, shorthaired. He wasn't big enough to make a meal of me, and I still had the Smith & Wesson, so while he was looking me over, I took a good look at him. He was lean, but he didn't look starved. He looked alert and curious. He sniffed the air, and I remembered that dogs were supposed to be oriented more toward scent than sight.[33]

While everyone else—particularly Aura Moss—becomes panicked at the sight of this wild dog, Lauren relies on her keen observations to try and make up her own mind. Here Butler continues the work of agitating symbolic gender rules by narrating the ways in which the Moss girls are at a disadvantage in contrast to Lauren. Because of their shelteredness as a result of being Richard's wives, their exposure to the outside world restricts their ability to accurately read the signs of their environment. Lauren's indifference and resistance to prescribed gender roles is what allows her to enthusiastically embrace an education about the outside world. Furthermore, she utilizes these learnings and skills in order to survive and preserve the time, ammunition, and energy she might otherwise waste being fearful. For Lauren, a panting-though-nonthreatening dog becomes an entity to be appreciated or learned from rather than feared and attacked.

In a later passage, Lauren's hyperempathy forces her to make a tough decision when a different wild dog does in fact pose a threat—though in a way one might not expect:

> One by one, we came abreast of the dog that had been shot and walked past it. It was a bigger, grayer animal than the one I had seen. There was a beauty

to it. It looked like pictures I had seen of wolves. It was wedged against a hanging boulder just a few steps up the steep canyon wall from us. It moved. I saw its bloody wounds as it twisted. I bit my tongue as the pain I knew it must feel became my pain. What to do? Keep walking? I couldn't. One more step and I would fall and lie in the dirt, helpless against the pain. Or I might fall into the canyon. . . . I thought I would throw up. My belly hurt more and more until I felt skewered through the middle. I leaned on my bike with my left arm. With my right hand, I drew the Smith & Wesson, aimed, and shot the beautiful dog through its head. I felt the impact of the bullet as a hard, solid blow—something beyond pain. Then I felt the dog die. I saw it jerk, shudder, stretch, its body long, then freeze, I saw it die. I felt it die. It went out like a match in a sudden vanishing of pain. Its life flared up, then went out. I went a little numb. Without the bike, I would have collapsed.[34]

Through its felt pain and death, Lauren's hyperempathy allows her, if even for a second, to become animal. It is important to note that my reading of Lauren's animality resists conceptions of animality that function at the level of analogy. For further elaboration on this distinction, I turn now to a brief critique outlined by Alexander Weheliye in *Habeas Viscus* that exposes some unfortunate trends that recur within the field of animal studies. As Weheliye notes,

> It is remarkable, for instance, how the (not so) dreaded comparison between human and animal slavery is brandished about in the field of animal studies and how black liberation struggles serve as both the positive and negative foil for making a case for the sentience and therefore emancipation of non-human beings. This sleight of hand comes easy to those critics attempting to achieve animal rights and is frequently articulated comparatively vis-à-vis black subjects' enslavement in the Americas.[35]

I highlight this moment in *Parable* and Weheliye's critique for a couple of reasons. To be clear, I am interested in investigating the way Butler theorizes different forms of relationality between humans and others. Included in that theorizing is an appreciation for and value of various forms of nonhuman life including plants and animals. I also have aimed to root those concerns within a diasporic black studies framework. Black studies discourse—particularly in the continental United States—has been extremely critical, if not outright resistant to, the use of analogy between black subjects (in this case, Lauren) and animals. As Christine Gerhardt points out, "Numerous

publications, mostly in the field of African-American studies, have emphasized how the symbolic association of blacks with wild, 'beastly' nature has
reinforced the exploitation of blacks in American history."[36] That said,
thinking through this moment at the level of analogy would be insufficient
and highly problematic—especially because the logic implies that blackness
(often understood to be always already bestial) when compared to animal
slavery signals devolution into animality.[37] This implied devolution, as well
as the hesitancy on the part of most scholars in black studies discourse to
engage notions of animality given its connection to the "reinforced exploitation of blacks," often forecloses the opportunity for productively theorizing different forms of relationality between humans / black subjects and
animals. That said, the productivity I seek to excavate becomes exemplified
in Wangechi Mutu's amalgamations of human and nonhuman animal symbols and also very clearly in this moment captured by Butler's narrative
where Lauren accounts: "The pain I knew [the dog] must feel became my
pain" and "I saw it die. I felt it die."[38] In this intimate moment, Lauren is not
like an animal, but instead becomes animal—opening her to a different set
of experiences that radically deepens her connection to another form of life.

Given her capacity for deeper connection, among other characteristics,
Lauren offers a conception of humanity unwed to white, male, patriarchal,
neoliberal, neoimperial conceptions of humanity. As I will now show, Lauren's disruptive gender performance and her hyperempathy syndrome, in
conjunction with her development of Earthseed, are the moments where
her ecological ethics cohere further. It is important to note that her development of Earthseed directly challenges many of the sentiments held by
those closest to her. Her immediate family and friends do not share Lauren's
beliefs in the slightest. To her best friend, Joanne, she explains how "three
books on survival in the wilderness, three on guns and shooting, two each
on handling medical emergencies, California native and naturalized plants
and their uses, and basic living: log cabin-building, livestock raising, plant
cultivation, soap-making—that kind of thing"[39] have undergirded her self-
fashioned education on survival and self-preservation. When Joanne makes
it clear that she thinks Lauren is crazy, Lauren retorts:

> I'm trying to learn whatever I can that might help me survive out there. I
> think we should all study books like these. I think we should bury money
> and other necessities in the ground where thieves won't find them, I think
> we should all make emergency packs—grab and run packs—in case we have

to get out of here in a hurry. Money, food, clothes, matches, a blanket . . . I think we should fix places outside where we can meet in case we get separated. Hell, I think a lot of things. And I know—I know!—that no matter how many things I think of, they won't be enough. Every time I go outside, I try to imagine what it might be like to live out there without walls, and I realize I don't know anything.[40]

Her plan for survival scares Joanne, and when Joanne betrays Lauren's trust and tells both their families about Lauren's line of reasoning, it causes problems for her and her father, Dr. Olamina. Her father is a man that has developed some sustainable ways for maintaining the safety of his family and himself, but his conversations with Lauren reveal that she does not entirely agree with his logic:

"I loaned a book about California plants and the ways Indians used them. It was one of your books. I'm sorry I loaned it to her. It's so neutral, I didn't think it could cause trouble. But I guess it has."

He looked startled, then he almost smiled. "Yes, I will have to have that one back all right. You wouldn't have the acorn bread you like so much without that one—not to mention a few other things we take for granted."

"Acorn bread . . . ?"

He nodded. "Most people in the country don't eat acorns, you know. They have no tradition of eating them, they don't know how to prepare them, and for some reason they find the idea of eating them disgusting. Some of our neighbors wanted to cut down all our big live oak trees and plant something useful. You wouldn't believe the time I had changing their minds."[41]

Dr. Olamina has clearly passed an appreciation for practical education to his daughter and even he has run into illogical resistance from uneducated peers regarding strategies for adaptation and survival. The difference between them, however, is that Lauren is not interested in using those strategies for adaptation for the purpose of improving her existing culture or hoping for its return to "better days." Lauren leans into the idea of her society's decay because of a desire to build something completely new from the destruction. Lauren's views contrast with those held by conservationists who seek to conserve environmental resources for the ultimate purpose of sustaining the economy and society as it presently functions. Though heavily centered on themes of ecology, *Parable* does not advocate for a romanticized—though ultimately exploitative—preservation of or "return to nature."

For Lauren, Earthseed becomes her blueprint for building a new world. Her new world unfortunately (but necessarily) costs her the comfort of the walled-in world she knows and many of the people in it. As she predicts, a number of tragedies plague her family: the disappearance and then death of her younger brother, the disappearance and presumed death of her father, and the total destruction of her Robledo community, including her step-mother and remaining younger brothers. The day she fears arrives and her preparation for it, though better than most, is still insufficient. The invasions and burning of her community sets her and the only other remaining members of her community—Richard Moss's youngest wife, Zahra, and her childhood friend Harry—on a journey north in search of a better life. On this journey up the coast of California, nearly everything they know becomes unfamiliar to them—including their understanding of the advantages and pitfalls of their various subject positions and gender presentations. Their journey calls to mind more insights from Spillers and her delineation of the (un)gendering that occurred for black subjects as a result of the Middle Passage. She writes,

> Those African persons in "Middle Passage" were literally suspended in the "oceanic," if we think of the latter in its Freudian orientation as an analogy for undifferentiated identity: removed from the indigenous land and culture, and not-yet "American" either, these captive persons, without names that their captors would recognize, were in movement across the Atlantic, but they were also nowhere at all. In as much as, on any given day, we might imagine, the captive personality did not know where s/he was, we could say that they were the culturally "unmade," thrown in the midst of a figurative darkness that "exposed" their destinies to an unknown course. Often enough for the captains of these galleys, navigational science of the day was not sufficient to guarantee the intended destination. We might say that the slave ship, its crew, and its human-as-cargo stand for a wild and unclaimed richness of possibility that is not interrupted, not "counted"/"accounted," or differentiated, until its movement gains the land thousands of miles away from the point of departure. Under these conditions, one is neither female, nor male, as both subjects are taken into "account" as quantities. The female in "Middle Passage," as the apparently smaller physical mass, occupies "less room" in a directly translatable money economy. But she is, nevertheless, quantifiable by the same rules of accounting as her male counterpart.[42]

The differences between the on-foot migration in *Parable* and the centuries-long Middle Passage that Spillers explains are many, but the two events do retain a few similarities that are helpful for theorizing these moments in Butler's text. In the nowhere-space of their journey, Lauren, Harry, and Zahra were "culturally 'unmade,' thrown in the midst of a figurative darkness that 'exposed' their destinies to an unknown course." As Lauren and her companions undergo cultural mutations, their respective genders and racial identifications shift. When strategizing for the journey, Lauren reveals, "I was thinking of traveling as a man," and everyone agrees that it is the safest bet for them given the material conditions under which they must travel and the "figurative darkness" they must combat. As Zahra explains of these conditions, "Mixed couples catch hell whether people think they're gay or straight. Harry'll piss off all the blacks and you'll piss off all the whites."[43] Lauren, recognizing these constraints, replies, "We [Zahra and I] can be a black couple and their white friend. If Harry can get a reasonable tan, maybe we can claim him as a cousin."[44] It is striking that Zahra makes an assumption that traveling together would engender suspicion that Lauren (while presenting as a man) and Harry might be gay—but that that would not be their biggest problem. Zahra is more concerned about the fact that they are a mixed-race group of travelers. Considering the rampant conservatism of their time-space, it is telling that queerness would be less of a problem than an interracial romantic pairing. The juxtaposition of these two concerns suggests that blackness (on a conceptual level) functions as a foremost and polarizing signifier in what Butler arranges. It is also telling that, despite her own observations and warnings, Zahra remains steadfastly against cutting her own hair and attempting to pass as a man like Lauren intends to—even as it might offer her more safety. That said, it is no small thing that Lauren welcomes, if not prefers, the opportunity to pass. The disruption is not arbitrary and it is not the only moment where Butler continues to unloosen maleness and femaleness from their symbolic principles.

Their first real challenge comes when the group has to kill an attacker in self-defense. Harry has a hard time adjusting, not only to what will be required of him in terms of his actions, but also in his role as subordinate to Lauren:

"Do you want to break off with us," Zahra asked, "go your own way without us?"

His gaze softened as he looked at her. "No," he said. "Of course not. But we don't have to turn into animals, for godsake."

"In a way, we do," I said. "We're a pack, the three of us, and all those other people out there aren't in it. If we're a good pack, and we work together, we have a chance. You can be sure we aren't the only pack out here."

He leaned back against a rock, and said with amazement, "You damn sure talk macho enough to be a guy."

I almost hit him. Maybe Zahra and I would be better off without him. But no, that wasn't true. Numbers mattered. Friendship mattered. One real male presence mattered.[45]

This moment is critical for all three characters. This is another moment where becoming animal does not signal devolution into animality but rather an appreciation for other animals from which survival skills might be learned. Moreover, Lauren's role as leader becomes solidified. This is not Harry's pack; it's Lauren's. She has the most resources, physical and mental strength, and willingness to make tough, quick decisions. Though male presence is appreciated, that maleness becomes disentangled from assumed leadership. Butler underscores this dynamic, as Lauren narrates,

Harry gave a wan smile. "I hate this world already," he said. "It's not so bad if people stick together."

He looked from her to me and back to her again. He smiled at her and nodded. It occurred to me then that he liked her, was attracted to her. That could be a problem for her later. She was a beautiful woman, and I would never be beautiful—which didn't bother me. Boys had always seemed to like me. But Zahra's looks grabbed male attention. If she and Harry get together, she could end up carrying two heavy loads northward.[46]

The contrast here between Lauren and Zahra is telling. Conceivably, both women are potential mates or sex partners for Harry, but in reality Zahra is the only viable option. There is no competition between the two, because the narrative demonstrates that Lauren, though she exhibits heterosexual desire, is disinterested and decidedly unavailable for a kind of partnering that would cause her to defer to the manipulations of the men in her life. This unavailability is not a result of arbitrary rebelliousness but instead reflects her need to protect her larger goals from any potential conflicts. Her dedication to her priorities, which aids in her leadership role, dismisses Harry before the inclination can be felt between either of them to be mates in this way. Additionally, Lauren's other encounters with men show that despite her heterosexual desires, complicity within normative gender performance is out of the question. Outside the walls of Robledo, in the desperate and dangerous conditions of their travels, she has even less incentive to compromise her resistance. For example, the potential burden of pregnancy that remains for Zahra once her attraction to Harry is revealed starkly contrasts the "heavy load" of Earthseed that gestates within Lauren as she carries it and gives birth to it on her journey northward.

Despite her disruptive gender performance, it is necessary to clarify that this reading of Lauren is based on her gender presentation rather than a suggestion of queer, same-gender loving desire. Unlike many of Octavia Butler's protagonists in her other novels, Lauren is emphatically hetersosexual. When meeting a man that becomes one of her new travel mates, Travis, Lauren waxes, "Looking at him makes me want to touch him and see how all that perfect skin feels. He's young, good looking, and intense."[47] Lauren's attractions are important. As Butler underscores the intensity of Lauren's desire, she points to the idea that although Lauren is not immune to her sexual cravings, she recognizes her circumstances and the ways that acting impulsively in response to her impulses might limit her larger goals for Earthseed. This self-discipline often allows room for further development of her independent thoughts, ideas, and responses to the rapidly changing landscape: "I felt alone between the two couples. I let them talk about their hopes and rumors of northern edens. I took out my notebook and began to write up the day's events, still savoring the last of the chocolate."[48] There is room for aloneness (though not necessarily loneliness), reflections, and pleasure in Lauren's queered solitude. The space she occupies between the two more conventional couples leaves room for self-creation and imaginative thoughts about a world to come.

As a leader, Lauren decodes outdated maps, discovers places of refuge, and is charismatic enough to rally her steadily expanding group of travelers. Throughout the novel, many of the spaces where her group retreats from the bleak realities of their voyage are in the "wilderness." Hidden by the cover of trees or next to the Pacific Ocean is where they talk, share, eat, relax, have sex, and debate about Earthseed together. Lauren accepts and confronts the realities of change in every single form of matter on Earth, and that acceptance allows her to articulate her religious beliefs that position humans as change agents. In the face of incredibly harrowing conditions, hopeful patience and liberal reform have never been viable options for improvement. Just as her hyperempathy syndrome allows her a deeper connection with animals and other humans, her attention to change allows her to develop an ecological ethics that respects the agency of other forms of matter as well as her relationship to those entities. Furthermore, her be-liefs, while self-authored, gestate in collaboration with other people's ideas and questions. She leads even as the hierarchical aspects of that leadership are troubled. Adam Johns sums up the effects of Lauren's Earthseed nicely, as he explains:

> To return to the most explicit of the *Parable* novels: change isn't merely powerful. It is ceaseless. We cannot be fixed, even if we are limited. Because we cannot be static, we can have at least some influence on the direction of change. To change our environment is to change our body, or the bodies of our descendants. Changing the environmental can, in some cases, even lead to genetic changes, which is precisely the subject of the *Parable* novels: a dystopian environment gives rise to genetic mutations, one of which [Lauren's hyperempathy syndrome] appears to be maladaptive, but turns out to be adaptive because of the religious-communitarian vision which it enables. The highly adaptive mutation helps, in turn, to establish a new environment, rich (although hardly saturated) with utopian possibilities.[49]

Johns's comments punctuate the notion that *Parable of the Sower* is about ecological ethics, yes—but an ethics that points to new and fundamentally different possibilities and not improvements of existing ones.

JOURNEYING WITH WANGECHI

Wangechi Mutu's work in many ways can be read as the visual counterpart to and representation of the kinds of "highly adaptive mutations" that Adam Johns describes above. In Mutu, we find another cultural producer imagin-ing new mutations of humanity and constructing new ecologies "rich with utopian possibilities" that reflect and audaciously critique the racial, spatial, and gendered ordering of our present world. Trevor Schoonmaker high-lights "the diptych *Yo Mama* created for the exhibition Black President: The Art and Legacy of Fela Anikulapo-Kuti at the New Museum of Contempo-rary Art" in 2003 and featured in her exhibition *Wangechi Mutu: A Fantastic Journey* as "one of Mutu's earliest and most overtly feminist works."[50] Schoon-maker goes on to point out that "this diptych retells the Christian story of Adam and Eve; this time, Eve defeats the conniving serpent and rules over her own kingdom."[51] Schoonmaker's reading helps us to excavate the kind of political work that Mutu engages. Slightly resisting Schoonmaker, I suggest that in *Yo Mama*, Mutu takes up a fundamental origin story in the tradition

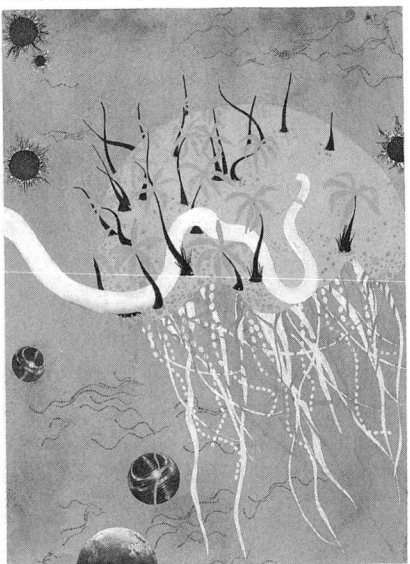

Figure 1. *Yo Mama,* 2003. Ink, mica flakes, pressure-sensitive synthetic. Polymer sheeting, cut-and-pasted printed paper, painted paper, and synthetic polymer paint on paper. Overall: 59.125 × 85 inches (150.2 × 215.9 cm). Courtesy of the artist.

of Western Judeo-Christian thought and not only provides a representation that omits Western "Man" as a primal figure but also displaces earth itself as an origin point for the whole of "humanity." Sure, the protagonist in *Yo Mama* could be a reimagining of Eve, but I wonder what thinking of this figure as something or someone a bit less familiar might yield for us. The geography, ecology, and "humanity" signaled in the diptych are just as familiar as they are strange. I aim to highlight how Mutu's critiques linger—not so subtly—in the interstitial familiar strangeness of blackness, spatial organization, and gender play, which is exactly where the concerns of this article lie.

It is quite extraordinary that Kenyan-born, Brooklyn-based Wangechi Mutu was featured prominently in the 2014 exhibition entitled *Earth Matters* at the National Museum of African Art located in the Smithsonian Institute in Washington, D.C. An accompanying publication of the same name featured a short essay by Mutu entitled "The Power of Earth in My Work."[52] Of the dozens of brilliant African artists featured in the exhibit and publication, Mutu was one of only four other artists selected to have their remarks appear alongside critical discussions of their art. In a welcome departure from the conventional wisdom that would have us believe that black people are unaware of or indifferent to issues regarding the environment, this *African and American*,[53] anointed by the Smithsonian Institute and the contemporary art scene, had indeed garnered enough recognition to speak authoritatively about nature. Mutu is the first contributor to appear in the volume and she is the only woman artist given a voice alongside three of her male contemporaries. The first words she offers in her essay are, "The people that I hail from are crop cultivators and landowners. We're farmer people."[54] Mutu's opening statement purposely invokes an intergenerational lineage that underscores her authority to know intimately and make art explicitly on her expertise—the land, the earth. Given Mutu's focus on land, constructions of nature, and earthliness more generally, I now turn to a deeper visual analysis of Mutu's visual work. With my readings, I seek to highlight some elements of a vital materialist ethics that can productively inform black feminist alternatives to Western environmental ethics.

A DIFFERENT MODE OF LOOKING

Mutu's 2006 piece *A Shady Promise* is displayed opposite. On the left there are the roots of a tree-like structure. Its hue is brown—reminiscent of bark—but a deeper, more penetrative gaze reveals that the tree bark seems to be made of something resembling stones—or perhaps storms? It isn't really clear what this tree bark is made from or if it is tree bark at all. Protruding—perhaps from the ground or maybe from the tree itself—are small grass-like structures with an iridescent quality reminiscent of metal. But, unlike what we might assume about an inertness or lifelessness of metal, these shiny grass-like structures move, sway, and swing through this uncanny environment.

Rather than growing straight upward—as many trees do in our continental U.S. climate—this tree-like structure grows from one panel to another and into the roots of the ground on the opposing end. The double rootedness of the tree calls into question associations of verticalness with growth, and with it the "natural" logic of hierarchy. Seated at the roots of the tree is a centered humanoid figure that I, following language offered by Mutu herself, will refer to as the protagonist. The protagonist wears a cool yet confrontational gaze and squats legs-splayed. Through the gestures and corporeal composition of the protagonist, a host of raced and sexed signifiers that we cling to in our "postracial" and "posthuman" moment are unsettled.

The lack of hair on the figure demarcates an inability to use it as a racial marker. It is a noticeable but also negligible omission in the rich sea of symbols Mutu infuses in her piece. The noticeable/negligible absence of

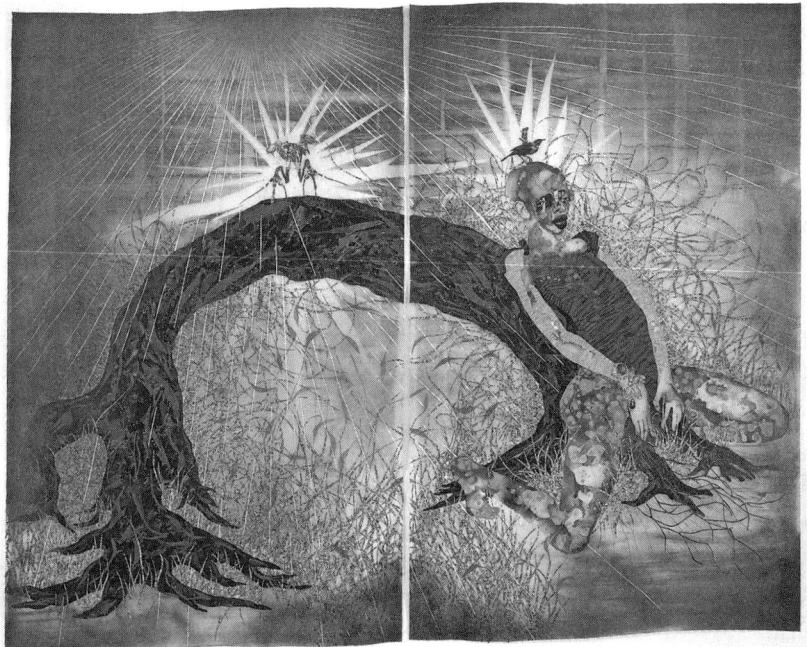

Figure 2. *A Shady Promise*, 2006. Mixed-media collage on Mylar. Overall: 87.5 × 108.75 inches (222.25 × 276.23 cm). Courtesy of the artist.

hair speaks to the absurdity or arbitrariness of using something like hair texture as a sufficient way to classify humans. Yet another marker of visualized black femininity can be found in the figure's lips—a key focus in the second panel. They are full and dark—signifying blackness, but it is also clear that the hue could be a matte lipstick by its texture. The lips further highlight the performativity and thus instability of blackness. Further, the figure is without skin—or at least the kind of thing we would readily identify as skin. Some parts of the body—the head, neck, bust, legs, and feet— appear to be covered in skin that has been flipped inside out. This perhaps signals the negligible differentiations—biologically speaking—between different races and ethnicities. Put differently, the ambiguity of the "skin" suggests that, "on the inside," humans are all the same. Or perhaps the skin is an alien form of skin—foreign to this world. As we try to place what skin the figure is in, we fall deeper into the world Mutu has constructed that is so profoundly unfamiliar. It becomes clear that even if we did know the skin color of the figure, this racial marker would no better help us to make sense of the "person" in question or the environment they occupy.

In *A Shady Promise*, Mutu constructs a world where the process of our viewing destabilizes the assumed necessity of racial markers. Part of the reason why the effect of Mutu's destabilizing process of viewing works so well is because of the way she layers unfamiliar symbols on top of or next to more familiar ones. Though the skin and hair of the figure are gone, other characteristics of the protagonist invite their comparison to current representations of visualized black femininity. For example, the way the figure is positioned with her legs splayed. From *King Magazine* to *National Geographic* to myriad magazine covers and billboards, black women are routinely positioned with their legs splayed or squatting or on all fours. Often the images focus on their complacent faces, sexually explicit and inviting gestures, and awkward (but repetitive and to some extent naturalized) "sexy" poses. The protagonist in *A Shady Promise* also sits on her knees with her legs splayed, but a bit awkwardly. The awkwardness draws our attention to the performative "unnatural" quality of the pose. At the same time, while the relaxed positioning of the upper body does not necessarily signal resistance, the protagonist's cool, calm, yet confrontational gaze does suggest a criticism of the oversexualization of black female bodies.

Just as Mutu's protagonist unsettles various markers that draw lines between ethnicities and genders, *A Shady Promise* also asks us to question markers of humanity, animality, vegetation, and other forms of materiality as well. Many strides in environmental discourse, animal studies, and biology have been made that demonstrate the interrelatedness of humans, plants, and animals, as theorists like Timothy Morton have begun to consider *ecological thinking* beyond the divisions that the idea of "nature" engenders.[55] Donna Haraway told us in 1985 that we were cyborgs, and many others—particularly those partial to theories of posthumanism—have long since accepted themselves as such.[56] Yet illusory and often misleading representations of nature and/or the environment have prevailed in terms of how we make sense of our relations with other forms of materiality. As hierarchy curses traditional environmental ethics (according to Bennett), Mutu asks us to consider the limitations of rigid hierarchy as well.

Though it remains unclear where the tree-like structure ends and where the protagonist begins, it is clear that their relationship to each other—in this constructed moment and perhaps even beyond it—is significant. From beneath the figure's splayed legs, the roots of the tree-like structure reach outward. As the figure's hands gently rest on the roots (or perhaps they are the tree's forearms) there is an intimacy or perhaps consent that can be read through the gentle touch the protagonist gives the tree's roots/forearms. Covering the protagonist's torso and arms could be either skin or clothing (a leotard perhaps) made of a bark-like substance but bears no resemblance to the tree-like structure in the background. Whether skin or clothing and whether the reference is to tree-bark or paper, the protagonist's clothing and positioning suggest boundary-blurring adjacency between plant and animal and human.

Finally, there is the presence of metal, or perhaps something formerly known as metal. The grass-like metal shines and splays about the tree lively and energetically from either the organic ground or from some built environment far away to which we have no access. Or perhaps the vitality of the shiny, metal-like grass that dances around the panels is a representation of the very alive shapes that our metals—in the way that they talk, act independently, and swirl all around us daily—have already taken. Something that could be metal is also attached to the figure's face in the shape of spectacles, but it is unclear whether the metal objects on her face are fashion, function, or prosthetic. The ambiguity again forces us to question whether these classifications matter. Mutu shifts our focus away from *why* particular classifications matter to *if* particular classifications matter—especially when it comes to "knowing" others and/or "knowing" our space.

Katherine McKittrick's concept of black women's geographies also provides much to an understanding of the interventions that Mutu engages. First, McKittrick alerts us to the idea that "the relationship between blacks and geography . . . allows us to engage with a narrative that locates and draws on black histories and black subjects in order to make visible social lives which are often displaced, rendered ungeographic."[57] The "ungeographic" rendering of black spaces calls to mind Trevor Schoonmaker's reading of Mutu's 2001 collage *Riding Death in My Sleep*.

Riding Death in My Sleep, for instance, sets the stage for Mutu's later explorations of cultural imbrication and displacement. She complicates notions of racial identity by creating a highly nuanced female figure: the skin is white; eyes, Asian, lips, full, perhaps African; and the hair as a key ethnic signifier, has been removed. Her body can be interpreted as being covered by a tight and psychedelic cat suit or diseased mottled skin. This fantastical woman perches on top of a mushroom-covered orb while hybrid bird-elephant and jellyfish-rabbit creatures fly above her head. As mushrooms are fleshy, fruit-bearing fungi that have no roots, do not require sunlight, and

Figure 3. *Riding Death in My Sleep*, 2002. Ink and collage on paper. 60 × 44 inches
(152.4 × 111.76 cm). Courtesy of the artist.

are neither plant nor animal, Mutu uses them in her work as a metaphor for immigration, as people separated from their own countries often settle— whether by necessity or force—in areas seen as intolerable by others.[58]

As Schoonmaker notes, mushrooms are a vital symbol for Mutu. What exactly is Mutu suggesting when she places a black woman, seductively and aggressively, centered on a mushroom and next to mushrooms, which are organisms that signify a challenging, intolerable, or inhabitable environment? McKittrick argues that "if identity and place are mutually constructed, the uninhabitable spatializes a human Other category of the unimaginable/native/black."[59] The title of the collage, *Riding Death in My Sleep*, is significant for thinking through the "uninhabitable spatial[izing] of a human Other." Mutu could be referring to death itself. Alternately, she could be cheekily playing with the idea of a "dead" African land. The knowing slight smirk Mutu's protagonist wears suggests that they know others might find this mushroom-rich environment uninhabitable or intolerable. For the protagonist, however, the land might be so easy to navigate (or rather she is so well equipped to handle the environment) that she can "ride it in her sleep." Mutu has publicly expressed her frustrations with stereotypical representations of Africa, and her training in fine art and anthropology offer her tools to address these frustrations formally in her work. When various documentaries profile Africa, particular regions are often described as "severe," conditions are described as "hellish," and the people, nonhuman animals, and vegetation are presented to the viewer through a tone of sheer awe at their biological and cultural "extremity." *Riding Death in My Sleep* offers an alternative understanding of the ways in which "the uninhabitable spatializes a human Other category of the unimaginable/native/black." Mutu's collage cleverly redeploys these assumptions. Ultimately, her depictions of humanity and representations of geography challenge the overrepresentation of "Man's geographies," which seek to classify various people and spaces as always already Other.

CONCLUSION: TROUBLING ECOLOGY

Butler's novel *Parable of the Sower* and Mutu's exhibition *A Fantastic Journey* offer a radically altered conception of ecological ethics and articulations of ecological relationality between different forms of materials. Across their extensive bodies of work, they challenge and trouble our assumptions regarding just about everything, leaving us with a posthumanist, poststructuralist, and postmodern understanding of our world and the categories within it. Obvious critiques of rigid hierarchy can be found across their work as their imaginings call for alternative visions of ecological relationality[60] that exceed the hierarchical myopia and politics of exclusion that have plagued environmental discourse—particularly in America—for the past century. I return to Bennett because this is where a vital materialist ethics, again, becomes useful. Bennett proposes:

> Vital materialists will thus try to linger in those moments during which they find themselves fascinated by objects, taking them as clues to the material vitality that they share with them. This sense of a strange and incomplete commonality with the out-side may induce vital materialists to treat nonhumans—animals, plants, earth, even artifacts and commodities—more carefully, more strategically, more ecologically.[61]

The "fascination by objects" of which Bennett speaks calls to mind a particularly crucial moment in *Parable of the Sower* where Lauren finally begins making progress in explaining and even converting her traveling companions to Earthseed. As Lauren narrates,

> Now we lounged in the shade of pines and sycamore, enjoyed the sea breeze, rested, and talked. I wrote, fleshing out my journal notes for the week. I was just finishing that when Travis sat down next to me and asked his question: "You really believe in all this Earthseed stuff, don't you?"
> "Every word," I answered.
> "But . . . you made it up."
> I reached down, picked up a small stone, and put it on the table between us. "If I could analyze this and tell you all what it was made of, would that mean I'd made up its contents?" . . . "Change is ongoing. Everything changes in some way—size, position, composition, frequency, velocity, thinking, whatever. Every living thing, every bit of matter, all the energy in the universe changes in some way. I don't claim that everything changes in every way, but everything changes in some way."[62]

In this moment, Lauren uses the object, the stone, and takes a clue from it to help explain the vitality (in this context understood as its capacity for change) that she shares with it. Placing Butler and Mutu's work in line with a vital materialist ethics highlights both their fascination with objects and, as I have shown, their "sense of a strange and incomplete commonality with the out-side." These political overtones seemingly place Butler's and Mutu's work squarely within—not an environmental stance—but rather a vital materialist one. This classification would be all well and good, save for the equally important black feminist overtones found in Butler's novels and Mutu's diptychs. As McKittrick eloquently points out, "Because female slave bodies [were] transformed into profitable sexual and reproductive technologies, they [came] to represent 'New World' inventions and are consequently rendered an axiomatic public object."[63] Or, in other words, via slavery—and I extend this to other diasporic colonial histories as well—black subjects, and specifically black women, have already been put in a position where their humanity has not been assumed because of the racialized and sexualized public functions they have served. So, for black women, their "questionable" humanity and illusory subject/object status has always already paved the way for their extreme instrumentalization. Several black scholars have argued for decades about the harmful effects of the instrumentalization of black female bodies. The objectification of black subjects it is not a debate or set of concerns that will dissipate anytime soon—particularly as slavery and its afterlife continues to shape all of our present lives and ooze into the future. So, even as Butler and Mutu can be read as offering a vital materialist ethics as an alternative to an environmental one, I argue that those readings are contingent on the troubling of that vital materialist ethics. Hierarchy and classifications are destabilized and reshaped, but they are not absent in the specific novels and diptychs I have highlighted here or across Butler and Mutu's work more generally. As we recognize their work for its ability to trouble our visual, spatial, and philosophical assumptions, it begins to take on a different mode of reception. As Spillers reminds us, "This problematizing of gender places [black female subjects], in my view, out of the traditional symbolics of female gender, and it is our task to make a place for this different social subject."[64] Engaging Mutu and Butler can aid in Spillers's call for a "different social subject." Furthermore, we can turn to Octavia Butler and Wangechi Mutu—not to decide whether or not environmentalism, or maybe even vital materialism, is the "best" form of ecological relationality for a black feminist political project. Butler and Mutu's work is less productive when read as a neat endorsement of environmentalism or vital materialism or as correctives to black women's discursive objectification—even as they both call attention to all these issues through their creative endeavors. But perhaps their aesthetic confrontations can be the guideposts to the to-be-named political theory in between.

CHELSEA M. FRAZIER is a PhD student in the Department of African American Studies at Northwestern University.

NOTES

1. Kimberly N. Ruffin, *Black on Earth: African American Ecoliterary Traditions* (Athens: University of Georgia Press, 2010). Consult the introduction for a breakdown of this racist and exclusionary rhetoric within mainstream environmental discourse.

2. Adam Johns, "The Time Had Come for Us to Be Born: Octavia Butler's Darwinian Apocalypse," *Extrapolation* 51, no. 3 (2010): 403.

3. Nasher Museum, "Wangechi Mutu: A Fantastic Journey," YouTube video (April 24, 2013) https://www.youtube.com/watch?feature=player_embedded&v=Q-x9mdk13ds.

4. Hortense Spillers, "The Idea of Black Culture," *CR: The New Centennial Review* 6, no. 3 (2006): 7–28. I use the phrase "black feminist critical culture" to acknowledge and extend Hortense Spillers's notion of black culture as "critical culture" in her 2006 essay, "The Idea of Black Culture."

5. Alexander Weheliye, *Habeas Viscus* (Durham: Duke University Press, 2014), 31.

6. Ibid.

7. Richard Iton, *In Search of the Black Fantastic* (New York: Oxford University Press, 2008), 200.

8. See Steven Stoll's *US Environmentalism since 1945: A Brief History with Documents* (Boston: Bedford's/St. Martin's, 2007). This text provides an overview of the ways in which environmental activism has pushed for liberal reform by staging interventions within the realm of mainstream political discourse.

9. Sylvia Wynter, "Unsettling the Coloniality of Being/Power/Truth/Freedom: Towards the Human, After Man, Its Overrepresentation—An Argument," *New Centennial Review* 3, no. 3 (2003): 260.

10. Katherine McKittrick, *Sylvia Wynter: On Being Human as Praxis* (Durham: Duke University Press, 2011), 26.

11. Wynter, "Unsettling the Coloniality," 261.

12. Jane Bennett, *Vibrant Matter: A Political Ecology of Things* (Durham: Duke University Press, 2010), 111.

13. Weheliye, *Habeas Viscus,* 31.

14. Bennett, *Vibrant Matter,* 13.

15. Ibid.

16. Sylvia Mayer, "Genre and Environmentalism: Octavia Butler's *Parable of the Sower,* Speculative Fiction, and the African American Slave Narrative," in *Restoring the Connection to the Natural World: Essays of African American Environmental Imagination* (Münster: LIT, 2003), 175.

17. Ibid.

18. Ibid.

19. Ibid.

20. Johns, "The Time Had Come," 401.

21. Rob Nixon, *Slow Violence and the Environmentalism of the Poor* (Cambridge, Mass.: Harvard University Press, 2011).

22. Octavia Butler, *Parable of the Sower* (New York: Time Warner Books, 1995), 9.

23. Wynter, "Unsettling the Coloniality," 261.

24. Lance Newman, *Our Common Dwelling* (New York: Palgrave Macmillan, 2005). Newman's notion of "material processes of exploitation" are explored further here.

25. Madhu Dubey, "Octavia Butler's Novels of Enslavement," *Novel: A Forum on Fiction* 46, no. 3 (2013): 357.

26. Hortense Spillers, "Mama's Baby, Papa's Maybe: An American Grammar Book," *Diacritics* 17, no. 2 (1987): 66.

27. Ibid., 72.

28. Ibid., 66.

29. Butler, *Parable,* 33.

30. Ibid., 37.

31. Ibid., 42.

32. Ibid., 38.

33. Ibid., 40.

34. Ibid., 45.

35. Weheliye, *Habeas Viscus,* 10.

36. Christine Gerhardt, "The Greening of African American Landscapes: Where Ecocriticism Meets Post-Colonial Theory," *Mississippi Quarterly* 55, no. 4 (2002): 520.

37. The argument is guided by conceptualizations of animality offered by Sharon Holland's forthcoming book project on distinctions/continuities between the human and the animal.

38. Butler, *Parable,* 45.

39. Ibid., 58.

40. Ibid.

41. Ibid., 64.

42. Spillers, "Mama's Baby, Papa's Maybe," 72.

43. Butler, *Parable,* 172.

44. Ibid.

45. Ibid., 183.

46. Ibid.

47. Ibid., 211.

48. Ibid.

49. Johns, "The Time Had Come," 410.

50. Trevor Schoonmaker, "Wangechi Mutu: A Fantastic Journey," in *A Fantastic Journey,* ed. Trevor Schoonmaker, Kristine Stiles, and Greg Tate (Durham: Duke University Press, 2013), 26.

51. Ibid.

52. Karen E. Milbourne, *Earth Matters: Land as Material and Metaphor in the Arts of Africa* (New York: Monticelli Press, 2014).

53. Wangechi Mutu's nationality is Kenyan and she was trained and resides/works in New York City.

54. Wangechi Mutu, "The Power of Earth in My Work," in Schoonmaker, Stiles, and Tate, *Earth Matters,* 91.

55. Timothy Morton, *The Ecological Thought* (Cambridge, Mass.: Harvard University Press, 2012).

56. Donna Haraway, *Simians, Cyborgs, and Women: The Reinvention of Nature* (New York: Routledge, 1991).

57. Katherine McKittrick, *Demonic Grounds: Black Women and the Cartographies of Struggle* (Minneapolis: University of Minnesota Press, 2006), x.

58. Schoonmaker, "Wangechi Mutu," 26.

59. McKittrick, *Demonic Grounds,* 130.

60. Jane Bennett's conception of "vital materialism" informs the argument here.

61. McKittrick, *Demonic Grounds,* 18.

62. Butler, *Parable,* 218.

63. McKittrick, *Demonic Grounds,* 46.

64. Spillers, "Mama's Baby, Papa's Maybe," 80.

Racial Violence, Mass Shootings, and the U.S. Neoliberal State

ANOOP MIRPURI

On June 17, 2015, a young white man walked into a Bible-study class at Emanuel AME Church in Charleston, South Carolina. Minutes later, he opened fire with a semiautomatic weapon and killed nine worshipers, including state senator and pastor Clementa C. Pickney. According to Felicia Sanders, who survived but lost her son in the massacre, the gunman proclaimed that his victims were "raping our women and taking over the country." In the aftermath of the atrocity, revelations about the gunman's white supremacist views and photographs of him posing with the confederate flag generated a requisite atmosphere of liberal nationalist condemnation, which quickly led to Southern penance at a bargain rate. A few weeks later, the governor of South Carolina gave the order to do what seemed previously unthinkable to many: remove the confederate flag from the statehouse grounds.

The widespread celebration of the flag's removal effectively ratified a general belief that a fringe white nationalist nostalgia for the Confederacy— evinced by a regional and vestigial reverence for the confederate flag—was the massacre's primary motivator. Encapsulated by calls to "take down the flag," the dominance of this view precluded a structural analysis that could locate the Charleston shootings not only within a long tradition of state-sanctioned antiblack violence, but also within a genealogy of U.S. settler-colonialism.[1] Indeed, the day after the shooting, in a much-celebrated monologue on *The Daily Show*, Jon Stewart captured the liberal nationalist ethos when he indignantly pointed out that "in South Carolina, the roads that black people drive on are named for confederate generals who fought to keep black people from being able to drive freely on that road." Inveighing against "the disparity of response between when we think people that are foreign are going to kill us, and killing ourselves," Stewart suggested that had this been "what we thought was Islamic terrorism," there would be no end to the material resources the U.S. state would marshal—including "torture" and "fly[ing] unmanned death machines"—in order to "keep Americans safe."[2] If Stewart's comments are read as a keen indictment of the state's unwillingness to protect black lives from gun violence, we should also ask why such a critique should depend on the trope of the Islamic terrorist threat. Indeed, this is precisely what enables Stewart's comparative distinction between foreign and domestic policy, between *warfare* and *politics*. What this distinction obscures, however, is that the state's biopolitical imperative to protect civilian life has consistently required the construction and articulation of racial threats as *enemy combatants*: the Indian, the slave, the terrorist, the criminal. Meanwhile, the contradiction he presents between *state action* and *inaction* forestalls the possibility of acknowledging that the U.S. settler-colonial state itself has from its inception struggled to reconcile the mutual constitution of state, extralegal, and nonstate violence: from "Indian removal" to slave patrols, border-control militias to lynching and firebombing, the militarization of urban policing and imperialist counterinsurgency to mass incarceration and the current war on terror. Put differently, the appeal for the inclusion of black life within the ambit of the civilian ("ourselves") ignores that the very demand to "keep Americans safe" has deputized whiteness, providing a discursive framework connecting settler-colonial and antiblack violence with imperialist warfare within and beyond U.S. borders.[3]

Looking at it from this view, the implication that the racial violence at Charleston was a particular instance of a supposedly broader phenomenon— the mass shooting of civilians—may have it backwards. If Stewart's insistence that "we" are "killing ourselves" naively imagines a "we" that never was, this essay suggests that the Charleston massacre forces a reckoning with the relation between mass shootings (which have prompted the discursive recognition that "we" are "killing ourselves") and racism (which persistently authorizes killing in the name of "ourselves"). How, then, should critical ethnic studies engage a contemporary formation in which the mass shooting as a form of nonstate violence has in recent years sought its victims across positivist categories of race and from populations whose civilian status have previously gone unquestioned? This essay treats the contemporary mass shooting as a simultaneously discursive and actual phenomenon, the evidently "intraracial" and "motiveless" (i.e., content-free) character of which has enabled its ideological compartmentalization as a distinct pathological form. I argue that its discursive recognition as such signals the prevalence of both liberal and white nationalist anxieties over the capacity of the state to protect the "nation" from violence, which together obfuscate a contemporary settler-colonial and antiblack formation that reproduces itself by regularly stripping entire populations of the protections of civilian status. Such anxiety is both the effect and instrument of recent imperialist wars that have figured Muslims as an internal and external threat and an increasingly privatized and fortified U.S. cityscape that has facilitated the militarized policing and criminalization of black surplus labor under neoliberalism. In turn, this essay suggests that the epistemological perspective animating the emergent field of critical ethnic studies provokes a challenge to the implicit nonracial designation of mass shootings that fit the profile of intraracial and pathological violence. Such designation is grounded in liberal positivist formulations of race, the institutionalization of which as racial knowledge inhibits critical efforts to understand how racism persists as an organizing feature of an officially antiracist state.[4] By contrast, I argue that actual instances of mass shootings—notwithstanding the racial identity of its victims—operate as privatized forms of sovereign power, the exercise of which under U.S. neoliberalism issues historically from the extralegal right to seize indigenous lands and the police power to criminalize black and anticolonial resistance to dispossession and enclosure.[5]

A reading of the phenomenal convergence of mass shootings under contemporary racial capitalism is necessarily an inquiry into the trajectory of civilian (i.e., racialized) life in the U.S. neoliberal state. If liberal universalism opposes the (raceless) civilian to the soldier, its most thoroughgoing critique within black studies has read modern civil society as an ontologically privileged space parasitic on a constitutive "state of exception" for the enslaved and colonized. At the same time, indigenous studies has identified "frontier" warfare and the violent land seizures of settler colonialism as the condition of possibility for liberal multicultural civil society.

This essay builds on scholarship that has understood both race and colonialism as foundational to modern social formations.[6] At the same time, I draw on and advance a materialist conceptualization of race as the historical outcome of a dialectic between race radical movements and a "resistance from above" that seeks to contain and compartmentalize their heterogeneity within liberal nationalist legal and epistemological frameworks.[7] In doing so, I put forward a reading of civilian life as the historically contingent possibility of corporeal integrity and flourishing—a fugitive capacity whose always provisional realization is at once the outcome of political struggles past and the potential ground on which future struggles take shape. On one hand, the biopolitical imperative to foster and protect the flourishing of "life itself" as the horizon of liberal political modernity ensures that the category of the civilian operates as a securitized domain that divides the planet, rationalizing violence against populations understood as threats to civil society.[8] On the other hand, it is critical for antiracist scholarship to register the methodological distinction between (while holding in productive tension) a formal analysis of power and the necessarily messy study of how differently racialized populations come to be positioned as civilian or enemy combatant through their constitution in histories of struggle and resistance.[9] To treat civilian life as a historical capacity, simultaneously under threat and subject to revocation, is to take account of how the privilege of being protected from violence accrues relationally to specific bodies and populations and the conditions under which it can be stripped from others. This demands an openness to thinking outside the frames of analogy and comparison, making visible the articulations between forms of violence that otherwise get treated as distinct, nonracial, or abstracted from the material conditions that shape them. As a contribution to the field of critical ethnic studies, this essay suggests that we might complicate our understanding of the relation among race, violence, and civilian life if we insist on a critique of mass shootings as a form of violence articulated through U.S. empire, antiblackness, and the spatial and political economy of late modern racial capitalism.[10]

Discussions of the relation between race and neoliberalism have yet to develop an account of the contemporary phenomenon of mass shootings. If it has been beyond their epistemological purview, this is in part due to the fact that the liberal positivist framework that has accompanied the institutionalization of racial knowledge makes it difficult to understand mass shootings in relation to the category of racial violence.[11] Alternatively, when there happens to be a clear "exception," it tends to be framed within a liberal antiracist discourse that treats such an event as unrelated to neoliberal state formation and regimes of capital accumulation.[12] On top of this analytical double bind, the widespread attention given to mass shootings in the media and the consequent debate about gun control that inevitably follows each instance helps reproduce the invisibility of the most common objects of gun violence in the United States: young black men.[13] Equally problematic is the propensity of these discussions to reify a heavily mediated form of violence as *exemplary of violence*, an epistemology that takes for granted a liberal theory of violence as corporeal, weaponized, spectacular, and operative outside (or in opposition to) the law.

The starting point for this analysis is that mass shootings should be treated neither as exceptional nor representative but rather should demand an account of the mechanisms articulating them to other forms of violence that shape and structure the U.S. neoliberal state. This includes targeted killing by U.S. military and police forces as much as it does widespread forms of quotidian terror and spatial fortification that result in the criminalization and incarceration of millions of people. Mass shootings should thus be understood as a phenomenon of racialized violence specific to the regime of accumulation and the affective structure of the neoliberal state. What unites them as a form are not the superstructural issues of firearm legislation or the accessibility and effectiveness of mental health treatment but the infrastructural convergence of racialization and "accumulation by dispossession" specific to late modern capitalism, which both state *and* non-state violence variably function to enforce.[14]

My hope is that reading the articulated violences of racial capitalism counters a structural tendency to interpret as *nonviolent* the routine forms of bodily and psychic constitution to which racially devalued bodies have been made consistently and differentially vulnerable. These include the whole array of legal and extralegal methods for keeping streets and neighborhoods "safe" that prevail under contemporary regimes of spatial privatization and enclosure. If this form of analysis contests the normalization of violence and degradation under the neoliberal sign of "freedom," at the same time it can bring into relief the social and discursive practices of freedom that such operations seek to control.[15]

U.S. EMPIRE, RACIAL KNOWLEDGE, AND THE OAK CREEK SHOOTINGS

Thinking about mass shootings as a form of racialized violence requires engaging the critique of a method that remains central to the analysis of race in legal practice and the social sciences: the positivist approach that takes as given an empirical distinction between *violence* and *racial violence*. Empirically, we determine certain violence to be racial (or not) based on evidence of motives and the presumed racial identity of its victims and perpetrators. But as critical race theorists have argued, the demand to establish the racism of an act by excavating racial motives is the product of and response to a broader positivist-legalist fetishization of (certain kinds of) evidence that works to singularize and abstract such instances from the wider social-discursive architecture that makes them possible and predicts their likelihood under particular conditions.[16]

To take this further, there is a consequential difference between a search for motives that tries to explain an act of violence with reference to the intent or psychology of the perpetrator and a materialist analysis of the accumulation regime shaping the affective logic that determines such violence. Part of what enables the confusion of these methods is that the latter often requires recourse to the subjective dimensions of a perpetrator's existence. The difference is that materialist analysis refuses to privilege such evidence as either autonomous or exhausting the act's meaning. But while scholarship in critical race and ethnic studies has often been suspicious of the imperative to know the racial identity and background of the perpetrator, a thoroughgoing materialism would need to bring the same skepticism to the demand to know and register the identity of the victims. It is critical to note that skepticism of the demand itself does not obviate the political necessity to know and register these identities. Indeed, such scrutiny need not be unwittingly tethered to neoconservative appeals to eradicate race reference from the law, nor should it be dismissively conflated with the anti-black claim that "all lives matter."[17] Rather, its vulnerability to these imputations indicates precisely the impasse in race theorizing that critical ethnic studies seeks to address. Instead of claiming that the racial identity of victims of violence is inconsequential, a materialist analysis helps complicate and revise how we understand violence as a subject of and for racial capitalism, expanding our conception of what is racial about violence and what counts as racial violence.

The mass shooting that recently occurred in Oak Creek, Wisconsin, is critical to engage in this discussion, not least because its racial specificity helps bring into view the differences between these approaches. On August 5, 2012, a U.S. Army veteran and avowed white supremacist, Wade Michael Page, shot and killed six people and wounded four at a Sikh temple, before exchanging gunfire with police and fatally shooting himself. On the surface, this appears as a straightforward example of racial violence. A cursory look into Page's background reveals a white man who played in several neo-Nazi rock bands and was part of a milieu of white supremacists playing and recording "hate music" celebrating white power and openly denigrating black and Jewish people in the crassest and most hackneyed of ways. His decision to target members of a racialized religious community is easily explained by this history, an act that has recent precedents in previous mass shootings at Jewish community centers in Los Angeles and Seattle. While the inability to know Page's exact motives may prevent these shootings from being legally classified as an act of terrorism, his more than casual association with white supremacist groups would be enough to indict it before a court of law as a racially motivated hate crime.

It quickly becomes clear, however, that the racial overdetermination of these shootings suggests that Oak Creek requires a more capacious understanding of what is racial about this violence than can be gleaned when limited to a positivist inventory of the shooter's motives. Given the increased incidence of violence against Sikhs apparently mistaken for Muslims in the United States after 9/11, many critics questioned whether Page *knew* he was targeting a Sikh temple, and further, whether he was even *aware* of the existence of Sikhism as a religion or identity. Indeed, after the shooting, there emerged widespread speculation over whether Page mistook the gurdwara in Oak Creek for a mosque, and thus whether he believed he was actually targeting Muslims. A number of commentators were quick to challenge the "mistaken identity" narrative for fear that the idea that Page targeted the "wrong people" (i.e., peaceful Sikhs) implicitly reproduced the stereotype of the threatening Muslim and the state narrative of an Islamic terrorist threat. At the same time, critics of Islamophobia have argued that an interrogation of this narrative is necessary for understanding and addressing the pervasive anti-Muslim rhetoric and sentiment that was a condition of possibility for Page's act.[18] Doing the work that mainstream discussions of Oak Creek were failing to do, for example, the liberal critic Wajahat Ali insisted not simply on pointing out the apparent racial elements of the shooting but placing them within the context of the rise of anti-Muslim hate crimes post-9/11 and the proliferation of right-wing hate groups following Barack Obama's election. Ali suggested that such trends place at risk not only "American Muslims" but also the bodies of people who signify as Muslim, such as "Arab American Christians, Iranian Jews and Sikh Americans."[19]

From Ali's perspective, the Oak Creek shootings are explained by the proliferation of "misinformation" about Islam among a right-wing fringe by an "Islamophobia network" of "pseudo-scholars, policy experts, politicians and media pundits."[20] If there is a material context for the rise of such beliefs, it is that a "lucrative cottage industry" is being fostered by a small group of funders exploiting the desire for "short-term political gain and publicity" among Republicans.[21] The "ill-gained profit" from such propaganda is shared among this network of organizations and individuals who have little regard for the fact that "extremist rhetoric inspires extremist violence."[22] I suggest that Ali's analysis be understood as exemplary of a liberal antiracist critique of Oak Creek specifically, and of racism as Islamophobia in general, effectively setting out the terms of debate for progressive discussions of race while appearing as the most radical limits of mainstream commentary on racial violence. For even as Ali provides a wider ideological context for Page's act, that context is reduced to the domain of ideas and abstracted from the political economy of U.S. empire.[23] This approach leads him to explain Oak Creek as an outcome of the production of false knowledge about Muslims and Sikhs. By contrast, I want to argue that we read Oak Creek as the effect of the violent material production of social truths (i.e., knowledge) that erode the phenomenological difference between Muslims and Sikhs.

My aim here is not to contest the factual basis of Ali's critique, which emerges from an illuminating study of Islamophobia by the Center for American Progress (CAP) (for which Ali was the lead author).[24] Indeed, the investigative work tracking the relation among financial organizations, donors, right-wing think tanks, scholars, and politicians has been critical in exposing the formation and circulation of common sense beliefs about Islam that function as knowledge in the university no less than in Washington, D.C. Rather, the problem is that explaining the Oak Creek shootings ("extremist violence") as an outcome of the circulation of false ideas ("extremist rhetoric") presumes that racial knowledge is the product of a war of ideas between reasonable people committed to empirical facts and ideologues spreading hate and propaganda. In this view, Islamophobia can be comfortingly thought of as the creation of an identifiable group of individuals and organizations that use financial power to incentivize the promotion of such ideas rather than the discursive instrument-effect of U.S. state-corporate military strategies for securing the conditions for capital accumulation in the Middle East and Central Asia. In the former explanation, there is a one-to-one correspondence between Islamophobic ideas and the organizations that produce them. In the latter, Islamophobia is understood not as a racist belief to which one may or may not subscribe but an endemic form of racism produced by material practices of warfare that simultaneously function to rationalize the global material inequalities and relations of domination such warfare secures.[25] As such, the question remains whether Islamophobia as a discursive practice can be adequately contested without an analysis of the material configuration of forces invested in resource extraction, weapons production, and the global construction of prisons, fences, walls, and other forms of securitization that enforce what Ruth Wilson Gilmore describes as "group-differentiated vulnerability to premature death."[26]

The central point is that in Ali's analysis, the social production of knowledge about race is insulated from the material conditions of possibility that give it life and make it meaningful. As a result, it obscures the productive function of race in naturalizing differential vulnerability to violence under capitalism, thus narrowing the possibility of conceiving what is racial about violence and what counts as racial violence. For Ali, if Oak Creek was an instance of a growing trend in anti-Muslim hate violence driven by cynical conservative politicians spreading misinformation, then the response should be the promotion and wide dissemination of multicultural education about the peacefulness of Islam. Since the legal standard for a hate crime is whether intent was based on either the victim's "perceived" or "actual" identity, what Page may or may not have been aware of matters less than his ignorance: his inability to perceive difference accurately and his probable belief in Islamophobic myths about the Muslim threat to Western society and norms. While this critique recognizes the way in which particular iterations of racist feeling can structure the vulnerability of bodies that do not belong to the group being discriminated against, it ignores the material conditions that produce Islamophobia as a social reality—indeed, that produce U.S. society *as* Islamophobic. It thus dissimulates Islamophobia's catalog of stereotypes as an inventory of personal racist beliefs, rather than an effect of materially produced social knowledge that shapes how we perceive bodies and populations. This allows it to proceed as if racism were a pathology of ignorance and that being exposed to more accurate knowledge about the other harbors inherent curative properties. But while such education may work to counter stereotypes, the liberal antiracist critique uncomplicatedly reproduces the assumption that an identity group's very status as a knowable object is unconnected from geopolitical relations of power, inequality, and imperialist violence. Indeed, such knowledge is made both possible and desirable by material conditions that secure, rather than contest, hierarchies of domination and subordination.[27]

It thus comes as no surprise that Ali's explanation of Oak Creek has nothing to say about drone warfare, CIA torture, and the U.S. military occupations for which Western knowledge about Islam serves both as alibi and rationale. The reification of racial identities as positively knowable prior to the materially produced knowledge procedures that bring them into being conceals how the social production of truth both *produces* and *erodes* socially visible differences between bodies and populations. Such material practices of race making activate not only the social perception of threat but also the social mobility of threat across given racial categories.

OAK CREEK AS A PARADIGM FOR MASS SHOOTINGS

The preceding analysis frames Oak Creek as the effect of practices of U.S. empire that produce particular bodies as threats and erode the phenomenological difference between identities whose social significance is otherwise taken for granted. The remainder of this essay develops this framework for an analysis of mass shootings as a contemporary form of violence animated by the motility of racial threat untethered from particular bodies and fastened to public space. It would be difficult to deny the suspicion that the mass shooting as a form is structurally understood as a more general, nonracial form of violence—nor is the form treated within studies of racial violence—because in most cases the victims tend to be identified as white.[28] But what happens once this relation between the general and the particular is inverted? That is, what kind of analytical effects are yielded once we no longer deduce the racial dimension of violence solely with reference to the identity of its victims? And further, what grounds exist for reading Oak Creek not as an exceptional mass shooting but as exemplary: a framework that enables a reading of the mass shooting as a specific form of racial violence ascendant within the U.S. neoliberal state?

The perspective that differentiates between what violence counts as racial and what is racial (or not) about violence based on the victims' identity cannot account for racial capitalism as a structure that enables the perception and proliferation of biopolitical threats unmoored from visible markers of race. This makes it difficult, if not impossible, to observe how historically and materially grounded categories of racialized threat—insurgent, criminal, terrorist—become the ground for new forms violence that, even as they work to reproduce historical ontologies of race, produce "differentiating effects at the point of [their] application."[29] Drawing on Gilmore's understanding of racism as the production and exploitation of premature death, Nikhil Singh has argued that a conception of racialization in which "violence takes precedence over ideological discourses" directs our attention to "the formation and institutionalization of structures and situations of protection and vulnerability" that invest specific populations with the differential capacity for bodily integrity and flourishing.[30] If violence is materially productive of such differential value and capacity, this is because the *productivity of violence* enacted against differentiated groups manufactures the facticity of race as an epistemological category, such that it may function alternately as a cause or a justification of that violence. The will to know certain forms of violence as racial (or not) can thus be understood as a complex dialectical outcome of race radical social movements at the same time as it functions as an epistemological perspective that has become central, if not necessary, to neoliberal racial capitalism. On one hand, as an artifact of early twentieth century campaigns against lynching and mid-century black and anticolonial freedom struggles, it has continued to provide conceptual and political ground for understanding the causes of violence and remains a critical tool in redressing and resisting the afterlife of slavery, colonialism, and genocide. On the other hand, when generalized as a will to know, it bears a tendency to abstract race and violence from their material and structural determinations, augmenting the "normative and rationalizing power" of official antiracisms "that have extended racialization procedures beyond color lines" under contemporary racial capitalism.[31]

It is not in itself problematic that the legal standard for determining Oak Creek as an act of racial violence requires evidence that Page perceived racial difference yet requires no evidence that he interpreted that difference correctly (i.e., that he knew his victims would be Sikh). Indeed, the inclusion of the provision for "perceived" difference in hate crime law is necessary to protecting vulnerable identities from violence insofar as it shifts the burden of proof from the violated to the violator. Within this framework, the victim does not have to demonstrate his or her difference, but only that a perceived difference was the cause of his or her violation. If a violated body is socially perceived as different, it can be presumed that the perpetrator perceives such difference whether or not he knows what that difference means. In the case of Oak Creek, the important point is that the shootings only *become* a racial matter once the fact of the Sikh victims' difference is socially registered, which is precisely and immediately what precipitates an exploration of Page's perception of difference, or what antidiscrimination law codifies as his racism. What he sees is less important than the fact that it is race *as it exhibits itself on the body* that motivated his act. It thus goes without saying that had the victims' racial difference not been registered socially, there would be no question of this being racial violence, and hence no need to excavate the racial causes of the act.

This has been the default approach not only to Oak Creek but to mass shootings in general and represents a tightly bound web of institutionalized assumptions about race, knowledge, interpretation, and individual/social perception. It takes for granted an epistemological and temporal distinction between raced bodies and their interpretation, as if perception were a given physiological capacity that precedes interpretation. Such an approach presupposes that all persons perceive the same thing when they see specific human bodies because what they perceive is a body's racial difference that is ontological, outside history, and not already the outcome of socially constituted interpretive practices. Insofar as a human body can be presumed to universally signify and exist outside of interpretation, the bodily signification of difference becomes naturalized, which functions as the effective disavowal— social constructionist or not—of the legal and social manufacture of bodies and interpretive practices that are presumed to exist in nature. But *if* we all perceive the same thing, it is not because perception is a natural physiolog-ical capacity but rather because practices of visuality are embedded in forms of disciplinary power and knowledge that teach us how to see by constituting the perception of what is presumed to exist outside of it.[32] Put differently, efforts to redress racial violence that mistake interpretation for perception ironically transmute the sociopolitical into the biological. The idea that interpretation sequentially follows perception, and as such is an individual matter of reading bodies that signify prior to such interpretation, simulta-neously naturalizes race while turning its hierarchical ordering into an aber-ration that can be educated out of existence.[33] But, as Jodi Melamed argues, race comes into being as an effect of "materially produced discourses that both constitute and are determined by the historically specific material cir-cumstances and geohistorical conditions for which they offer comprehen-sion and sense making."[34]

By implicitly endowing race with a prediscursive life, the positivist ap-proach risks implicitly naturalizing the violence it often seeks to contest by identifying race as its *cause,* according to which race functions as an expla-nation rather than a formation and epistemology that needs to be explained.[35] This is not to contest an insight central to work in critical race studies: that racial signification automatically grants or precludes access to civilian status that produces not just differential capacities for life and death but also differ-ential grounds for political struggle. It is rather to suggest that—however vex-ing within struggles against racism, colonialism, and genocide—materialist accounts of violence that do not rely on race as cause (even when we *know* race to be the cause) are necessary for constituting forms of critical analysis and political struggle adequate to contemporary formations of racial capital-ism, whose capacities for endless value extraction depend on the production, commodification, and naturalization of the very differences understood to precede it.

By way of exemplification, it is worth examining the Oak Creek shoot-ings in relation to a far more publicly mediated mass shooting that occurred just five months later. On December 14, 2012, after shooting and killing his mother in her home, Adam Lanza killed twenty children and six staff mem-bers at Sandy Hook Elementary School in Newtown, Connecticut. Despite their temporal proximity, some observers avoided discussing the shootings in relation to one another, in part not to conflate the differences between instances of violence understood to be different in kind: on one hand, a racially motivated hate crime, and on the other, a more difficult to explain instance of abhorrent and pathological mass gun violence. For many anti-racist activists and commentators, however, it was precisely the differences between them that demanded recognition. In this view, the proximity of the Newtown shootings and the attention they received elided the specificity of what happened at Oak Creek. Not only did the attention paid to Newtown preclude the possibility of making connections between militarism, Islamophobia, racial violence, and U.S. foreign policy. Making matters worse, the public and media focus on Newtown at the cost of Oak Creek effectively functioned as a denial of the persistence of U.S. racism—in the forgetting of the Sikh victims of white supremacist violence—and a typical enactment of racism—in the privileged valuation of white lives as more worthy of grieving.[36]

Accordingly, in the wake of the Newtown shootings, antiracist critique was generally concerned with exposing and resisting the tendency to allow a focus on Newtown (and the phenomenon of mass shootings more generally) to obscure the racially differential vulnerability of people of color to gun violence.[37] I point this out not to suggest that either the elision of differential vulnerability to violence or the differences between these shootings are insignificant. Neither do I wish to contest the claim that the murder of white children at Newtown gave many an alibi for ignoring the difficult questions raised by Oak Creek. Instead, my interest is in how the claim that Oak Creek is exceptional replicates the liberal nationalist narrative that distinguishes between the particularity of racial violence and the general character of mass shootings as a problem for all civilians. This does not mean we should deracialize Oak Creek so that it can be compared with Newtown as a more general form of violence. Rather, it means that we rethink the racialized structural and affective conditions of possibility that articulate the shootings at Oak Creek and Newtown. In other words, making the epistemological choice to examine mass shootings as a problem of racial capitalism requires us to read the latter through the former, putting on hold a reading that distinguishes between them on the basis of their racial or nonracial character. It asks us to generalize racial violence as a hermeneutic category, which allows us to bring into focus the historically contingent character of civilian life.

Once we place under scrutiny the analytic function of racial violence as a positivist descriptor, we are forced to adopt a different perspective. It is not that neither of these acts was racist, but that such forms of mass violence in the contemporary moment—Newtown no less than Oak Creek, but Oak Creek for different reasons than might be expected—cannot be other than instances and outcomes of racial capitalism. If the critique of the "mistaken identity" explanation for Oak Creek brings into relief the material convergence of U.S. empire, war making, and Islamophobia, reading Oak Creek and Newtown relationally requires bracketing what we know about the identity of the victims. In this way, the suspension of racial perception/visibility as a causal explanation can bring into view *race* as the articulating mechanism that makes such massacres possible while uniting them as a form. One useful way of doing so would be a materialist analysis of the affective structure of Page's racism. However, rather than a search for individual motives to explain the cause of Page's act—which in Lanza's case would lead us nowhere—such an analysis attempts to excavate the wide proliferation of its affective structure as material *social* consciousness by situating it within the accumulation regime that makes it possible.

While the Islamophobia harbored by a U.S. military veteran provides a clue to understanding why Page would plan his shooting at a gurdwara, there is a wider set of interlocking anxieties capturing Page's consciousness, suggesting that the affective structure of the mass shooting both overdetermines and outstrips its particular instantiation at Oak Creek. Far less discussed than Islamophobia after the shooting was Page's documented antipathy toward *blackness*: that is, not simply hatred of black people, but antagonism toward blackness as a capacious racial threat whose infiltration of the state has augured the state's delinking from the (white) nation. In other words, if the law demands a motive, an equally compelling explanation is that the shootings were driven by Page's revanchist anti-statism. Mobilized by and as resistance to the black freedom struggle, this can be understood as an ethos of white masculinist victimhood against the perceived special treatment received by black people as represented by anti-discrimination law, the legal protection of racial and sexual identities in hate crimes law, and more generally the mythical power of black people and Muslims in manipulating the levers of an officially multicultural state, from affirmative action to the implementation of sharia law.[38] And while it is undeniable that each of these accounts is necessary to thinking through the determinants of Oak Creek, the affective structure that undergirds Page's act should be understood as constituted by a dense social articulation of antiblackness and anti-Muslim racism that is itself made possible by U.S. settler-colonial sovereignty. In other words, what becomes clear is that when limited to a view that reads Sikh people as potential victims of violence because they appear as Muslims, antiblackness and U.S. empire as material and affective determining structures become obscured from analytical purview.

Likewise, if we take for granted that as a military veteran Page believed he was doing the work of the U.S. state by killing Muslims, we ignore that Oak Creek fits into a long tradition of state *and* nonstate violence against indigenous and black people that has functioned to draw the boundaries of civil society by designating who would be abandoned to its outside.[39] Indeed, we need not rely on a white nationalist manifesto or the lyrics of a song by a neo-Nazi rock band to make the strong claim that Page understood himself as a self-conscripted soldier, defending the racial nation against threats to its freedom and health, imagining that he was doing the work of which the multicultural U.S. state was incapable.[40] This form of anti-statism has deep material sources, and it cannot be reduced to the libertarian wing of the Republican Party or the Cato Institute's wealthy donors anymore than it can be individualized as Page's.[41]

If the affective disposition of a single mass shooter might be elaborated as the normative outcome of materially produced social knowledge about race, then we need to understand the specific articulation of anti-statism, antiblackness, and empire as a structure of feeling, an "actively lived and felt" social experience.[42] Only by conceptualizing this articulation as a social and historical phenomenon can we begin to understand how it operates as a condition of possibility for mass shootings in relation to, and no less than, the quotidian "life support systems that sustain terror and bare life [and] which frequently appear in more benign forms of political control."[43] By the same token, reading mass shootings in their structural relation to violence under racial capitalism provides an important framework for apprehending what is specific about the affective structure of race in the U.S. neoliberal state. In this formation, the articulation of antiblackness and anti-statism under the U.S. settler-colonial empire conjures figures of threat to an ideal biopolitical flourishing. Such flourishing is not only seen as no longer guaranteed by the state. It is understood as actively harmed by the state insofar as the state is corrupted by race: a broad conception that articulates and refashions an array of threats—most crucially blackness, indigeneity, and Islam—into a figure of the enemy combatant. Contemporary anti-statism as a discursive practice of dispossession evokes the endless search for, and thus the perception and mobility of, racial threats to the nation. Such threats might adhere not only to a variety of racially marked bodies but also the public spaces inhabited by them, including persons whose previously protected civilian status goes unrecognized by a form of private sovereignty enacting the history and logic of antiblack and settler-colonial violence. Mass shootings should thus be understood as a phenomenon of racialized nonstate violence that both ramifies and throws into crisis the accumulation regime and affective structure of the U.S. neoliberal state.

ANTIBLACK ANTI-STATISM AND PRIVATIZED SOVEREIGNTY

In developing an understanding of mass shootings as a nonstate form of violence that bears a structural relation to the neoliberal state, I point to four fundamental transformations that organize contemporary spatial-social life in the United States—the historical emergence of which can be dated across the years 1968 and 1979. First, the expansion of the capacity and technology of state violence by the U.S. military, the police, and the criminal justice apparatus. Second, the successes of the attack on the Keynesian state's capacity to provide for the social welfare, economic security, and ideal flourishing of its population, achieved through the uneven privatization of public space and institutions that were previously understood as a measure of commitment to a "common good"—even if the common good has itself always been an exclusive category. Third, the spatial reorganization articulated on these shifts that has facilitated the circulation of violence and degradation between gentrifying urban ghettoes and a growing network of prisons and jails both everywhere and entirely hidden from view. Fourth, the seemingly increasing frequency of mass shootings of civilians committed by civilians and other nonstate actors.[44] There has been an invaluable field of scholarship that has worked out the relation between the first three elements.[45] Building on this work, I suggest the importance of thinking these elements together as having a structural relationship, one in which race operates not simply as a by-product or justificatory procedure but as its central articulating mechanism.

Gilmore has argued that the first three elements—the expansion of the state's capacity for violence, the attack on the state's social functions, and the militarized reordering of space—constitute the basic characteristics of the neoliberal state, or what she generatively calls the "anti-state state."[46] The racialized attack on Keynesian forms of social investment, suburban tax revolts, and resistance to racial remediation, combined with the 1970s debt crisis, generated a surplus of state capacity, the legitimate deployment of which was found in the increasing militarization of municipal police forces and the eventual explosion in prison construction. Because the postwar liberal state had for upward of two decades been incentivizing and subsidizing a perversely self-regenerating cycle of suburban migration and urban isolation, such surplus state capacity was not just unevenly distributed spatially and racially. The militarization of police forces by the late 1960s and the ensuing run on prison construction in the 1980s and 1990s became central to the ongoing process of spatially and racially reconstructing cities, suburbs, and rural hinterlands all over the United States, fortifying the boundaries between enclaves of capital investment and abandonment; between what Loïc Wacquant calls the "prison-ghetto nexus" and the privatized spaces of luxurious consumption increasingly sprouting not just in suburbs but in urban districts formerly marked for "renewal."[47]

Even at the time, it was clear to many that this emergent transformation and recalibration of state power was a new racial and spatial project elaborated as an appeal to law and order, authority, and traditional values. It was launched in the face of radical and revolutionary struggles manifesting in a multitude of novel forms of social collectivity, organization, and imaginative visions of alternative ways of flourishing—what Stefano Harney and Fred Moten describe as "an operation from above designed to break up the means of social reproduction and make them directly productive for capital."[48] That is, the U.S. neoliberal state as a contradictory and dialectical formation emerged out of the racialized criminalization of black political militancy, cross racial movements against U.S. colonial and imperial power, and working-class struggles for economic justice, security, and basic human flourishing.

As a counterinsurgency, it was mobilized and sustained by the post–civil rights success at figuring the state as undone from the nation—as corrupted by race and black in its corruption—even as black communities were increasingly being devastated by all that seemed left of the state: a bloated and nightmarish criminal justice apparatus and the largest prison construction project in the history of the world.[49] But the conflation of race and the state was not simply a dissimulation of the state's vicious criminalization of blackness. By representing black protest and resistance as extortionist, it functioned as a revanchist discursive force that helped fashion what Stuart Hall termed the "exceptional state," a hegemonic form whose emergent coherence was grounded in a cross-class belief that blackness and the heterogeneous social movements for which it came to stand were existential threats to social order.[50] This anti-state state generalized criminalization as the preeminent form of racialized class power undergirding a new era of capital accumulation, producing coercive new forms of surveillance, containment, and population management as necessary to the defense of an increasingly privatized and atomistic vision of civil society.

Bearing a dialectical relation with the midcentury black freedom struggle, antiblack anti-statism has long been an effective force of economic and political management and control, crystallizing at decisive moments in legal and political history: accruing significant cultural power following the Supreme Court's 1954 desegregation order and achieving so powerful a materialization in the context of civil rights legislation that it became a constitutive element of neoliberal white masculinity. Chester Himes adroitly captures the irony of this productive dissimulation in *Cotton Comes to Harlem* (1965). Early in the novel, two white New York Police Department officers patrol a "back to Africa" rally of black folk in a fenced-in and denuded vacant lot in Harlem, when one officer casually offers a by then common sense diagnosis that seems more than blatantly at odds with the scene on display: "This country is being run by niggers."[51] Three years later Lyndon B. Johnson signed into law what was at the time the most significant federal crime legislation in U.S. history, the Omnibus Crime Control and Safe Streets Act (1968), an officially antiracist biopolitical measure that provided millions of dollars for the rationalization and militarization of federal and municipal police forces across the United States.

The emergence of this formation as a racially articulated conjuncture can be productively situated if we locate contemporary nonstate mass shootings within a genealogy that includes a watershed episode of state killing whose rationalization helped usher in and manufacture the legitimacy of the antistate state. On September 13, 1971, New York state troopers stormed the Attica Correctional Facility and opened fire, killing twenty-nine prisoners and ten prison guards. Simultaneously *mass shooting* and *counterinsurgency op,* this move came in response to an impasse following the takeover of the prison four days earlier by a multiracial coalition of prisoners demanding the state's acknowledgement of their political subjectivity. In the words of the state commission charged with investigating Attica, "with the exception of Indian massacres in the late 19th century, the State Police assault which ended the four-day prison uprising was the bloodiest one-day encounter between Americans since the Civil War."[52] As I have suggested elsewhere, with this deployment of "exception," the commission unwittingly located Attica within the long history of efforts to constitute U.S. state and civil society through the managed exclusion of those that have been understood as exceptions to the norms of liberal governance: the Indian and the slave.[53]

Indeed, in the scramble to rationalize the massacre, state actors on the scene circulated a fabricated story in which the prison rebels had castrated the white prison guards and stuffed their genitals into the guards' mouths before slaughtering them, "Mau Mau style" (in the words of New York's deputy commissioner of corrections).[54] Framing prisoners as primitives and savage barbarians, unable to abide by the rules of civilized warfare, this story effortlessly evoked a narrative structure for reading criminality as auguring a state of exception, a narrative that has been continuously deployed to rationalize U.S. territorial conquest and imperialist warfare, from Indian removal on the Western frontier to Cold War counterinsurgency in Southeast Asia, Africa, and Central America, according to which it was the "savages" who raped, tortured, scalped, and mutilated.[55] It was not simply that the state categorically refused to recognize the prisoners as political subjects, but rather that their claim to such status was sufficiently threatening to justify the invocation of emergency conditions that had already effectively been in place, from which perspective the state was authorized to kill without regard to legal and civil protections.

Antiblack anti-statism should be conceptualized as a flexible and materially effective discursive practice of neoliberal state formation: the frontline instrument that would literally clear space for the construction of a new state-capital formation, the fulcrum for what David Harvey refers to as accumulation by dispossession. This perspective allows us to revise the dominant account of the relation between prison growth and neoliberalism. It is not that the militarization of the police and the proliferation of prisons emerged historically in order to contain the fallout of deindustrialization, transnational free-trade agreements, and the massive dispossession and upward distribution of social wealth constitutive of the structural adjustment of the U.S. state. It is rather that the historical and material conditions of possibility for neoliberalism reside in the mass criminalization and confinement of the populations most deeply affected and displaced by the privatization of public spaces and institutions.[56]

The immense surge in the use of bodily immobilization and confinement as a primary form of global social exclusion is the single most critical example of how racism operates, not as an unfortunate symptom or residual element of the uneven neoliberalization of the state, but as the foundation on which such a state formation depends. The ability of race to sustain the class divisions this state formation constitutes is dependent on the social invisibility of race as an active and materially effective force of wealth and value distribution. Anti-statism's reliance on race is precisely what enables the naturalization of material inequalities organized by capital, producing a pernicious idea of blackness as parasitic on the state and the social body, symbolized most potently by the twin figures of the criminal and the welfare queen.[57]

While the dense figuration of blackness as simultaneously (illegitimate) power, corruption, and threat has sustained the neoliberal state and its regime of privatization and mass incarceration, it might also be understood as the structure of feeling animating recent killing sprees at Oak Creek, Charleston, as well as Newtown. Insofar as it is understood as a form of *social experience,* viewing antiblack anti-statism as a structure of feeling places critical analysis on the terrain of social "meanings and values as they are actively lived and felt."[58] This is to say that mass shooters are more than simply racist. They are vectors of and for contemporary racial capitalism, whose uncontrollable violence dialectically elicits the state's liberal nationalist claims to protect "civilian life" through the strengthening of its police and military powers. Viewing mass shooters as such forces us to think about mass shootings as a phenomenon having a historically specific social subjectivity in which the vigilante or rogue as nonstate actor necessarily takes "his motive to the grave."[59] The frantic search for a motive that cannot be found is what obscures the social logic of violence. This is not to argue that racist beliefs or optics are unimportant but that they are not the only (or the most effective) way of conceptualizing the racialized dynamics of mass shootings. To say that Oak Creek and Newtown share a social subjectivity is to say that Oak Creek has as much in common with Newtown as a specific form of violence emergent within the contemporary social formation as it does with traditional forms of racist violence, such as lynching and firebombing.

The decisive difference is that mass shootings are a nonstate or illegitimate form of violence that the law actively seeks to punish, insofar as it infringes on the state's monopoly on violence, whereas most violent forms of racial boundary maintenance have historically been state-sanctioned (even when extralegal). Rather than viewing this violence as a disturbing trend having to do with America's romance with guns or the lack of attention to mental health, we might instead read mass shootings as examples of a kind of redistribution of power in which private citizens are increasingly invested with the capacity for sovereign violence—the power to decide who should live and who should die, for demarcating zones of protection and vulnerability, thus assuming the task of martially defending a biopolitical flourishing that the state, in its racial corruption, is actively felt as incapable of securing.

It may be the case that this capacity to decide on the life and death of others has much to do with guns and mental illness, but not necessarily because Americans have a primordial attachment to guns or from a failure to treat the mentally ill.[60] From a materialist perspective, rather, this privatized sovereign violence is enabled by an uncanny convergence between a massive supply of firearms (and thus their almost unrestricted availability); a veritable epidemic of mental illness driven as much by the pharmaceutical industry as by the anomic conditions of life under neoliberalism; and an antiblack anti-statism that has facilitated a frontal attack on the existence— indeed the very idea—of public space and public institutions. The attack on public space has taken a variety of material and epistemological forms, but what the recent spate of school shootings shares with urban gentrification, "stop and frisk," "broken windows," and "zero tolerance" policing, and the transformation of inner city schools from institutions of normalization to mass-criminalization, is the *arrogation of the right of incursion* on the lives and livelihoods of the people who depend on and dwell in such spaces. The arrogation of this right is productive of the quotidian fear and terror experienced in racialized space, which may never be admissible as evidence or testimony to the routine practices of violence attendant on policy.[61]

If it is possible and permissible to think of Eric Garner's cry before his legal murder at the hands of the NYPD—"I can't breathe"—as the most literal testimony to such arrogation possible, then we might think of this arrogation itself as the political unconscious of the protest movement against police brutality that has taken up Garner's cry as a refrain. It would be a mistake to imagine as accidental that an era in which the privatization of public space and institutions has been a central imperative of neoliberal state formation has also been witness to a new generalized vulnerability to violence experienced on urban sidewalks, in public institutions from schools to prisons, and in spaces of religious and community gathering.[62] Crucially, this felicitous convergence has elicited calls for the increased *fortification* of such spaces, which tends to further blur the distinction between public and private, and between civilian, police, and soldier. Just as the discourse of so-called "black-on-black violence" has facilitated a neoconservative antiracism that demands more muscular police presence in the ghetto and the right to disperse the gathering of individuals in public spaces, one of the major responses to the Newtown massacre has been the call to arm the faculty and staff of public schools as a means towards *preventing* violence.[63]

Like mass shootings in general, privatized sovereignty as a mode of policing and fortifying space is in itself not new. It is a recalibration of Marx's "so-called primitive accumulation" as the ongoing condition of racial capitalism. On one hand, it is a derivation of the violent seizure and enclosure of indigenous land, which invested settlers with a sovereign capacity to kill if it could be proven (i.e., asserted) after the fact that the peoples holding prior claims to the land exhibited resistance that could be construed as having unofficially declared war. On the other hand, it is a reconfiguration of the police power under slavery, according to which freepersons were de facto deputized and invested with the sovereign right to kill if they could prove ex post facto that it was in the interest of self-defense, protecting property, or that the victim was suspected of being a slave.[64]

As the discursive criminalization of Garner, Sandra Bland, Michael Brown, Trayvon Martin, and Walter Scott reminds us, it is not that the capacity of the state to protect civilian life has yet to be fully extended to the most vulnerable among us. Rather, the formation of the U.S. state has historically constituted such vulnerability as an outcome of "the practical concern: how to both defend and legitimate a social order built on ongoing murder and dispossession, that is, the theft of black labor and indigenous lands."[65] Indeed, how does one make sense of the fact that these particular state-sanctioned killings could command national attention as exemplary instances of racial violence without the corresponding ability to legally redress them as such, except to conclude that violence inflicted on black bodies is always already sanctioned by the law: that the logical presumption of guilt embedded in the law's discursive architecture turns the victims into threats and the killers into victims?

But while the history of racial domination accrues in the constitution of sovereign power as whiteness, the too-easy slippage between race and ontology can elide as much as it illuminates about the conjunctural determinations of violence.[66] More precisely, it obscures the complex and often contradictory process through which post–civil rights legal norms, police power, and racial identities themselves have been constituted both as an effect of, and in resistance to, the necessarily protracted black radical and anticolonial struggles to expose premature death as a historical condition of racialized embodiment. The insistence on the dialectics of this transition is crucial if we are to elaborate forms and methods of analysis that appreciate the specific ways the resistance struggles of the oppressed have persistently shaped the constitution of power, such that we might appreciate both the granularity of social change and the specific conditions of the present moment. If a materialist antiracism is to move effectively beyond legalistic and moralizing claims about racist individuals and toward a strategic approach that seeks to engage power rather than disdain it as criminal or malevolent, then historical time cannot be understood as a zero-sum game illustrating either transcendent moral progress or the persistent replication of domination in novel frameworks, but instead as a brittle accumulation of victories and defeats that are always provisional and uncertain. And as the Black Lives Matter movement has most recently demonstrated, the capacity to achieve the legal recognition of the value of black life depends on struggles that are irreducible to law or policy. In other words, it is one part of a broader communizing struggle over the development and defense of the means, spaces, and material capacities to be able to do more than just live in the first place.[67]

RESISTING THE EXCEPTIONALISM OF RACIAL VIOLENCE

It is fair to recognize that this inquiry places critical race analysis on thorny terrain. It would be dangerous to gainsay the everyday lived reality for specifically targeted populations in the United States today, the subjects of which are forced into a persistent reckoning with how to comport themselves in such a way so as to avoid becoming the object of violence as a result of their racial, gender, and/or sexual identity. Complicating matters is that just as identity-based social movements have succeeded in diminishing the prevalence of certain forms of state-sanctioned violence, the proliferation of state and nonstate violence affecting black, indigenous, brown, and trans people today can be understood as a reaction to such success—indeed, an effect and index of the massive resistance to liberal nationalist forms of inclusion. It is also critical to acknowledge that the shootings at Oak Creek reflect the fact that a similar danger to that faced by black people and Muslims has also been experienced by Sikhs, members of a small but highly visible racialized religious community that has been increasingly subject to "hate violence" since 9/11. Indeed, in the wake of Newtown and the more recent resurgence of an openly aggrieved and wounded white nationalism among the poor and working class, claims about the excessive vulnerability to violence of black people, Sikhs, Muslims, and others that signify as South Asian and Middle Eastern, are likely to be dismissed in some contexts as, at best, irrationally race-conscious, and at worst, racist. But even if it is the dismissal of these claims that antiracist analysis should work to contest, this essay has suggested that such a contestation cannot be successful if it is content to rely on empirical evidence demonstrating such claims.

Indeed, a recognition of the intensification of "group-differentiated vulnerability to premature death" in the post–civil rights U.S. neoliberal state is inhibited not by a lack of evidence or knowledge but by a legalistic and progressive vision of the history of the last forty years to be a series of social achievements in tolerance and inclusion—a widening of the orbit of civil society—rather than one of increased poverty, criminalization, urban apartheid, spatial fortification, and both generalized as well as group-differentiated precarity. That this liberal nationalist vision participates in precisely the same disavowal of dispossession as does antiblack anti-statism suggests that they are equally animated by a racialized structure of feeling that is insulated from facts and, as such, perversely reads abjection as power. As a result, I have been arguing that an emphasis on making the facts of racial violence empirically visible without attention to the affective dimensions of antiblackness and U.S. empire that structure and frame such knowledge might be seen as the discursive constraint of a politics that, in the words of Barbara Jeanne Fields, seeks "the reallocation of unemployment, poverty and injustice rather than their *abolition*."[68]

By the same token, any dismissal of the historically shifting, contingent, and complex articulation of antiblackness, U.S. empire, anti-Muslim racism, and anti-Sikh violence can only take place if one imagines race ontologically as a fixed structure across modernity, rather than as an active formation itself productive of new orders of violence and histories of struggle. Nonmaterialist accounts that obscure the *relational precariousness* of racialized life are belied by the fact that we live in an era in which the U.S. state itself has become increasingly committed to using violence on its own as well as on foreign populations, while the state's capacity for protecting even the most narrow vision of the social from violence, suffering, and deprivation has not just receded under the weight of global ecological crises but has come under vicious and willful attack. It thus comes as little surprise that all types of racially differentiated bodies and populations may be more vulnerable to violence than they were forty years ago. Under such conditions, even as the violence inflicted on and the value exacted from black and brown bodies continues to structure the material, social, and spatial ordering of the U.S. state, one of the shifts that the recent proliferation of mass shootings as a form of violence demonstrates is that even signifying as white does not guarantee one's civilian status under contemporary racial capitalism.

To claim the historical specificity of race as an articulating mechanism and structuring force requires the consideration of how historical struggles against racism have reshaped the operations of racial capitalism and the procedures through which the dialectic of biopolitical flourishing and premature death are effected and rationalized in the contemporary United States. In the case of gun violence, at issue today is to what extent, and according to what means and rationalities, does privatized sovereignty constitute new orders of protection and vulnerability that exceed all normative injunctions and legal imperatives of a *formally antiracist state*. It may be that what we have been witnessing as the neoliberalization of the U.S. state is a biopolitical transformation in which the growth in the state's capacity for total violence to foster zones of flourishing on a global scale is paradoxically shadowed by, even productive of, its inability to control the terms by which legitimate violence is defined and enacted. And if there is an instructive difference between the mass shootings at Oak Creek and Newtown that finally needs to be accounted for, it might be seen in light of this paradox, which puts a new angle on what Chandan Reddy has described as "the limits of violence to foreclose, obliterate, or fully encompass that upon which it manifests."[69]

Many have argued that the Oak Creek victims did not receive the same kind of attention as those at Newtown because Sikhs are thought of as outside the imagined community of the nation. The implication is that the national response to the shootings was a subtle but unequivocal replication of the racist optic of the shooter. But perhaps we should consider that the muted response to the shootings evinces instead a generalized anxiety with the vision of a white racial nation that Page was attempting to defend—a liberal nationalist anxiety that by no means signals the end of white supremacy, and indeed is likely to facilitate the production of new hierarchies of value according to novel categorizations of the deserving and undeserving. Even so, it may well be the case that Page never gave up his identity as a soldier, that his racial optic was shaped by his experience in the military, and that he saw himself as performing the mission of which a multicultural state was incapable. In this sense, what Oak Creek exposed is the overdetermination of such acts of violence within the context of U.S. empire and the complicity between discourses of racial nationalism and liberal multiculturalism by which it is constituted. If Oak Creek was in this sense an exceptional mass shooting, then the response to Oak Creek suggests a disavowal that certain groups have been rendered vulnerable to such violence by the practices of U.S. empire. But it is also clear that Oak Creek—like the massacre at Emanuel AME Church—is an exception to the generality of racism in U.S. culture, precisely because it can be legally and positively identified as racism. There tends not to be handy a psychotic white supremacist with which to explain realities such as differences in life expectancy, wealth inequality, residential segregation, disparities in educational achievement, and mass incarceration. And more often than not, those on whom legitimate state violence is exercised are not understood as objects of violence because of their racial identity but because of their legal or political status: criminal, terrorist, insurgent, Islamist. If most forms of racism are not legible to the law, Oak Creek is exceptional insofar as the racism of the massacre can hardly be denied.

On one hand, Oak Creek is exceptional from other iterations of gun violence, and on the other, it is exceptional from other forms of racism. This double exceptionalism is finally what it shares with the most recent spate of state-sanctioned killings by police, which is distinct not in its frequency but rather in the publicity it has garnered at a moment in which the U.S. state form is increasingly in crisis. The fact of their exceptionalism is crucial to acknowledge because it demonstrates the slipperiness of an antiracist politics grounded in a liberal positivist conception of racial violence. Taking Oak Creek or antiblack police violence as demonstrative of the persistence of racial violence in the United States puts us at risk of facilitating the erasure of the antiblack and settler-colonial foundations of the U.S. neoliberal state that have been the condition of possibility for the shootings at Newtown no less than they were at Oak Creek. Not only does such an approach facilitate a reading of what constitutes racial violence as self-evident and in no need of theorization outside of liberalism's legal and political categories. It also reifies the operations of a particular kind of violence as something unconnected to quotidian forms of social constitution and bodily degradation under neoliberal racial capitalism. Such moves unwittingly risk ratifying a broader tendency to neglect the capacity of racial capitalism to shape the lives of everyone at the most fundamental levels of existence: from how we feel, to where we dwell, whether we can exist in public without being detained and searched, whether or not we will spend much of our life in a cage, and when and under what conditions we live and die.

Clearly, this is not to argue that "exceptional" forms of violence do not deserve the attention of critical ethnic studies. Instead, we might continue to construct forms of analysis and response that resist their exceptionalism. Rather than see Oak Creek as exceptional to the shootings either in Newtown or on the streets of Chicago on any given day, we might more effectively revalue its victims while advancing the purview of critical ethnic studies if we think about what articulates these forms of violence. Rather than thinking through the lenses of analogy or comparison, we might work toward theorizing what common conditions give rise to them and what knowledge systems, ways of thinking, and epistemological orientations obscure these articulations from view. Rather than thinking about the mass murder of civilians as abstracted from the myriad ways in which racial capitalism differentially structures everyday life, we might think about Oak Creek *and* Newtown in their articulation not only to the everyday of racial subjection under U.S. empire but also in the everyday of mass incarceration and the regime of spatial privatization and enclosure that regularly strips persons of their social and civilian status. Such realities may at first seem unrelated, only available to comparison or analogy, but opening up the question of their articulation might yield insights for which we were not prepared and offer an important perspective for abolitionist and antiviolence struggles. And because this is a knowledge practice invested in forming social articulations rather than reproducing the very differentiations that such violence enacts, a collaborative project of resisting such exceptionalism might allow us to experience unexpected moments of flourishing.

ANOOP MIRPURI is assistant professor of English and affiliate faculty in black studies at Portland State University.

NOTES

1. Ta-Nehisi Coates, "Take Down the Confederate Flag—Now," *Atlantic,* June 18, 2015, http://www.theatlantic.com/politics/archive/2015/06/take-down-the-confeder ate-flag-now/396290/.

2. Emily Yahr, "Read Jon Stewart's Blistering Monologue about Race, Terrorism and Gun Violence after Charleston Church Massacre," *Washington Post,* June 19, 2015, https://www.washingtonpost.com/news/style-blog/wp/2015/06/19/read-jon-stew arts-blistering-monologue-about-race-terrorism-and-gun-violence-after-charles ton-church-massacre/.

3. While the conception of whiteness as *deputized* builds on Nikhil Singh's understanding of the relation between whiteness and the police power, the formulation itself is indebted to the work of Frank Wilderson. This essay, however, follows Singh's conceptualization of whiteness as a formation irreducible to white people. Nikhil Pal Singh, "The Whiteness of Police," *American Quarterly* 66, no. 4 (2014): 1091–99; Frank B. Wilderson III, "The Prison Slave as Hegemony's (Silent) Scandal," in *Warfare in the American Homeland: Policing and Prison in a Penal Democracy,* ed. Joy James (Durham: Duke University Press, 2007), 25.

4. On the U.S. state and "official antiracisms," see Jodi Melamed, *Represent and Destroy: Rationalizing Violence in the New Racial Capitalism* (Minneapolis: University of Minnesota Press, 2011).

5. Inderpal Grewal has made the connection between mass shootings and what she calls "racial sovereignty." While this essay complements her central claim, it departs from her in two ways. First, it highlights the centrality of antiblackness and settler colonialism to anti-statism as a structure of feeling. Second, it emphasizes the nonstate character of mass shootings and thus the importance of *nonstate violence* in constituting racial governance in the United States as an officially antiracist state. See Inderpal Grewal, "Racial Sovereignty and 'Shooter' Violence: Oak Creek Massacre, Normative Citizenship and the State," *Sikh Formations* 9, no. 2 (2013): 187–97.

6. As Walter Benjamin suggests, the category of the civilian is grounded in distinctions organizing political modernity: between law and violence, civil society and states of exception, politics and warfare. While the critique of these distinctions emerges almost as soon as their founding, anticolonialism and black radicalism has sought less to theorize their indistinction than their necessary coexistence and spatial/ontological division of colonial modernity. See Walter Benjamin, "Critique of Violence," in *Reflections*, trans. Edmund Jephcott (New York: Schocken Books, 1986); Ned Blackhawk, *Violence Over the Land: Indians and Empires in the Early American West* (Cambridge, Mass.: Harvard University Press, 2006); Jodi Byrd, *The Transit of Empire: Indigenous Critiques of Colonialism* (Minneapolis: University of Minnesota Press, 2011); Franz Fanon, *Wretched of the Earth* (New York: Grove Press, 1993); Achille Mbembe, "Necropolitics," *Public Culture* 15, no. 1 (2003); Jared Sexton, "People-of-Color-Blindness: Notes on the Afterlife of Slavery," *Social Text* 28, no. 2 (2010): 36–37; Frank B. Wilderson III, *Red, White & Black: Cinema and the Structure of U.S. Antagonisms* (Durham: Duke University Press, 2010).

7. Stefano Harney and Fred Moten, *The Undercommons: Fugitive Planning and Black Study* (New York: Minor Compositions, 2013); Melamed, *Represent and Destroy*; Chandan Reddy, *Freedom with Violence: Race, Sexuality, and the US State* (Durham: Duke University Press, 2011); Nikhil Singh, "Racial Formation in an Age of Permanent War," *Racial Formation in the Twenty-First Century*, ed. Daniel Martinez HoSang et al. (Berkeley: University of California Press, 2012), 276–301.

8. Michel Foucault, *"Society Must Be Defended": Lectures at the College de France, 1975–1976*, trans. David Macey (New York: Picador, 2003), 254; Michel Foucault, *The History of Sexuality: An Introduction, Volume 1*, trans. Robert Hurley (New York: Vintage, 1990), 88–89, 92–102.

9. Jodi Melamed, "Racial Capitalism," *Critical Ethnic Studies* 1, no. 1 (2015): 76–85.

10. Drawing on a rich tradition of black and critical race Marxism, this approach is a contribution to the collective project of theorizing how a twentieth-century history of race radical struggles has altered the relation between the historical capacity for flourishing and positivist conceptions of race. See Barbara Jeanne Fields, "Slavery, Race, and Ideology in the United States of America," *New Left Review* 181 (May–June 1990): 95–118; Ruth Wilson Gilmore, *Golden Gulag: Prisons, Surplus, Crisis, and Opposition in Globalizing California* (Berkeley: University of California Press, 2007); Robin D. G. Kelley, *Race Rebels: Culture, Politics, and the Black Working Class* (New York: Free Press, 1996); Cedric Robinson, *Black Marxism: The Making of the Black Radical Tradition* (Chapel Hill: University of North Carolina Press, 1983); Nikhil Pal Singh, *Black Is a Country: Race and the Unfinished Struggle for Democracy* (Cambridge, Mass.: Harvard University Press, 2004).

11. The argument can be made that mass shootings might not be understood as a phenomenon without the vast media attention given to them; that their cultural significance is far greater than their historical or sociological significance. There is in fact no consensus on whether there has been an increased frequency of mass shootings over time. The important point is that mass shootings should not be assumed to have the same determinants across history simply because they can be

classified as a specific kind of violence with a specific name. In other words, the question of their relative frequency across time (though empirically demonstrable) is less important than the need to understand and interpret the particularity of their incidence in any given conjuncture. Significantly, studies that demonstrate either an increased frequency or no significant rise in mass shootings both tend to examine available data over the last forty years. Since this is precisely the conjuncture this essay seeks to examine, data regarding year-to-year variability in incidents are not especially useful. See J. Pete Blair and Katherine W. Schweit, *A Study of Active Shooter Incidents, 2000–2013* (Washington D.C.: Texas State University and Federal Bureau of Investigation, U.S. Department of Justice, 2014); Jesse Signal, "Why You Shouldn't Fear the Rise in Mass Shootings," *New York,* September 26, 2014, http:// nymag.com/scienceofus/2014/09/why-you-shouldnt-fear-the-mass-shooting-rise .html.

12. Recent "exceptions" include the 2012 Oak Creek shootings (which this essay discusses) as well as the 2014 Isla Vista shootings near the University of California, Santa Barbara, in which a "half-white" identified Asian American male composed a manifesto detailing his sexual rejection by white women and avowal to get revenge. The racial, gendered, and sexualized elements of this massacre have been widely discussed, as have been the sexualized dimensions of the shooter's antiblackness. For the shooter, antiblackness was a structure of feeling that determined his relationship with humanity as such, and white women in particular, who eventually became his targets and victims. However, it is one thing to call the shooter racist and misogynist, and even to say that race played a role in the killings, but it is telling that nowhere in the commentary have I found this massacre described as racial violence.

13. According to a recent study released by the Center for Disease Control and Prevention, black people are ten times as likely to die in a gun-related homicide than whites, while mass shootings constitute a tiny fraction of gun homicides in the United States. See Dan Keating, "Gun Deaths Shaped by Race in America," *Washington Post,* March 22, 2013, http://www.washingtonpost.com/sf/feature/wp/2013/03 /22/gun-deaths-shaped-by-race-in-america/; Alan I. Leshner et al., eds., *Priorities for Research to Reduce the Threat of Firearm-Related Violence* (Washington, D.C.: National Academies Press, 2013).

14. David Harvey, *A Brief History of Neoliberalism* (New York: Oxford University Press, 2005), 159.

15. Even Wendy Brown, who has done much to advance our theorization of neo-liberalism, tends to read the social and subjective transformations it has augured as primarily nonviolent. My own reading is indebted to Saidiya Hartman's understanding of the relation between the spectacular character of black suffering and the quotidian exercise of violence and terror. See Saidiya Hartman, *Scenes of Subjection: Terror, Slavery, and Self-Making in Nineteenth-Century America* (New York: Oxford University Press, 1997), 14; Wendy Brown, *Undoing the Demos: Neoliberalism's Stealth Revolution* (New York: Zone Books, 2015).

16. Kimberlé Crenshaw and Gary Peller, "Reel Time / Real Justice," *Denver University Law Review* 70, no. 2 (1993): 283–96.

17. George Yancy and Judith Butler, "What's Wrong with 'All Lives Matter,'" *New York Times,* January 12, 2015, http://opinionator.blogs.nytimes.com/2015/01/12/whats-wrong-with-all-lives-matter/?_r=0.

18. Moustafa Bayoumi, "Did Islamophobia Fuel the Oak Creek Massacre?," *Nation,* August 10, 2012, http://www.thenation.com/article/169322/did-islamophobia-fuel-oak-creek-massacre#; Dawinder S. Sidhu, "Lessons on Terrorism and 'Mistaken Identity' from Oak Creek, with a Coda on the Boston Marathon Bombings," *Columbia Law Review* 113 (2013): 76–87; Mehnaz M. Afridi, "The Gurdwara Sikh Killings: Domestic or Global Taxonomy of Terror," *Sikh Formations* 9, no. 2 (2013): 215–25.

19. Wajahat Ali, "Wade Michael Page: Islamophobia Unleashed," *Salon,* August 7, 2012, par. 4, http://www.salon.com/2012/08/07/wade_michael_page_islamophobia_unleashed/.

20. Ibid., par. 7.

21. Ibid., par. 7, 19.

22. Ibid., par. 20.

23. Nishant Upadhyay, "Pernicious Continuities: Un/settling Violence, Race and Colonialism," *Sikh Formations* 9, no. 2 (2013): 263–68.

24. Wajahat Ali et al., *Fear, Inc.: The Roots of the Islamophobia Network in America* (Washington, D.C.: Center for American Progress, 2011).

25. Keith P. Feldman, "Empire's Verticality: The Af/Pak Frontier, Visual Culture, and Racialization from Above," *Comparative American Studies* 9, no. 4 (Winter 2011): 325–41; David Harvey, *The New Imperialism* (New York: Oxford University Press, 2005); Junaid Rana, *Terrifying Muslims: Race and Labor in the South Asian Diaspora* (Durham: Duke University Press, 2011); Nikhil Singh, "The Afterlife of Fascism," *South Atlantic Quarterly* 105, no. 1 (2006): 71–93.

26. Ruth Wilson Gilmore, "Race and Globalization," *Geographies of Global Change: Remapping the World,* ed. R. J. Johnson et al. (New York: Wiley-Blackwell, 2002), 261.

27. Byrd, *Transit of Empire,* xvii; Melamed, *Represent and Destroy,* 4–15; Edward Said, *Orientalism* (New York: Vintage, 1979); Gayatri Chakravorty Spivak, "Can the Subaltern Speak?," *Marxism and the Interpretation of Culture,* ed. Cary Nelson and Lawrence Grossberg (Urbana: University of Illinois Press, 1988), 271–313.

28. When the issue of mass shootings does emerge within antiracist critique, the fact that they are often perpetrated by white men is used to counter stereotypes that frame black people and Muslims as supposedly more violent. The question is asked: what allows whiteness the privilege of freedom from being represented by the violent or criminal act of one white person, while people of color have never been granted the privilege of such individuality? This is one of the more enduring ways that W. E. B. Du Bois's question from over a century ago ("How does it feel to be a problem?") has been taken up politically. However, in contrast to the radical philosophical implications of Du Bois's formulation, the above question takes the existence of race for granted, rather than investigating the way racial identities are themselves constructed in and through the mediation and definition of violence. At the same time, the question takes the category of crime for granted, ignoring the

way social and legal understandings of crime are historically shaped in relation to conceptions of race, class, and the preservation of social hierarchy. See Khalil Gibran Muhammad, *The Condemnation of Blackness: Race, Crime, and the Making of Modern Urban America* (Cambridge, Mass.: Harvard University Press, 2011).

29. Singh, "Racial Formation," 284.

30. Ibid., 284–85. Singh writes: "Forms of past racial ordering are only partially predictive of racial (or nonracial) futures, particularly when we recognize the extent to which racial meaning crystallizes in the course of ongoing political struggles and across periods of vast social and economic change. The important point is that social differentiations that come to be known as racial have been and continue to be produced *in advance* of stable orders of racial reference and in contexts in which fields of racial reference are actively destabilized" (285).

31. Melamed, *Represent and Destroy*, 3; Etienne Balibar, "Is There a Neo-Racism?," *Race, Nation, Class: Ambiguous Identities* (London: Verso, 1991), 19.

32. Osagie Obasogie, *Blinded by Sight: Seeing Race through the Eyes of the Blind* (Stanford: Stanford University Press, 2013).

33. To say that bodies come to signify (be perceived) as an effect of socially constituted interpretive practices—which is to say, materially produced knowledge—does not mean that *all* persons will interpret a body the same way, any more than a normative implication that biophysical sense perception precedes interpretation suggests that all interpretation is personal and not shaped by ideology. The production of social truth and dominant knowledges never goes uncontested by the production of knowledges by racialized subjects within contexts of domination and subordination. Indeed, if the capacity and value that accrue to group-differentiated populations are themselves the outcome of processes of historical struggle, then to make claims about the formation and effects of a dominant epistemology is itself part of a practice of exposing its contingency.

34. Melamed, *Represent and Destroy*, 12.

35. Fields, "Slavery, Race, and Ideology," 101–4.

36. The dominant critical tendency following Oak Creek was to emphasize the Americanness of the Sikh victims and criticize the lack of media attention toward the victims and their community. For example, see Naunihal Singh, "An American Tragedy," *New Yorker*, August 13, 2012, http://www.newyorker.com/online/blogs/newsdesk/2012/08/an-american-tragedy.html?mobify=0.

37. A revealing instance is the series of comments posted online by a Thai restaurateur in Texas, critical of the media attention paid to the victims of Newtown at the expense of racialized victims of gun violence and Palestinian children who become victims of Israel's bombing of schools in Gaza. The author of these comments was quickly vilified as racist. Cavan Sieczkowski, "Thai Noodle House Restaurant in Hot Water after Racist Sandy Hook Shooting Comments," *Huffington Post*, December 18, 2012, http://www.huffingtonpost.com/2012/12/18/thai-noodle-house-sandy-hook-shooting-racist-comments_n_2322081.html.

38. Erica Goode and Serge F. Kovaleski, "Wisconsin Killer Fed and Was Fueled by Hate-Driven Music," *New York Times*, August 6, 2012, http://www.nytimes.com/2012/08/07/us/army-veteran-identified-as-suspect-in-wisconsin-shooting.html?

hp; "Academic Who Knew Sikh Shooter Wade Michael Page Says Neo-Nazi Soldiers, Musicians Shaped His Hatred," *Democracy Now,* August 9, 2012, http://www.democ racynow.org/2012/8/9/academic_who_knew_sikh_shooter_wade.

39. Anoop Mirpuri, "Oak Creek and the End of Civil Society," *New Black Man (in Exile),* August 16, 2012, http://newblackman.blogspot.com/2012/08/oak-creek -and-end-of-civil-society.html.

40. Eventually the mass shooter's white nationalist manifesto did appear, apparently penned by the perpetrator of the Charleston massacre.

41. An influential libertarian think tank, the Cato Institute was originally founded in 1974 as the Charles Koch Foundation. Charles and David Koch run the multinational corporation Koch Industries and are major underwriters of libertarian knowledge production and conservative candidacies for political office in the United States.

42. Raymond Williams, *Marxism and Literature* (New York: Oxford University Press, 1977), 132. In addition to Williams's "structure of feeling," influential in my account is the concept of "libidinal economy," developed by Frank Wilderson in his engagement with the work of Saidiya Hartman and Jared Sexton. Wilderson, quoting Sexton, discusses libidinal economy as "a dispensation of energies, concerns, points of attention, anxieties, pleasures, appetites, revulsions, and phobias capable of both great mobility and tenacious fixation." See Wilderson, *Red, White & Black,* 7. However, while Wilderson suggests that the symbolic dimension of race can be separated out from economy, I use Williams's term to accent my own emphasis on the historical shifts and material relations that shape particular affective structures—in this case, the specificity and distinctiveness of antiblackness under neoliberalism.

43. Alexander G. Weheliye, *Habeas Viscus: Racializing Assemblages, Biopolitics, and Black Feminist Theories of the Human* (Durham: Duke University Press, 2014), 72.

44. The relation between racialization and the proliferation of mass shootings has recently been noted in an *American Quarterly* forum on whiteness. See Cynthia A. Young and Min Hyoung Song, "Forum Introduction: Whiteness Redux or Redefined?," *American Quarterly* 66, no. 4 (2014): 1074.

45. For example, see Jenna Loyd et al., eds., *Beyond Walls and Cages: Prisons, Borders, and Global Crisis* (Athens: University of Georgia Press, 2012).

46. Gilmore, *Golden Gulag,* 245.

47. Jason Hackworth, *The Neoliberal City: Governance, Ideology, and Development in American Urbanism* (Ithaca: Cornell University Press, 2006); Douglas S. Massey and Nancy A. Denton, *American Apartheid: Segregation and the Making of the Underclass* (Cambridge, Mass.: Harvard University Press, 1998); Robert O. Self, *American Babylon: Race and the Struggle for Postwar Oakland* (Princeton: Princeton University Press, 2005); Loïc Wacquant, "Deadly Symbiosis: When Ghetto and Prison Meet and Mesh," *Punishment and Society* 3, no. 1 (2001): 95–133.

48. Harney and Moten, *The Undercommons,* 77. See also Dan Georgakas and Marvin Surkin, *Detroit: I Do Mind Dying; A Study in Urban Revolution* (Boston: South End Press, 1999); Jack O'Dell, "The July Rebellions and the Military State," *Freedomways* 7, no. 4 (Fall 1967): 288–301, reprinted in O'Dell, *Climbin' Jacob's Ladder: The Black Freedom Movement Writings of Jack O'Dell,* ed. Nikhil Pal Singh

(Berkeley: University of California Press, 2010); Reddy, *Freedom with Violence*, 28; Nikhil Pal Singh, "The Black Panthers and the Undeveloped Country of the Left," *The Black Panther Party [Reconsidered]*, ed. Charles Jones (Baltimore: Black Classic Press, 1998).

49. Gilmore, *Golden Gulag*, 5. Also see Dan Berger, *Captive Nation: Black Prison Organizing in the Civil Rights Era* (Chapel Hill: University of North Carolina Press, 2014); Dylan Rodriguez, *Forced Passages: Imprisoned Radical Intellectuals and the U.S. Prison Regime* (Minneapolis: University of Minnesota Press, 2006).

50. The year 1971 marks a decisive turning point in the coalescence of a hegemonic cross-class antiblack anti-statism. Stuart Hall and his colleagues described this formation as the "exceptional state" to explain how the post-postliberal British state managed its crisis of legitimacy coincident with the demise of the Fordist-Keynesian consensus. In order to secure this legitimacy and represent coercive police power as the product of a cross-class consensus, "the state [becomes] the bureaucratic embodiment, the powerful organizing centre and expression of the disorganized consensus of the popular will. So, whatever the state does is *legitimate* (even if it is not 'right'); and *whoever threatens the consensus threatens the state*. This is a fateful collapse. On the back of this equation, the exceptional state prospers." Stuart Hall et al., *Policing the Crisis: Mugging, the State, and Law and Order* (New York: Palgrave Macmillian, 1978), 310. See also Naomi Murakawa, "The Origins of the Carceral Crisis: Racial Order as Law and Order in Postwar American Politics," *Race and American Political Development*, ed. Joseph Lowndes et al. (New York: Routledge, 2008), 243.

51. Chester Himes, *Cotton Comes to Harlem* (New York: Vintage, 1988), 8.

52. New York State, Special Commission on Attica, *Attica: The Official Report of the New York State Special Commission on Attica* (New York: Praeger, 1972), xi.

53. Anoop Mirpuri, "Mass Incarceration, Prisoner Rights, and the Legacy of the Radical Prison Movement," *The Punitive Turn: New Approaches to Race and Incarceration*, ed. Deborah McDowell et al. (Charlottesville: University of Virginia Press, 2013), 131–55.

54. Herman Badillo and Milton Haynes, *A Bill of No Rights: Attica and the American Prison System* (New York: Outerbridge & Lazard, 1972), 98.

55. If, as Jodi Byrd argues in *Transit of Empire*, "the Indian is the original enemy combatant who cannot be grieved . . . the ontological ground through which U.S. settler colonialism enacts itself as settler imperialism," with this narrative the state made "'Indian' those peoples and nations who stand in the way of U.S. military and economic desires" (xviii, xx).

56. If this argument pushes against the tendency of otherwise illuminating accounts of neoliberalism to read mass incarceration as a symptom of (or incidental to) deeper political-economic shifts, it also challenges nonmaterialist accounts that read mass incarceration as a mutation cum replication of seemingly past modes of domination. For an influential example of the former, see Wendy Brown, "Neoliberalism & the End of Liberal Democracy," *Theory and Event* 7, no. 1 (2003): 1–19; and of the latter, see Michelle Alexander, *The New Jim Crow: Mass Incarceration in the Age of Colorblindness* (New York: New Press, 2012).

57. Wahneema Lubiano, "Like Being Mugged by a Metaphor: Multiculturalism and State Narratives," *Mapping Multiculturalism,* ed. Avery Gordon and Christopher Newfield (Minneapolis: University of Minnesota Press, 1996), 64–75.

58. Williams, *Marxism and Literature,* 132.

59. This is one of the most common ways of talking about a mass shooter who either commits suicide or dies in a gunfight with the police. The *New Yorker*'s "annals of psychology" are not immune to this language. See Andrew Solomon, "The Reckoning," *New Yorker,* March 17, 2014, http://www.newyorker.com/magazine/2014/03/17 /the-reckoning.

60. David Kopel, "Guns, Mental Illness and Newtown," *Wall Street Journal,* December 18, 2012, http://online.wsj.com/news/articles/SB10001424127887323723104578185271857424036; Lucinda Roy, "Even after Newtown, Americans Will Resist Obama's Call to Tighten Gun Laws," *Guardian,* December 16, 2012, http://www.the guardian.com/commentisfree/2012/dec/16/newtown-americans-resist-obama-gun -laws.

61. In *The Undercommons,* Harney and Moten remind us that policy functions as "correction, forcing itself with mechanical violence upon the incorrect, the uncorrected" (78).

62. Samuel R. Delany, *Times Square Red, Times Square Blue* (New York: New York University Press, 1999); Christina B. Hanhardt, *Safe Space: Gay Neighborhood History and the Politics of Violence* (Durham: Duke University Press, 2013); Jamie Peck, "Liberating the City: Between New York and New Orleans," *Urban Geography* 27, no. 8 (2006): 681–713; Loïc Wacquant, *Punishing the Poor: The Neoliberal Government of Social Insecurity* (Durham: Duke University Press, 2009).

63. Molly Redden, "Meet John Lott, the Man Who Wants to Arm America's Teachers," *New Republic,* December 19, 2012, http://www.newrepublic.com/blog /plank/111263/meet-john-lott-the-man-who-wants-teachers-carry-guns#.

64. See Lisa Ford, *Settler Sovereignty: Jurisdiction and Indigenous People in America and Australia, 1788–1836* (Cambridge, Mass.: Harvard University Press, 2010); Bryan Wagner, *Disturbing the Peace: Black Culture and the Police Power after Slavery* (Cambridge, Mass.: Harvard University Press, 2009).

65. Singh, "The Whiteness of Police," 1093. See also Blackhawk, *Violence over the Land,* 9.

66. Singh, "The Whiteness of Police," 1096. See also Fred Moten, "Black Op," *PMLA* 123, no. 5 (2008): 1743–47.

67. Alicia Garza and L. A. Kauffman, "A Love Note to Our Folks," *n+1,* January 20, 2015, https://nplusonemag.com/online-only/online-only/a-love-note-to-our -folks/; Barbara Ransby, "The Class Politics of Black Lives Matter," *Dissent* (Fall 2015), https://www.dissentmagazine.org/article/class-politics-black-lives-matter.

68. Fields, "Slavery, Race, and Ideology," 118. Emphasis mine.

69. Reddy, *Freedom with Violence,* ix.

Nations, Nationalisms, and *Indígenas*

The "Indian" in the Chicano Revolutionary Imaginary

LOURDES ALBERTO

T he 1960s and 1970s were a dynamic time for people of Mexican descent in the United States. Emboldened by the advances of the African American civil rights movement, Mexican American youth sought to attain civil rights and improve their social and economic status. Led by Cesar Chavez and Dolores Huerta, farm workers organized as the UFW (United Farm Workers) to remedy the exploitative working conditions of agricultural laborers and their children.[1] By 1968, Chicano and Chicana student protesters in Los Angeles took to the streets in the first of several major student walkouts, followed by protests at the Democratic National Convention against the Vietnam War and the draft.[2] *El Movimiento* sought to address economic and civil opportunities that led Mexican Americans to experience poor educational and health access, impoverished living conditions, and exploitative labor practices in the United States.

Invigorated by the reforms and protests of the civil rights movement, a wave of Chicano and Chicana writers, performers, and artists initiated a cultural renaissance that was instrumental in engendering the political ideologies and cultural identities of the Chicano movement. Playwright Luis Valdez, the Teatro Campesino, and radical poets Alurista and Corky Gonzalez created a cultural reservoir through the selective elevation and celebration of an indigenous ancestry, forging a Chicano history, culture, and identity steeped in pre-Columbian aesthetics—what I will refer to as "Chicano" and/or "Chicana indigenism." The continued presence of Aztec history, culture, and iconography since *El Movimiento* through the new millennium reveals the centrality of indigeneity in constructing political identity for Chicanos and Chicanas. Mesoamerican history became crucial in engendering Chicano political thought and identity, serving as a counternarrative to the oppressive experience of Mexican Americans in the United States. Much like the political movement itself, Chicano indigenism

sprang from cultural nodes throughout the Southwest with no central organizing machinery, yet indigenist aesthetics soon permeated every aspect of
Chicana/o political life and culture and remains a vibrant component of
contemporary Chicana/o identity. Chicano indigenism can be divided into
two major waves. During the first wave (the early and more militant years
of the Chicano movement), a masculine, cultural nationalist configuration
of indigeneity predominated. Thus, throughout this essay, "Chicano indigenism" will refer to this early nationalist formulation of Chicano indigeneity, which has had a lasting impact on contemporary Chicana/o cultural
identity. The second major wave, what I will refer to as "Chicana indigenism," refers to the feminist revisions and practices whose hallmarks were
theories of mestizaje that echoed Chicano indigenisms, but with significant
revisions and critiques. While Chicana indigenism was most visible in the
1980s, its antecedents are visible during the Chicano movement. This essay
focuses on the Chicano nationalist uses of indigeneity and what I argue is
the incorporation of Mexican *indigenismo*.

Indigenism was not a phenomenon exclusive to the Chicano movement.
On the contrary, indigenism has a long history throughout Latin America,
forged predominantly in the 1920s. *Indigenismo* in Mexico encompassed a
range of governmental policies, educational reforms, land redistributions,
artistic movements, intellectual movements, and racial frameworks insti-
tuted during the early twentieth century as a strategy to bring cohesion to
the emerging nation. The multiple aims of *indigenismo,* as governmental
policy as well as cultural production, facilitated the formation of a modern
Mexican nation by creating a myth of origin through the selective incorporation of indigenous history—while at the same time excluding actual
indigenous people through assimilation programs and land dispossession.
The colonial legacies of *indigenismo* continue to fuel the national imaginary
and produce the cultural context (which animates the political context) that
indigenous Mexicans formulate and (re)imagine as their identities—a process that is heightened in diaspora as they travel to places like California,
Oregon, and increasingly the Midwest and East Coast. Thus, from my vantage point as a Chicana/o and indigenous studies scholar and an indigenous
Zapotec woman, I am compelled to try to understand why it is that at the
moment in which Chicanos and Chicanas participated in a paradigmatic
shift in the meaning of citizenship, belonging, and nation, they invoked
a Mexican indigenist aesthetic that had been largely responsible for dismantling indigenous culture and society through its assimilationist policies
throughout the Americas. Precisely because the apparatus of indigenism

remains a threat to indigenous culture, indigenous history, indigenous epistemologies, and indigenous self-determination, by adopting indigenist poetics, Chicanos' and Chicanas' uses of indigeneity is viewed as an extension of a colonial practice. Rather than creating a simple binary between Chicana/o and native peoples, however, I explore the cross-border forms of indigenism in Chicano and Mexican culture to understand the uneven legacies of colonization, especially in relation to land and place. The recovery of lost lands through the myth of Aztlán was central to early Chicano anticolonial movements—with the lack of territory to take hold of, indigeneity gives life to the mythic geography that Chicanos were so desperately in search of. For indigenous Mexicans, land is also at the heart of their autonomy, cosmology, and history (their sense of Indianness), thus indigenist policies were often implemented through land reform and dispossession. I hope to provide a nuanced discussion of how indigenist cultural practices imprint and ultimately constitute Chicano and Chicana revolutionary epistemologies.

CHICANO INDIGENISM: INVENTING "CHICANONESS"

The (re)making of the "Indian" in Mexican national discourse and culture has not been a closed trajectory; after all, Mexicans inherited visions of the native by earlier colonists and European empires. Thus, the strategic deployment and uses of the Mexican *indio* and *india* (gendered male and female terms for Indian, respectively) have continued to inform and constitute (indigenous and nonindigenous) political identities, movements, and cultures outside of Mexico. Most significantly for this study, Mexican *indigenismo* was imported and reimagined by Chicano intellectuals and writers of the civil rights movement to engender a Chicano national culture. Early on, poets, performers, and writers such as Rodolfo "Corky" Gonzales, Luis Valdez, and Alurista created a lexicon of pan-indigenous, pre-Columbian mythology. While Gonzales, Valdez, and Alurista do not represent the full scope of Chicano revolutionary writing, they each drafted texts that occupy a central place in Chicano nationalist thought and writing. Gonzales authored the indelible poem *Yo Soy Joaquin* (1967); Alurista helped draft what became the foundational text of the Chicano Movement, a kind of Chicano declaration of independence, *El Plan Espiritual de Aztlán* (1969); and Valdez, who would go on to become the most visible Chicano playwright,[3] published *Aztlán: An Anthology of Mexican American Literature* (1972). Together, these texts forged a Chicano ethos that evolved into a counterhegemonic discourse of the Chicano movement while also giving rise to ethnoracial theories of race, nation, and gender. Culture became the terrain on which the Chicano nation was elaborated and indigenism became the topography of that terrain. Indigeneity, in the form of indigenism and through the logic of nationalism, functioned as succor for Chicanos within a U.S. ethnoracial framework that had enacted a long history of violence against Mexican Americans, including mass deportation, lynching, quotidian racism, land dispossession, language elimination, nativism, and police abuse. While Chicano nationalist discourses resulted from strategies of empowerment, nationalism gathered its rhetorical legitimacy from indigenist practices; thus, Chicano nationalism was formulated under the shadow of the complex negative history of *indigenismo* in Latin America. The paradoxes of such a pairing make the study of Chicano indigenism an exciting and a potentially volatile field.[4] Situating Chicano nationalist impulses within Daniel Alarcon's paradigm of the palimpsest[5]—the apparition of Aztlán, the resurgence of La Malinche, and the invocation of *la raza cosmica*—allows us to consider names, language, imagery, narrative, and geographic remappings (Aztlán) as indigenist impulses—portals that make visible the relationship to Mexico and the multiple, contested discourses of indigenism.

MEXICAN *INDIGENISMO*: THE ROOTS OF CHICANO INDIGENISM

The starting point for Chicano cultural nationalism can be found in a much earlier nationalism: Mexican nationalist rhetoric of the 1920s. Separated by over fifty years and the U.S.–Mexico border, I turn to this postrevolutionary period of Mexican history as the starting point of the Chicano and Chicana revolutionary imagination.[6] Mexican *indigenismo* emerged during the 1920s in postrevolutionary Mexico as a set of policies, cultural practices, and desires mobilized to remake Mexico into a modern nation. *Indigenismo* was not a singular practice or discourse but an ideology disseminated by the nascent government through educational, economic, agrarian, and social policies targeted at indigenous populations, while a concomitant cultural agenda reclaimed and reimagined specific forms of indigeneity through art, music, museums, and celebrations, and various other patriotic symbols.[7] In 1920, at the end of the Mexican Revolution, Mexican officials were faced with the challenge of nation building—identifying its new citizenry and modernizing them into an appropriate body politic.[8] Charged with the project were *indigenistas*, Creole elites and intellectuals who were to devise and implement ways of extending governmental authority over the newly formed nation. *Indigenistas* focused on Indians as a unique Mexican natural resource that could be manipulated to remake Mexico into a nation with its own cultural and political trajectory. Thus, *indigenistas* wanted to distinguish the "new" Mexico from its previous European model as a colony while, ironically, retaining the ideas of progress and racial purity disseminated by Europe. Indigeneity and the "Indian" were readily identified as optimal vehicles for the project of nationalism and nation building in the twentieth century. While it can be argued that many *indigenistas* worked with indigenous populations with altruistic visions, indigenous culture and history were reworked to further the psychic separation between Mexico and Europe. During the nineteenth century, Mexico was invaded four times by foreign powers: Spain in 1829, France in 1838 and again in 1861, and the United States in 1846. The invasions and subsequent wars generated a kind of patriotism rooted in the defense of the land and against the foreign.[9] Spearheaded by nonindigenous intellectuals—Jose Vasconcelos, Manuel Gamio, Franz Boaz, Moises Sanz, and many others[10]—*indigenismo* "recast national history as a popular struggle against invasion, subjugation, and want" and located the Indian at the center of national desire.[11] But before the Indian could take its place as national hero, indígenas had to be rehabilitated into suitable Mexican citizens.

For indigenistas, the process of reimagining Indians as suitable citizens occurred along several distinct lines—education, arts, social sciences, agrarian reform, and health. Such projects first required the dismantling, or at least the refashioning, of previously held racist beliefs about Indians as irrevocably degenerate subjects who could never be assimilated into Mexican society, government, or future.[12] For the purposes of this study, I will focus on the cultural developments, since it is the cultural components that were incorporated into Chicana/o literature and culture. Mexican intellectuals began redefining *Mexicanness* by focusing on pre-Columbian cultures. While one branch of the social sciences worked directly with assimilating indigenous populations, another branch of the social sciences worked on creating a national culture by transforming indigeneity into an object.[13] Anthropologists focused on Mesoamerican ruins, archaeological statues, and symbols to create a mythology about the Mexican character as essentially linked to what they described as the warrior-like culture of the Aztecs. Dark figures such as Huitzilopochtli, the Aztec god of war, began to figure prominently in Mexican nationalism; the display of the Huitzilopochtli statue in the Mexican National Museum was instrumental at this time in the public imagination, creating a common national culture.[14] Indians became increasingly refigured as part of a distant past, facilitated in large part by the collapse of indigeneity with objects of the ancient past, which had the effect of closing off possible future trajectories of indigenous people as dynamic and living subjects. Thus, *indigenismo* ultimately ensured the disappearance of contemporary indigenous populations, as they were no longer seen as a part of Mexico's present and future; rather, they were frozen in an ancient past symbolizing Mexico's raw ethnic roots. Furthermore, the public representations of indigeneity increasingly followed the logic of evolution. Indians were the origin, leaving behind, for modern Mexicans, specific characteristics and abilities of strength, cunning, and physical prowess. Ironically, the founders of *indigenismo* were not in fact indigenous or mestizo but rather of European descent.

Yet by claiming a universal link to ancient cultures, *indigenistas* also laid the groundwork for mestizaje, a racialized identity based on the mixture of Spanish and Indian blood. Championed most famously by Jose Vasconcelos in *La Raza Cosmica (The Cosmic Race),* the logic of racial hybridity increasingly became the only way in which Mexican elites could find a place for indigenous populations in Mexico's future. Under the minister of education Jose Vasconcelos, mestizaje was indelibly linked to revolutionary citizenship with the publication of *La Raza Cosmica* in 1925.[15] He argued that the Latin American mestizo constituted the race of the future, bringing together all of the strengths and virtues of the major races: black, white, yellow, and red.[16] As scholars have argued, the most effective national(ist) institutions have been centralized educational agencies; thus, as minister of education, Vasconcelos's indigenist projects and ideologies had the widest reach. Vasconcelos's idea of the *raza cosmica* continues to be taken up again and again in Chicano nationalism and is continually invoked as a multicultural utopia in contemporary Mexican and Mexican American culture.

Racial mixture became the guiding philosophy of Mexican policy and rhetoric. The political project of mestizaje established the boundaries of indigenous identity in the national imaginary even as actual indigenous people were the target of assimilation projects. Indigenous people were recast either as peasants or as a working-class group and no longer by cultural or ethnic difference. While nationalism incorporated Indian difference as a source of historical and cultural pride, mestizaje subsumed the contemporary Indian in the ancient past and within the biology of the contemporary Mexican citizen. As Sheila Contreras points out, "It was non-Indians who devised *indigenismo* . . . post-Revolutionary *indigenismo* represented another formulation of the 'Indian' problem . . . an exercise in subjugation through which the dominant white/mestizo population was able to solidify and extend its control over Indigenous communities."[17] Thus, the process of *indigenismo* involved the disciplining of Indian bodies, while at the cultural level it involved the reeducation of the mestizo and Creole citizenry. Pierre Nora reminds us that national pedagogies "mobilize the past in order to move the individual into a particular future.... As much as they create affiliations, they generally order them into hierarchies reflecting differences in class, race, gender, and national space."[18] As indigenous peoples underwent de-Indianization, were nonindigenous people being trained to envision their fellow citizens not only as unnecessary but also as an obstacle to Mexican success and economic power? As an indigenous Zapotec woman, living in diaspora and thus situated between Chicano and Mexican indigenisms, I take up Alcida Rita Ramos's call to expand our understanding of the concept of indigenism beyond official governmental policies to the vast realm of the popular and learned imagery.[19] It is the dynamism of popular culture that also reveals the dynamism of indigenism, complicating its uses in the Mexican national imaginary and its importation across the U.S.–Mexico border. Thus, the multiple appropriations of the "Indian," the continual evacuation of it as a signifier, the construction of it as an object, and its reified formulation as a racial category, have collectively and continually served as the platform from which revolutionary Chicana/o imagination is formulated in the United States.

In an effort to disentangle these lines of inquiry, I turn to Alarcon's theoretical paradigm of the palimpsest. He explains that palimpsests are "sites where texts have been superimposed onto others in an effort to displace earlier or competing histories." But, more significantly, he argues that "displacement is never total; the suppressed material often remains legible, however faintly, challenging the dominant text with an alternative version of events."[20] Thus, this critical indigenous study explores how the "Indian" has operated as a symbol, racial category, and myth—a kind of palimpsest that has been written and rewritten in an effort to anchor revolutionary imaginaries in the Americas. It is necessary to underscore that while I focus on discursive practices between nation and indigeneity, because indigenous people predate the practice of indigenism, their bodies, cultures, and histories remain the site in which such reinscriptions are centered.[21] In other words, nationalist pedagogies fossilize native and indigenous people within a previous temporality, a time before modernity. Within the linear telling of Western history, native peoples are celebrated as absent even though they exist very much in the present; they are always imagined as a myth of origin, but seem unimaginable as contemporary subjects.[22] The daily lives of indigenous communities at home and in diaspora are structured by this discursive trapping between temporalities—the ancient past and the modern present—which establishes artificial measures of indigeneity. Invented within such a temporal disjunction, Indianness is determined by abstract notions of racial and cultural authenticity. Thus, when indigenous people do appear, they are often urged to conform to and perform static notions of indigeneity, artifacts on which the nation can define itself: "Successfully[,] nationalisms presume some prior community of territory, language, or culture, which provide the raw materials for the intellectual project of nationality."[23] While indigenous communities have predated the nation, these "prior communities should not be 'naturalized,' as if they existed in some essential way, or have simply prefigured a history yet to come." Rather, these "religious, linguistic, ethnic, and regional communities are themselves always already in the process of historical formation and change. What looks from the outside and from a distance as a bounded group appears much more divided and contested at closer range."[24] Indigenous decolonization efforts have thus centered on this issue of authenticity and temporality.

CHICANO *INDIGENISM*: MASCULINITY, RACE, AND MYTH

Chicanos and Chicanas gravitated to Mexican *indigenismo* emerging out of a previous nationalist period in postrevolutionary Mexico, a time in history viewed as the height of Mexican, and by extension Mexican American, self-determination. Chicanos could lay claim to both a successful social revolution and a modern nation outside the United States, but such early notions of Chicano identity were cast as Indian and decisively gendered male.[25] Consequently, and in keeping with this revolutionary Mexico, two main sites of Chicano culture were reimagined to construct Chicanos as indigenous subjects by Chicano writers: Chicano quotidian culture (including food, music, family structure, and the barrio) as "residual" forms of indigenous culture, and the racialization of Chicanos as biologically indigenous. Significantly, these reimaginings of Chicano ethnoracial identity and Chicano culture repeatedly reinstated patriarchal gender relationships.

In *Yo Soy Joaquín,* Gonzales takes up the work of narrating Chicano oppression and systematic marginalization. He writes, "I am Joaquín, lost in a world of confusion, caught up in the whirl of a gringo society, confused by the rules, scorned by attitudes, suppressed by manipulation, and destroyed by modern society."[26] Gonzales's epic poem resonated with Chicanos' and Chicanas' political consciousness because Gonzales captures the sentiment that had framed the Mexican American experience: they held a second-class status in U.S. society both as citizens and laborers. Gonzales's poem is a retelling of the Chicano experience in the spirit of self-determination. He reminds us that the initial successes of the Chicano movement began with the farmworkers' organization and their challenge to agribusiness, what was largely seen as the triumph of David over Goliath.[27] When the poem begins, Joaquin, the Chicano everyman, is merely a reflection of the dominant society's disdain for him; and he, in turn, cannot exert his autonomy as a result of this construction. Chicano activists and writers believed that Chicano self-determination was intimately tied to economic and political opportunities. Given the historical and social conditions of Mexican American disenfranchisement, it is clear why Chicanas/os gravitated to a battle cry like the one Gonzales offered. Yet as the calls to action and activism in poetry grew, Chicano poetics increasing relied on the glorification and uplifting of an ancient indigenous ancestry to undo their "confused, scorned, suppressed and destroyed" experiences. Chicana/o movement texts narrated the tension Chicano writers identified between the Mexican American experience and the U.S. nation-state: linguistic anxieties and political and cultural self-determination. The ancient Indian figure and Mesoamerican culture were resuscitated as the sources of resistance and as a common history that all Mexican Americans shared or could share as they came into a political awakening.

Embracing and celebrating a common indigenous past was an avenue through which they could begin to rewrite their status as a conquered people. In *Yo Soy Joaquín*, Joaquin begins as a meek and denigrated figure, but through the invocation of his Indian ancestors he becomes empowered:

I am the mountain Indian,
superior over all.
The thundering hoof beats are my horses. The chattering machine guns
are death to all of me:
Yaqui
Tarahumara
Chamala
Zapotec
Mestizo
Español.[28]

Joaquin not only embraces his indigenous ancestry but also becomes Indian himself. Becoming Indian was the first strategy employed by early writers, establishing an ancient indigenous ancestry regardless of their actual historical relationships to a tribe, people, language, or custom. Gonzales positions Joaquin as a valiant "mountain Indian" riding a horse, imbued with a superiority that is linked to the land, the mountain. Indigeneity is positioned as organic wildness ("thundering hoof beats" and mountain) against the mechanization of colonization ("chattering of machine guns") that results in the death of a range of indigenous peoples (Yaqui/Tarahumara/Chamala/Zapotec) contained in the singular "me." Multiple identities are subsumed into an indigenous and revolutionary collectivity and into a male narrator. Through the construction of indigeneity as linked to the land, Chicano indigenism, similar to Mexican *indigenismo,* subsumed indigenous people (historic and contemporary) into a national figure not by absolute erasure or elimination but through a process of assimilation that forced Indians to relinquish their actual ties to the land. Specific tribes and pueblos, languages, places, and struggles for autonomy are absorbed into a generic "mountain Indian" that can then be put forth, moving transnationally, in the service of constructing a radical mestizo as the central subject of decolonization in the United States. To be part of the national imaginary, or in this case a revolutionary, required an assimilation of Indian difference.

Even as Gonzales advances the cry for revolution in the poem through the invocations of the "I," the temporality of race and genealogy seems odd: "Zapotec, Mestizo, Español." Colonization and modernity signal the end of "all of him," indigenous (Zapotec), the modern Mexican subject (mestizo), and the colonial (Español). The issue of temporality and indigeneity captures the paradoxes of colonization for indigenous people and its persistence in the Chicano imaginary. Indigenous people were relegated to the past but were also a necessary revolutionary figure of the present and thus constantly invoked. But Gonzales does not culminate with the mestizo or Indian figure but with the Spanish (it is the colonial figure that closes the genealogy of indigeneity), thus one can see the depth of the struggle Chicanos psychically faced and the faultiness of indigenism, with its propensity for producing an overdetermined racial category that ultimately could not meet the psychic needs of Chicano nationalists. Despite calling on a rich indigenous history, that history could not eliminate or even displace the Spanish, the colonial, which continues to persist.

The voice projected as "the" Chicano voice is clearly gendered male and moves easily through time and space. The "males who inform Chicano cultural identity have names (Cuauhtemoc, Moctezuma, Juan Diego, and so on), but the females are nameless abstractions."[29] Chicanos are positioned as any and all historical indigenous subjects. "Yaqui, Tarahumara, Chamala, Zapotec" are subsumed in the figure of "the mountain Indian."[30] The invocation of the Indian self extends the construction of a Chicano community:

> La Raza!
> Mejicano!
> Español!
> Latino!
> Hispano!
>
> Chicano!
> or whatever I call myself
> I look the same
> I feel the same
> I cry
> and
> sing the same.
>
> I am the masses of the people and
> I refuse to be absorbed.[31]

Unbeknown to Gonzales, the practice of creating the singular category of "Indian" in which "mestizo, raza, Mexican, Spanish, Latino, Hispanic, and Chicano" could be contained, and having the "Indian" (Yaqui, Tarahumara, Chamala, Zapotec) continue on as Chicanos in the United States, forecloses the historical developments and trajectories of those very groups. The Latin American indigenous people, history, and culture (Yaqui, Tarahumara, Chamala, Zapotec) that he names and imagines serve as classes and groups that are read as simple prehistories of Chicanos. In invoking a broad ethnoracial category of Indian, Gonzales's poem does the very thing it sets out to undo: create naturalized categories. Early nationalist writings aimed to deconstruct the racist constructions of Mexican history, language, and culture through the political subject of the Chicano. Yet, through its masculinist constructions, Chicano nationalist writings narrated Chicano oppression by creating an Indian subject with deep ethnic fixity. In other words, Mexican Indianness was imbued with ethnoracial continuity so that Chicanos could create a dynamic past and future in the United States. As postcolonial scholars have reminded us, even such claims to "ethno-racial authenticity can be unmasked as contingent historical creations or claims."[32]

In the inner city, Chicano indigenism took on a new valance through "residual forms of indigeneity"—that is, all aspects of contemporary day-to-day Chicano life are in one way or another traced back to Indian roots. The circuitous evolution of Chicano culture that Valdez presents in *Aztlán: An Anthology of Mexican American Literature* establishes Chicanos as "authentic" Americans through traces of indigeneity, superseding the Anglo presence in the Americas and infusing Mexican American cultural practices with authority through a myth of origin.[33]

Chicano barrio culture is similarly recast as indigenous:

> The presence of the Indio in La Raza is as real as the barrio. Tortillas, tamales, chile, marijuana, la curandera, el empacho, el molcajete, atole, La Virgen de Guadalupe—these are hard-core realities for our people. These and thousands of other little human customs and traditions are interwoven into the fiber of our daily life. América Indigena is not ancient history. It exists today in the barrio, having survived even the subversive onslaught of the twentieth-century neon gabacho commercialism that passes for American culture. . . . Frijoles and tortillas remain, but the totality of the Indio's vision is gone.[34]

In Valdez's representation of Mexican American barrio culture (the Mexican American urban ghetto), "Américan Indígena" is only a *residual* Indian identity. That is, when Valdes identifies indigeneity within the Mexican American context, it is in cultural objects, in iconography, and only in opposition to Anglo society. As Rodriguez y Gibson reminds us, this kind of "indigeneity functions as a reactive and oppositional category of identification—its most powerful meanings lie in opposition to something it is not. Because it is reactive, it is flawed as an indication of authenticity which is itself a flawed anti-colonial strategy."[35] Within the Chicano imaginary, indigeneity is locked into a triangulation with authenticity and decolonization; thus, indigeneity is limited/regulated by Chicano uses. Furthermore, indigeneity, as it appears in Valdez's political writings, is continually collapsed with Chicano, making aspects of the Chicano inner city aspects of indigenous life. While such a laundry list of indigenous things helped convince Chicanos that *they* were in fact the reservoirs of Mexican indigeneity, and therefore the purveyors of indigenous cultural patrimony, Valdes in fact reveals a stark blindness Chicanos possessed in relation to actual indigenous people. While Valdes presents a kind of residual indigeneity in objects and practices, there is no sense that they came from actual indigenous people (even as he exclaims, "América Indígena in not ancient history") but only persist in mestizo forms as lineages. The presence of these indigenous "hardcore realities" of barrio life neglect to acknowledge the way in which these knowledges and practices that permeate Mexican culture demonstrate the lasting contemporary contribution of indigenous peoples to national culture. The identification of indigenous presence should not be a sign of residual indigenous culture; rather, indigenous culture should be recognized as the dominant culture attached to actual villages, places, and people. Unfortunately, Mexico and Chicanos refuse to see this presence—the dominance doesn't translate into a recognition of indigenous peoples today but rather reflects a blindness toward them. The scholarship on critical indigenous Latino studies since the turn of the century has shown that indigenous people have been a significant presence in every major wave of Mexican labor and immigration— Zapotec laborers can be traced to all the waves of the bracero programs and began to settle in Los Angeles in significant numbers since the 1970s, after the student massacre and political upheaval in Mexico in 1968.

As a political strategy, indigeneity has liberatory potential as long as Chicanos assert themselves as indigenous—a claim that is continuously refuted by actual native peoples. Thus, Chicano indigenism does not provide us a nuanced understanding of indigeneity; rather, it exposes the links to Mexican indigenism and the polemics of nationalist identities. For Chicanas, it was clear that such nationalist desires located women as another source of indigenous authenticity. The sites of barrio indigeneity (tortillas, tamales, chile, marijuana, la curandera, el empacho, el molcajete, atole, La Virgen de Guadalupe) refer in one way or another to the domestic sphere, primarily in the form of food and other consumables. Chicano indigenism had the additional effect of fastening gender relationships to heteronormative structures of the home under the guise of authenticity.

While the aims of such cultural texts were meant to unite Chicanos by crafting their own modes of self-representation, scholars Rosa Linda Fregoso and Angie Chabram suggest that "this representation of cultural identity postulated the notion of a transcendental Chicano subject at the same time that it proposed that cultural identity existed outside of time and that it was unaffected by changing historical processes."[36] When it came to indigeneity, specifically, Chicanos could not see that their "mimetic notion or representation obfuscated the fact that the naming of cultural identity was not the same thing as cultural identity."[37] As the Chicano movement seemed to import and celebrate pre-Columbian Aztec culture as a liberatory strategy, when examined through a critical indigenous studies lens, the limits of mimesis become visible. Gonzales's characterizations of Benito Juarez, Mexico's pre-revolutionary president, are especially revealing. He writes:

> I fought and died for Don Benito Juarez, guardian of the Constitution.
> I was he on dusty roads on barren land as he protected his archives
> as Moses did his sacraments.
> He held his Mexico in his hand on
> the most desolate and remote ground which was his country.
> And this giant little Zapotec gave not one palm's breadth
> of his country's land to kings or monarchs or presidents of
> foreign powers.[38]

Gonzales continues in the tradition of mythologizing history's "great men." In Mexico's national imaginary, Juarez, an Oaxacan Indian, is Mexico's beloved leader of the Reform period, resisting French occupation and instituting a new republic.[39] Attuned to Juarez's significance as a political and cultural figure in the Mexican national imaginary, Gonzales positions Chicanos alongside Juarez as guardians of justice and democracy ("I fought and died for Benito Juarez"). Mexico's new constitution and forefather embody the possibility of new citizenship in Mexico and cast Chicanos as discerners of such righteousness. In the Chicano quest for political representation, Juarez is a father figure from whom the spirit of a new country can be inherited. Through Juarez we gain access to important cultural artifacts, the constitution, and his nebulous archives that facilitated the invention of Chicano nationalist culture. Most fundamentally of all, through Juarez Chicanos "attempt to manufacture and manipulate a particular view of the past, invariably as a myth of origins which is meant to establish and legitimate the claim to cultural autonomy and eventually to political independence."[40] Yet Chicanos appear oblivious to the actual historical context of Juarez's presidency and land reforms—a well-documented set of policies. Guided by European liberalism, he broke up "the ancient communal landholdings of indigenous communities which ultimately facilitated the creation of a landless rural work force and the concentration of rural lands in the hands of the primarily Spanish-descendant oligarchy."[41] He laid down the foundations for "progress and development," which required the subordination of indigenous worldviews and practices to the rule of state power and liberal property rights law.[42] The paradox of Chicano indigenism is that even as it celebrates the Indian forefather of Mexico, such celebration simultaneously relies on racialized tropes of the Indian to endear Juarez to the reader, even though Juarez worked to dismantle and assimilate indigenous cultures.

It is the reference to Juarez as the "giant little Zapotec" that ultimately marks him as Indian. While Gonzales readily identifies him as Zapotec, an indigenous group from Oaxaca, it is his use of "smallness" that readily signifies "Indian." In Mexico, the diminution of Oaxacans is a common practice to racialize them as being Indian. Indians from southern Mexico are stereotypically thought of as short (or little), and terms such as *Oaxaquita*, or little Oaxacan, circulate throughout Mexican vernacular. Gonzales elevates Juarez in part because of his indigenous status, but he simultaneously resuscitates racialized tropes of indigeneity to imbue him with power. In describing him as a "giant little Zapotec" who fights off foreign powers, Gonzales is compelled to idealize him, yet mark him as Indian, a discursive strategy that renders him the familiar "noble savage." As Juarez serves as a kind of Chicano forefather, another myth of origin, Aztlán, simultaneously emerges as an indigenist narrative. Benito Juarez and Aztlán exemplify the contradictory impulses of Chicano indigenism. Chicanos lay claim to Benito Juarez as founding father of the Mexican nation while also laying claim to Aztlán, a mythic homeland that precedes the formation of Mexico. Aztlán represents a uniquely Chicano revision of Mexican *indigenismo*. Most significantly, Valdes appropriates Juarez as if he were part of the Aztlán history he is mapping out, when of course he is not. Rather, he is a Zapotec Indian from Oaxaca, indigenous people from southern Mexico and distinct from the Aztecs. In the conflation of Juarez and Aztlán, we see precisely the reification of indigenous past as monolithic!

CHICANO INDIGENISM AND THE MYTH OF AZTLÁN

The concept of Aztlán entered Chicano discourse with "El plan espiritual de Aztlán," drafted at the Denver Youth Conference in 1969. Although officially drafted by committee, Alurista is largely acknowledged as the primary author of "El plan."[43] It states,

> Brotherhood unites us and love for our brothers makes us a people whose time has come and who struggle against the foreigner "Gabacho," who exploits our riches and destroys our culture. With our hearts in our hands and our hands in the soil, We Declare the Independence of our Mestizo Nation. We are a Bronze People with a Bronze Culture. Before the world, before all

of North America, before all our brothers in the Bronze Continent. We are a Nation, We are a Union of free pueblos, We are Aztlán.[44]

More so than any other nationalist concept or practice, Aztlán embodied the multiple longings, the aspirations, and the poetic allure of the Chicano movement; it spoke to the desire for connection and unity, homeland, and the condition of diaspora, while contesting the notion of Chicanas/os as outsiders or foreigners. For university students across the United States, it continues to capture a revolutionary potential. As an indigenist practice, the concept of Aztlán functions primarily as a myth of origin, possessing all the hallmarks of Mexican *indigenismo*. In a retelling by Valdez, the myth of Aztlán was for the Aztecs a mythic homeland that lay to the north of Mexico City. He recounts:

> We have been in América a long time. Somewhere in the twelfth century, our Aztec ancestors left their homeland Aztlán, and migrated south to Anáhuac, "the place by the waters," where they built their great city of México-Tenochtitlan. . . . Aztlán was left far behind, somewhere "to the north," but it was never forgotten. Aztlán is now the name of our Mestizo nation, existing to the north of Mexico, within the borders of the United States. Chicano poets sing of it, and their *flor y canto* points toward a new yet very ancient way of life and social order, toward new yet very ancient gods.[45]

While Aztlán was a recognizable component of Mexican *indigenismo* it did not occupy the central place in Mexican nationalism that it does in Chicano revolutionary thought. Thus, the advancement of Aztlán and its incorporation into a political imaginary is a distinctively Chicano phenomenon. As Natividad Gutiérrez's fieldwork reflects, the myth of Aztlán and Aztec history and culture do not have any validity or any kind of significance for the Mixtecs, Zapotecs, or Mayas.[46] In the United States, Chicanos seized on the narrative, resignifying the reference to the "north" as the U.S. Southwest and rewriting the myth of Aztlán not as a Mexican myth of origin but as a Chicano myth of origin, potentially bypassing Mexico altogether as the only point of origin for Mexican Americans.

Seizing on the nationalist potential of such a narrative, Chicano indigenists employed the Aztlán myth to legitimate their presence in the United States by arguing that they were residing in their ancestral homeland and thus could not be called out as "illegal" or "alien" to the land.[47] Similarly, Chicanos sought legitimacy and power through the Treaty of Guadalupe

Hidalgo. The treaty ensured that Mexican land grants would be honored and that Mexicans would be granted full citizenship during and after U.S. annexation of the Southwest. Together these claims make up the core of Chicano historical primacy; but as Contreras has pointed out, this logic is fundamentally contradictory. She writes,

> Rather than complementing each other, [these claims to the Southwest] contradict and compete, despite the idea of historical primacy that lies at the foreground of each. . . . On the one hand, Aztlán is an assertion of land rights based on an Indigenous myth, and, on the other, the treaty rights afforded by the Treaty of Guadalupe Hidalgo are mestizo claims based upon a Mexican national identity and the settler privilege bestowed by Spanish and Mexican land grants.[48]

Similarly, Rafael Perez-Torres has famously argued that "rather than evoke a bridge beyond history, Aztlán reveals the discontinuities and ruptures that characterize the presence of Chicanos in history."[49] The single term "Aztlán" operates as an empty signifier, able to simultaneously call up the struggle by Chicanas/os to contest their racialization in the United States as foreigners, contestations of the U.S.–Mexico border and Chicano Southwest, and the feminist opposition by Chicanas to the machismo and nationalism of the Chicano movement. In an effort to bring an additional layer to the discussion of Aztlán, I thus explore how Aztlán was refigured when put in dialogue with contested histories of indigenous people and the legacy of Mexican *indigenismo* in Chicano nationalism. In particular, the concept of Aztlán opens up another avenue to mestizaje as the counterpart to indigenism. At the end of the Chicano movement, Chicanos and Chicanas increasingly used mestizaje in conjunction with indigenism to theorize Chicana/o subjectivity in the United States. The "contradictory impulses" exposed in the use of Aztlán are the result of the rise of mestizaje as a way of claiming indigeneity.

CONCLUSION

The co-opting of Mexican *indigenismo* in the United States forces us to contend with the uses of indigeneity in Chicano nationalism and revolutionary thought during the civil rights movement. The emergence of *Chicano indigenism* points to the dynamic interplay between the Mexican national discourse of indigeneity in the emerging Mexican state and its U.S. masculinist appropriations by Chicano nationalists. The field of critical ethnic studies is particularly suited to take up indigeneity within transnational contexts precisely because its methodology is grounded in comparative approaches. Tracing the transnational routes of indigenism alerts us to the uneven terrain of the "coloniality of power," employing Quijano's concept—that is, how does the specter of colonialism continue to animate indigenous/nonindigenous interactions vis-à-vis Mexican and Chicano indigenism? What are the implications of such indigenist dependencies/overlaps for indigenous, Chicano, and native studies? Put another way, critical ethnic studies' focus on indigenous peoples *and* race prompts us to explore the following questions: How is it that within the Mexican context indigenism appears as a neocolonial practice responsible for the disenfranchisement of indigenous people, yet it reappears in the U.S. context, opening up the possibility of postcolonial resistance in the Chicano Movement? And where within the genealogies of indigenism do U.S. North American and Latin American indigenous people appear, resist, and persist?

Furthermore, the study of Chicano indigenism also begs further investigation into the feminist revisions of it. Mexican *indigenismo* and Chicano indigenismo is further turned on its head as both nationalist deployments are undermined and refashioned by Chicana feminists used as a tool to disrupt heteronormative imaginings of the Chicana/o experience.[50] Indigenism reveals itself to be a kind of palimpsest, "sites where texts have been superimposed onto others in an effort to displace earlier or competing histories," only to reappear as suppressed material, remaining legible, however faintly, challenging the dominant text with an alternative version of events.[51] Thus, this work explores how the "Indian" has operated as a symbol, racial category, and myth, a kind of palimpsest that has been written and rewritten in an effort to anchor revolutionary imaginaries in the Americas. Underscoring the practices of nation and indigeneity are indigenous people who predate the practice of indigenism and thus their bodies, cultures, and histories remain the site in which such reinscriptions are centered.[52] Both the Chicano nationalist impulse toward *indigenismo* and its Chicana feminist revisions continue to potentially re-create the uneven power relationships between Indian and nation. Present-day indigenous peoples were thus seen as relics of an ancient world impeding the progress of the new Mexican state and therefore relegated outside the nation. With the growth of indigenous studies and the growing complexity of ethnoracial relationships between native/Indian and Chicana/o histories, literatures, and intellectual inquiry, this is another front which must be explored. The question remains, what is the possibility of taking signs, seemingly revolutionary, and resignifying them from colonial constructs to signs and signifiers of resistance against colonial and neocolonial structures of history? In forming a modern Mexican nation, early Mexican nationalists envisioned Aztec culture and indigeneity as a past that could be safely celebrated while mestizaje could be embraced as the future. It is mestizaje that continues on as the greatest legacy and contested terrain of Chicana/o subjectivity.

LOURDES ALBERTO is an assistant professor of English and ethnic studies at the University of Utah and the author of *Mexican American Indigeneities* (forthcoming).

NOTES

1. Rodolfo Acuña, *Occupied America: A History of Chicanos* (New York: Harper and Row, 1981); Maylei Blackwell, "Contested Histories: Las Hijas De Cuauhtemoc, Chicana Feminisms, and Print Culture in the Chicano Movement, 1968–1973," in *Chicana Feminisms: A Critical Reader,* ed. Gabriela F. Arredondo et al. (Durham: Duke University Press, 2003).

2. Carlos Muñoz Jr., *Youth, Identity and Power: The Chicano Movement* (London: Verso, 1989); Ernesto Chavez, *!Mi Raza Primero¡: Nationalism, Identity, and Insurgency in the Chicano Movement in Los Angeles, 1966–1978* (Berkeley: University of California Press, 2002).

3. Valdez went on to author and direct *Zoot Suit, La Bamba,* and *Yo Soy Joaquin,* and really launched Edward James Olmos's career.

4. Curtis Marez, "Signifying Spain, Becoming Comanche, Making Mexicans: Indian Captivity and the History of Chicana and Chicano Popular Performance," *American Quarterly* 53 (2001): 267–307. Marez calls this practice "indigenism of the antique."

5. Daniel Cooper Alarcon defines the palimpsest as "[the] unique structure of competing and interwoven narratives that challenge the way we think of cultural identities and its representations as well as enabling a study of history, cultural identity, ethnicity, literature and politics, *in relationship to one another,* providing a new vantage point on the relationship between the US and Mexico at a time when they are more intimately linked than ever." Daniel Cooper Alarcon, *The Aztec Palimpsest: Mexico in the Modern Imagination* (Tucson: University of Arizona Press, 1997), xvi.

6. My turn to Mexico to understand Chicano indigenism has been fueled by the work of many Latin American scholars who have pointed to the complicated manifestations of Latin American indigenismo in U.S. literature and culture. They include Walter Mignolo, Robert Irwin McKee, Kristen Silev Gruez, Juan Poblete, Stefano Varese, Jose Rabasa, and Beatriz Gonzalez Stephan.

7. Mary Kay Vaughan and Stephan E. Lewis, *The Eagle and the Virgin: Nation and Cultural Revolution in Mexico, 1920–1940* (Durham: Duke University Press,

2006); Eric Hobsbawn and Terrance Ranger, *The Invention of Tradition* (New York: Cambridge University Press, 1983).

8. Alan Knight, "The Mexican Revolution: Bourgeois? Nationalist? Or Just a 'Great Rebellion'?," *Bulletin of Latin American Research* 4, no. 2 (1985): 1–37.

9. Vaughan and Lewis, *The Eagle and the Virgin*; Benedict Anderson, *Imagined Communities: Reflections on the Origin and Spread of Nationalism* (London: Verso, 1983).

10. For a more extensive discussion of Mexican indigenistas, please see Alexander S. Dawson, *Indian and Nation in Revolutionary Mexico* (Tucson: University of Arizona Press, 2004). Mexican indigenismo was a three-decade national project with various intellectuals and projects throughout its history.

11. Vaughan and Lewis, *The Eagle and the Virgin*, 1.

12. There is a vast field of research by Latin American scholars on Mexican indigenism.

13. Dawson offers an exhaustive account of how the social sciences, in particular Franz Boaz and his student Manuel Gamio, were instrumental in using scientific methods to justify racist approaches to assimilating indigenous populations.

14. J. Franco, "The Return of Coatlicue: Mexican Nationalism and the Aztec Past," *Journal of Gender Studies* 13, no. 2 (2004): 205–19.

15. M. J. Saldaña-Portillo, "Reading a Silence: The 'Indian' in the Era of Zapatismo," *Nepantla: Views from the South* 3, no. 2 (2002): 287–314.

16. José Vasconcelos, *La raza cosmica: La mission de la raza iberoamericana* (Barcelona: Espasa Calpe, 1925).

17. Sheila Marie Contreras, *Blood Lines: Myth, Indigenism, and Chicana/o Literature* (Austin: University of Texas Press, 2008), 26.

18. Pierre Nora, "Between Memory and History: Les Lieux de mémoire," *Representations* 26 (1989): 7–25 (7, 16).

19. Alcida Rita Ramos, *Indigenism: Ethnic Politics in Brazil* (University of Wisconsin Press, 1998), 4–5.

20. Alarcon, *The Aztec Palimpsest*, xiv.

21. Saldaña-Portillo, "Reading a Silence," 287–314; Guillermo Bonfil Batalla, *Mexico Profundo: Una Civilización Negada* (Mexico City: CIESAS, 1987); Hector Díaz Polanco, *Indigenous Peoples in Latin America: The Quest for Self-Determination* (Boulder, Colo.: Westview Press, 1997); Edward McCaughan, "Social Movements, Globalization, and the Reconfiguration of Mexican/Chicano Nationalism," *Social Justice: A Journal of Crime Conflict and World Order* 26, no. 3 (Fall 1999): 59–78.

22. Gerald Vizenor, *Fugitive Poses: Native American Indian Scenes of Absence and Presence* (Lincoln: University of Nebraska Press, 2000).

23. Geoff Eley and Ronald Grigor Suny, *Becoming National: A Reader* (New York: Oxford University Press, 1996), 9.

24. Ibid., 9–10.

25. José F. Aranda, *When We Arrive: A New Literary History of Mexican America* (Tucson: University of Arizona Press, 2003).

26. Rodolfo "Corky" Gonzales, *I Am Joaquin / Yo Soy Joaquin: An Epic Poem* (Denver: Totinem, 1967), 3.

27. Yolanda Broyles-González, *El Teatro Campesino: Theater in the Chicano Movement* (Austin: University of Texas Press, 1994).

28. Gonzales, *I Am Joaquin*, 9.

29. McCaughan, "Social Movements," 59–78.

30. Gonzales, *I Am Joaquin*, 9.

31. Ibid., 20.

32. Eley and Suny, *Becoming National*, 172.

33. Such claims are continuously invoked by slogans such as "We didn't cross the border, the border crossed us!"

34. Luis Valdez, ed., *Aztlán: An Anthology of Mexican American Literature*, ed. Stan Steiner (New York: Vintage Books, 1972), xvi.

35. Eliza Rodriguez y Gibson, "Imagining a Poetics of Loss: Notes toward a Comparative Methodology," *Studies in American Indian Literatures* 15, nos. 3–4 (2003): 23–50.

36. Rosa Linda Fregoso and Angie Chabram, "Chicana/o Cultural Representations: Reframing Alternative Critical Discourses," in *Chicana/o Cultural Studies Reader*, ed. Angie Chabram-Dernersesian (New York: Routledge, 2006), 28.

37. Ibid.

38. Gonzales, *I Am Joaquin*, 7, 9.

39. Juarez was from San Juan Guelatao in Oaxaca, Mexico.

40. Eley and Suny, *Becoming National*, 8.

41. McCaughan, "Social Movements," 59–78.

42. Ibid.

43. The version of "El plan" I reference here is Valdez's publication in *Aztlán: An Anthology of Mexican American Literature*.

44. Valdez, *Aztlán*, 403.

45. Ibid., xxiv.

46. Natividad Gutiérrez, *Nationalist Myths and Ethnic Identities: Indigenous Intellectuals and the Mexican State* (Lincoln: University of Nebraska Press, 1999).

47. Alarcon, *The Aztec Palimpsest*; Genaro Padilla, "Myth and Comparative Cultural Nationalism: The Ideological Uses of Aztlán," in *Aztlán: Essays on the Chicano Homeland*, ed. Rudolfo Anaya and Francisco Lomeli (Albuquerque: University of New Mexico Press); Raphael Perez-Torres, "Refiguring Aztlán," *Aztlán: A Journal of Chicano Studies* 22, no. 2 (Fall 1997): 13–41.

48. Contreras, *Blood Lines*, 33.

49. Perez-Torres, "Refiguring Aztlán," 13–41.

50. Norma Alarcón, "Chicana Feminism: In the Tracks of 'the' Native Woman," *Cultural Studies* 4, no. 3 (1990): 248–56.

51. Alarcon, *The Aztec Palimpsest*, xiv.

52. Saldaña-Portillo, "Reading a Silence," 287–314; Bonfil Batalla, *Mexico Profundo*; Díaz Polanco, *Indigenous Peoples*; McCaughan, "Social Movements," 59–78.

Americans in the Pacific

Rethinking Race, Gender, Citizenship, and Diaspora at the Crossroads of Asian and Asian American Studies

MICHAEL JIN

In early September 1928, nineteen-year-old Walnut Grove, California, native Toshiko Inaba arrived at the Port of San Francisco via a trans-Pacific vessel from Japan. At the age of three, Inaba had been sent to Kumamoto Prefecture to be raised by her uncle's family. After spending sixteen formative years of her life in Japan, Inaba decided to return to her country of birth with the intention to resettle permanently. However, her reentry to the United States was denied by the U.S. immigration authorities, who determined that Inaba had lost her American citizenship while living abroad. Without permission for readmission to the United States, Inaba found herself detained at the Angel Island Immigration Station across the bay from the city of San Francisco.[1]

As Inaba awaited her deportation order at the Angel Island Immigration Station, her family in California hired lawyers to appeal the decision by the U.S. Bureau of Immigration to deny her admission. However, a series of hearings conducted by the U.S. Labor Department's Board of Special Inquiries did nothing to grant Inaba admission to U.S. soil. Inaba refused to give up and filed a petition in the U.S. District Court for her admission as an American citizen. As the hearings on her case dragged on, Inaba would remain imprisoned on Angel Island for over a year before her eventual deportation to Japan in January 1930. Her sixteen-month detention made Inaba the longest detainee from Japan in the history of the Angel Island Immigration Station.[2]

Toshiko Inaba was not a Japanese immigrant but a U.S. citizen with proper paperwork who wanted to resettle in her hometown in Sacramento County.[3] What, then, caused her detention and deportation? Inaba's fate was a result of complex legal and judicial developments in the 1920s that had shaped U.S. policies on citizenship and immigration. As Mae M. Ngai has noted, the exclusionary U.S. immigration and naturalization policies during the 1920s, such as the 1924 Immigration Act, manifested the racialization of Asian immigrants as inassimilable foreigners.[4] However, Inaba's case demonstrates that these restrictive legal and judicial measures in the 1920s not only excluded foreign-born Asian immigrants but also had serious implications on the citizenship status of fifty thousand second-generation Japanese Americans *(Nisei)* who had spent various amounts of time abroad as migrants, students, workers, travelers, and sojourners.

This article examines how complex and unexpected legal and sociopolitical developments in and between the two competing Pacific empires placed this heavily understudied group of U.S.-born transnational migrants at the crossroads of Asian and Asian American history. By the eve of the Second World War, thousands of second-generation Japanese Americans, who were U.S. citizens by birth, had lived and traveled outside the United States. Many of them had been sent to Japan at young ages by their first-generation *(Issei)* parents to be raised by their relatives and receive a Japanese education. Others accompanied Issei return migrants who resettled permanently in Japan or Japanese colonies in Asia when the Great Depression compounded many Japanese immigrant families' survival in the United States during the era of intense anti-Asian sentiment and legal exclusion. Many Nisei also sought opportunities for employment or higher education in a country that represented an expanding colonial power in Asia, especially during the 1930s. Some of these Nisei returned to the United States before the outbreak of Pearl Harbor and became known as *Kibei* (literally, "returned to America").[5]

Japanese Americans who migrated to Japan at young ages and those who embarked on subsequent journeys to Japan's colonial world in the Pacific before World War II rarely appear in popular narratives of Asian American history. A U.S.-centered immigrant paradigm has confined the history of Japanese Americans to the interior of U.S. political and cultural boundaries. Moreover, because the Japanese American internment during World War II and the emphasis on Nisei loyalty and nationalism have been dominant themes in the postwar scholarship and public history of Japanese Americans, there has been little room for the examination of the Nisei transnational experience in Japan and its colonial world.[6] However, as Eiichiro Azuma's work on Japanese immigrants and their Nisei children on both sides of the Pacific has shown, there were critical intersections between the history of Japanese colonialism in Asia and the history of racial exclusion in the United States before World War II in the Japanese American experience that necessitate meaningful transnational and interdisciplinary approaches.[7]

While the history of Nisei who lived in the Japanese Empire remains a difficult topic to pursue because of the demands of bilingual and transnational research, it nevertheless offers important and meaningful alternatives to a dichotomous U.S. immigrant paradigm. The fifty thousand or so Nisei who traversed the Pacific in the first half of the twentieth century were a group of second-generation migrants that defy the notion of the United States as the final terminus of immigrant history. Their experiences also challenge the concept of the United States as the "host nation" of immigrants; to Nisei migrants in Japan, the United States represented the "sending nation." More accurately, their history complicates linear and predictable notions about "sending" and "receiving" societies. Transnational movements of Japanese Americans before, during, and after World War II also defy the notion of a singular migration, transmigration, or settlement pattern. Instead, their lived experiences must be examined in the context of fluctuating social, cultural, and political histories and movements between the United States and Japan.

Although many works in Asian diasporas have examined the multifaceted experiences of return migrants, transmigrants, and diasporic subjects across countries and regions, the transnational movements of U.S.-born Nisei migrants to Asia-Pacific further complicate the geographical, conceptual, and spatial boundaries of Asian American studies. Recent works on Asian migration have offered multiple diasporic localities as a norm rather than the exception in the broad outlook of migration history. They have emphasized the complex formations of transnational families, communities, and networks through shared identities and connections.[8] However, the history of American-born Nisei in the Pacific require an analytical approach beyond the concept of diasporic experience as one defined essentially by ancestral origin or determined by the site of localization.

Responding to Shelly Chan's call for a "temporal approach" to the diasporic experience, I examine the emergence of the Japanese American diaspora as a process contingent upon complex, unpredictable, and unexpected convergences of multiple social realities across national borders.[9] Japanese American migrants made their trans-Pacific journeys to Japan at a critical intersection between U.S. immigration history, the history of Japanese colonial expansion, and Asian American history. Government records, periodicals, and personal accounts in both Japanese and English reveal that the presence of U.S.-born Japanese Americans in Japan had significant diplomatic implications on the increasingly deteriorating U.S.–Japan relations from the 1920s to the 1940s. Employing both spatial and temporal approaches to understanding the Japanese American diaspora at these critical moments demonstrate how the Nisei transnational generation on both sides of the Pacific confronted, negotiated, and articulated their legal and cultural citizenship.

NISEI TRANSNATIONAL MIGRATION: RETHINKING RACE, GENDER, AND CITIZENSHIP IN ASIAN AMERICAN STUDIES

The Toshiko Inaba case reveals complex gendered implications of U.S. immigration and citizenship laws on the lives of Nisei transnational migrants. Upon Inaba's arrival at San Francisco in 1928, the immigration officers reviewing her papers discovered that she had married and divorced Torao Yamamoto, a Japanese national, during her sixteen-year residence in Japan.[10] Unbeknown to Inaba at the time of this marriage, the U.S. government in 1922 had enacted the Married Women's Independent Nationality Act, better known as the Cable Act. This law forced American women marrying "aliens ineligible to citizenship" to forfeit their U.S. citizenship.[11] In the same year Congress passed the Cable Act, the U.S. Supreme Court ruled in *Takao Ozawa v. United States* that Japanese nationals did not qualify for naturalization rights reserved for "Caucasians" or "free whites" and formally established Japanese nationals as "aliens ineligible to citizenship."[12] Thus, the immigration officers at the Port of San Francisco and Angel Island interpreted Inaba's marriage history as the legal ground on which she had ceased to be an American citizen vis-à-vis the Cable Act of 1922.[13]

If the Cable Act of 1922 and *Ozawa v. United States* worked in tandem to strip Inaba of her U.S. citizenship, the Immigration Act of 1924 served as the legal measure that directly contributed to the U.S. Bureau of Immigration's denial of her return to the United States. The 1924 Immigration Act effectively halted Japanese immigration by imposing permanent limitations on the entry of immigrants from Asia. As someone who had lost her U.S. citizenship by marriage to a Japanese national, Inaba became a stateless individual. For the purpose of immigration proceedings, the U.S. immigration officers reclassified her as a Japanese citizen and an immigrant. The officers at the Port of San Francisco then used the racialized quota system established by the 1924 Immigration Act to deny her admission to U.S. soil. In the eyes of the immigration officers, Inaba had become a Japanese citizen and an immigrant no longer eligible for admission to her country of birth.[14] This sudden change of Inaba's national identity was not by her choice, but by the mandate of law and the High Court of the United States that had changed her legal and racial status of Japanese while she was away from home.

Thus, the U.S. legal and judicial enactments designed to exclude immigrants from East Asia in the 1920s also redefined the citizenship and national identity of Japanese Americans who resided overseas before the Pacific War. The 1920s marked the beginning of what is commonly regarded in U.S. immigration history as the "exclusion era." Immigration historians and Asian American scholars have illuminated the critical impact of exclusionary legal and judicial measures on the history of U.S. citizenship and naturalization. They have focused on the landmark decision in *Ozawa v. United States* as a race-specific interpretation of naturalization rights that excluded Asian immigrants from American citizenry. Similarly, studies have focused on the 1924 Immigration Act as a exclusionary policy designed to prevent the influx of an unwanted population from Asia as well as southern and eastern Europe.[15] In other words, only foreign-born migrants were thought to be legally subject to these exclusionary measures.

However, the Inaba case exposed an unexpected consequence of exclusionary U.S. immigration and naturalization laws when U.S.-born Japanese American migrants in the Japanese Empire also became *legally* subject to these immigration and naturalization laws of the 1920s. The changes in legal status of Issei in the United States, in fact, had serious implications on the citizenship of Nisei who resided abroad. Thus, the history of Nisei in prewar Japan can shed new light on the exclusionary U.S. immigration and naturalization policy against Asian immigrants before World War II.

This case also reveals how the Japanese American women who were in Inaba's plight had to negotiate both Japanese and American legal and cultural institutions to articulate, reassert, and preserve their citizenship, lest they face permanent separation from their families and communities back in the United States. The reason for Inaba's extended incarceration before she was sent back to Japan was that she chose to fight her way home by filing a series of court appeals from Angel Island. In her appeals, she argued that her marriage to Yamamoto should have been null and void in the first place because the said marriage had not been in accordance with Japanese marriage law. Inaba claimed that the marriage had taken place "without her own knowledge and without the consent of her parents," which was required by law in Japan in order for a marriage to be legally recognized. Moreover, she claimed that she found out about her alleged marriage to Yamamoto in September 1927, four months after a marriage certificate had been filed by her relatives without her consent. Upon discovering that she had been married off to Yamamoto, she asserted, she promptly resorted to what she viewed as something any good, independent young American woman would do. She "caused her family record to be changed so that she would no longer be a member of Yamamoto's family, but a member of her own family." This act, according to Japanese laws existing at the time, constituted Inaba's "complete and absolute" release from the alleged marriage.[16]

Inaba's strategy was thus twofold: she emphasized the illegitimacy of her marriage in Japan on legal grounds, and she emphasized her cultural citizenship as an independent American woman who had kept her American identity intact despite her upbringing in a Japanese household across the ocean from her hometown in California. She and her lawyers hoped that this approach would convince the U.S. federal court to honor and restore her U.S. citizenship by birth.

However, the opinion of the presiding American judge was hardly sympathetic to Inaba's plight. Judge Franklin H. Rudkin of the U.S. Ninth Circuit Court of Appeals upheld the Board of Special Inquiries decision for Inaba's deportation. He insisted that Inaba's marriage to Yamamoto, arranged or not, provided enough legal grounds to strip her U.S. citizenship. As to Inaba's claim that the marriage had taken place without her knowledge, Rudkin responded that the "only evidence of coercion was the fact that her husband was selected for her by her relatives, according to Japanese custom." "If such coercion will invalidate a marriage between Orientals," the judge added, "it is a matter of common knowledge that few, if any, of such marriage [*sic*], will result, or can result, in expatriation."[17] Rudkin's opinion was thus based primarily on racialized perceptions of Asian "culture" and his insistence that arranged marriages without women's consent were common in Asia. He thus dismissed the legality of Inaba's annulment in the Japanese legal system. Inaba's appeal to her American citizenship, both legal and cultural, proved to be of little avail in Rudkin's court, which effectively upheld racially coded U.S. citizenship and immigration laws of the 1920s. Inaba's experience revealed that as long as these exclusionary legal institutions existed, Nisei women living abroad constantly faced the possibility that they would not be allowed to return to their homes in the United States upon their marriage to Japanese men.

ANTI-JAPANESE SENTIMENT AND NISEI CITIZENS IN JAPAN

Inaba's story had far-reaching transnational implications on the issue of Nisei citizenship in U.S.–Japan relations before World War II. Before this case, officials at the Japanese Foreign Ministry already had foreseen that the increase in U.S. exclusionary legal measures against Japanese immigrants would potentially affect the citizenship status of their U.S.-born children living abroad. As U.S.–Japan relations began to sour in the 1920s and especially in the 1930s with Japan's military aggression in China, the presence of American citizens of Japanese ancestry in Japan became a diplomatic issue that neither of the two governments had dealt with before. Japan's high diplomats became increasingly mindful of the presence of American citizens of Japanese ancestry in Japan. They understood that these laws not only affected the lives of Japanese nationals in the United States but also might require the Japanese government to reevaluate the administration of a significant population of American citizens who could lose their citizenship and settle permanently in Japan and Japanese colonies.[18]

However, it was not until Inaba's arrival in San Francisco in 1928 and the ensuing court cases that Japanese diplomats and American legal experts grasped the complex gendered impact of exclusionary laws in the United States on the lives of Nisei women living in Japan. In 1926, Vice Consul K. Tsurumi in Los Angeles consulted the Japanese Consulate General's legal advisor Ray E. Nimmo's opinion about the citizenship problem of Japanese Americans residing in Japan. In a letter, Tsurumi asked Nimmo whether Japanese Americans in Japan would face the danger of losing their U.S. citizenship as a result of their extended stay abroad.[19] Nimmo's legal opinion, based on his research on U.S. citizenship cases, was that for Nisei in the Japanese Empire to lose their American citizenship they would have to voluntarily foreswear their allegiance to the United States. Based on Nimmo's explanation, the only realistic cause for Nisei to lose U.S. citizenship would be service in the Japanese military, as it would require them to swear allegiance to the Japanese Emperor.[20]

The Japanese Foreign Ministry's concern at this time focused mainly on Nisei men's citizenship in Japan, as their potential military records in Japan and its colonies in Asia seemed to be the only viable evidence of their voluntary expatriation.[21] In reality, however, the number of adult Nisei dual citizens in Japan in the early 1920s was insignificant.[22] Nisei military service in Japan would become a more realistic problem once Japan entered a full-fledged war against the Allied forces during World War II and conscripted Japanese American men living in Japan. Many Nisei men in Japan would reach military age by then and indeed lose their U.S. citizenship as a result of their service in Japan's war against the United States.[23]

It was not until Japanese diplomats in the United States learned of Toshiko Inaba's detention on Angel Island, her appeals cases, and her eventual deportation to Japan, that they finally realized that Nisei women were more likely to face the possibility of losing their U.S. citizenship.[24] They paid close attention to the Inaba case and reported to their superiors in Tokyo on the proceedings of her appeals. At the same time, the Japanese Foreign Ministry and Home Ministry began an effort to find out more about the whereabouts of Nisei residents in Japan. However, new administrative measures to manage the Nisei population in Japan proved to be far from organized, nor was it ever a high administrative priority in the Japanese government. Moreover, the government could not even manage to determine how many Nisei were actually present in Japan. In 1929, the Japanese Ministry of Foreign Affairs estimated that the number of Nisei from the continental United States and Hawaii in Japan had reached thirty thousand. This report claimed that these Nisei were present in Japan for "educational purposes."[25] However, the ministry's estimate did not include those Nisei residing in Japan who were not of school age or those who had gone to Japan for reasons other than a pursuit of education.

The Ministry of Foreign Affairs and the Home Ministry made an attempt to gather more comprehensive data in 1932. In Tokyo, the Metropolitan Police determined that there were 450 Nisei from North America present in the capital. Evidence suggests that the Tokyo Metropolitan Police attempted to keep close watch on the activities of the Nisei in Tokyo in the 1930s. Official reports on the number of Nisei submitted by prefectural offices were far from reliable, however, as they were rather hastily prepared from various sources without effective means of confirmation. Many of these census reports were based on voluntary registrations of families with Nisei living in their households, local school enrollment records, and the estimates prepared by "overseas associations" (kaigai kyōkai) in some prefectures. Moreover, none of the reports provided accurate information about the movements and whereabouts of the Nisei in Japan. It is unclear, for example, how many of the 450 Nisei in Tokyo were students and workers who had moved to the capital from other prefectures.[26]

What actually concerned the Ministry of Foreign Affairs officials more than the census data was the impact of the Nisei presence in Japan on growing anti-Japanese sentiment in the United States. In the 1930s, reports from the consuls general in California particularly alarmed the ministry officials because leading anti-Japan and anti-immigration activists in the United

States, who actively penned criticism of Japan's colonial expansion, began to make specific reference to the Nisei in Japan.[27] For instance, long after Toshiko Inaba's deportation in 1930, California Joint Immigration Committee leader and anti-immigration activist V. S. McClatchy thought the Immigration Act of 1924 was not exclusive enough to stop the influx of all individuals of Japanese race.[28] Throughout the 1920s McClatchy had authored anti-Japanese articles, such as "Guarding the Immigration Gates" and "The Japanese Problem in California." In the 1930s, he began to pay closer attention to the existence of second-generation Japanese Americans in Japan and incessantly warned the American public of what he alleged was Japan's plan to dispatch fifty thousand Kibei—Nisei returnees from Japan—to the U.S. West Coast and Hawaii as spies. For instance, in a widely circulated article in 1937, McClatchy claimed that the Japanese government had harbored Nisei saboteurs in Japan and indoctrinated them with the "duties and loyalty of Japanese citizenship." McClatchy argued that these Nisei would then be sent back to North America to lead Japan's effort to invade the United States by "forc[ing] entrance for her emigration." McClatchy also claimed that those Kibei already in California freely infiltrated into the Japanese American Citizens League (JACL), an emerging Nisei community and civil rights organization on the U.S. West Coast, and had thus added logistical and organizational prowess to their operation as Japanese agents.[29] In his effort to disseminate his message of warning against the alleged Kibei espionage in the United States, McClatchy effectively utilized his personal connection with anti-immigration groups in California as well as leading newspapers, such as the Hearst-owned *San Francisco Examiner* and his family's *Sacramento Bee*.[30]

The anti-Japanese sentiment and the negative public perception of Japanese Americans educated in Japan before World War II had far-reaching transnational consequences. McClatchy's commentaries caught the attention of Japanese American community newspapers as well as the Japanese government–run Domei News Agency, which fed translations of McClatchy articles to local newspapers in Japan. In the first half of 1937, these stories of McClatchy's anti-Kibei messages were often accompanied by a report that the U.S. government had an immediate plan to ban the return of all Japanese Americans residing in Japan. The report warned that the U.S. Congress planned to enact a bill that would require all Japanese Americans residing in Japan to register themselves with U.S. diplomatic missions. The failure to do so would cost the Nisei in Japan the right to return to their homeland.[31]

In May 1937, the Hiroshima Overseas Association reported to the director of the Japanese Foreign Ministry's America Division that McClatchy had written his support for such a bill. This bill would force U.S. citizens who had spent more than two years overseas without registering with the U.S. Consulate to lose their citizenship.[32] This kind of report was so widely circulated by the Japanese press that the Ministry of Foreign Affairs in Tokyo soon received a number of requests for confirmation of the news, as well as for instructions to Japanese Americans living in Japan on the proper course of action. In a letter to the Minister of Foreign Affairs on June 28, 1937, the governor of Wakayama Prefecture demanded clarification of an account in an *Osaka Mainichi Shimbun* report earlier that month on the alleged U.S. bill banning the return of Kibei to their country of birth. The paper reported that the United States had launched a legislative campaign to block the return of Japanese Americans from Japan as a response to the ongoing return migration of Kibei to the U.S. West Coast in the 1930s. This legal measure would go into effect as early as July of that year, according to the paper, which admonished local Nisei residents to report to the U.S. Consulate General to register their American citizenship and denounce any intention to seek permanent residence in Japan.[33] In Kobe in western Japan, an emigration brokerage company ran an advertisement offering to file registration paperwork on behalf of Nisei residents in Japan. The ad quoted the Domei News Agency report on the alleged anti-Nisei/Kibei bill and urged the Nisei in Japan to begin the process of registration with the local U.S. Consulate General.[34]

In the end, it turned out that the reports on the U.S. banning of overseas Nisei had actually started out as a rumor that spread rather quickly. A report from the Japanese consul general in Los Angeles later that year clarified the matter; no evidence was found of any immediate activism to enact such an exclusionary law.[35] However, the impact of this rumor in Japan proved significant, as it revealed the centrality of the issue of citizenship among the Nisei in Japan. The potential loss of their U.S. citizenship and the consequent expatriation of thousands of American-born Nisei would become a critical diplomatic issue at a time of growing tension between the United States and Japan. This incident also demonstrated that Japanese American residents in Japan had experiences that were deeply embedded in legal and political institutions in the United States and Japan, as well as anti-Japanese sentiment in the United States.

The clarification by the Japanese consul general in Los Angeles about the rumor, and even the repeal of the Cable Act in 1936, far from ended the overseas Nisei's fear of the potential loss of their U.S. citizenship. In early 1939, about 150 Nisei residents in Japan from nine organizations under the flagship of the League of Young Japanese Americans convened in Tokyo for a special meeting. According to a Tokyo Metropolitan Police report, the league had organized the gathering to provide a one-day information session on Nisei citizenship. The meeting's purpose was to help ease the anxiety within the Japanese American community in Japan about the possible loss of their U.S. citizenship while residing overseas.[36]

The keynote speaker at this meeting was Tetsuichi Kurashige, a Nisei journalist who had resided in Japan for ten years. A graduate of the University of Oregon School of Law, Kurashige had written articles for the Tokyo-based *Japan Times Weekly* on the issue of Nisei citizenship. A self-proclaimed legal expert in citizenship laws, Kurashige fielded heated questions from the audience about the matter of Nisei citizenship and marriage. The speaker offered textbook answers: first, Japan's 1924 Nationality Law allowed Nisei to choose between U.S. and Japanese citizenship; and second, one could lose his or her U.S. citizenship by becoming a naturalized citizen of another country or formally pledging allegiance to the government of another country. He also assured the audience by explaining that a Nisei woman would not lose her U.S. citizenship by marrying a Japanese man, since the Cable Act had long been repealed.[37]

Hardly more informative than what the Nationality Law had already stipulated, this meeting in Tokyo nevertheless showed that many Nisei in Japan had to live with varying degrees of fear that the life choices they made while living overseas might strip them of their citizenship. Almost a decade after Toshiko Inaba's deportation from San Francisco, legal measures designed to regulate the immigrant generation (Issei) still had equally significant implications on the lives of American citizens of Japanese ancestry living abroad. Furthermore, anti-Japanese activists in the United States were now targeting them as the enemy.

THE NISEI TRANSNATIONAL GENERATION AND THE MAKING OF THE JAPANESE AMERICAN DIASPORA

Despite these critical legal and diplomatic implications, little has been written about the 50,000 second-generation Americans of Japanese ancestry living in prewar Japan who potentially faced Toshiko Inaba's fate. An important political reason has contributed to the Japanese American scholarship's dominant domestic framework and its suppression of the history of Japanese

Americans in the Japanese Empire. Few scholars in the United States before the proliferation of transnational research in the 1990s were willing to come to grips with the history of Nisei who lived, studied, and worked in pre–World War II Japan. The postwar Japanese American scholarship focused heavily on the injustice of the U.S. government's incarceration of Japanese immigrants and Japanese American citizens during the Pacific War and many scholar-activists found it difficult to write about the Nisei educated in Japan. It was particularly difficult when "Nisei as Americans first" was the dominant political motto that drove the postwar movement for redress as well as the history of unquestioned Nisei loyalty to the U.S. government.[38] Many of the 20,000 Kibei who returned from Japan before the war subsequently experienced the wartime internment (1941–46) along with the rest of the 110,000 or so Japanese and Japanese Americans from the West Coast. These Kibei have become controversial figures both in the Japanese American community and in scholarship. Many of them, because of their education in Japan, have been stigmatized as pro-Japan elements in the internment camps. At the same time, the U.S.-centered immigrant paradigm has largely overlooked their experiences in prewar Japan and other locations in the Pacific.[39]

Even the critics who challenged the dominant postwar image of Nisei as a quiet, patriotic model minority took caution against potentially damaging the movement for redress and reparations in the 1980s. The most telling example is the pioneering historian Yuji Ichioka's decision to deliberately delay the publication of an article critical of the history of Nisei loyalty until 1997.[40] In this article, Ichioka presented the case of Kazumaro Buddy Uno, a Nisei who had spent part of his childhood in Japan, returned there later as a young journalist, and then worked for the Japanese military during World War II. Uno's resentment of racial discrimination in America turned him into a sympathizer of Japan's war against the United States and made him radically hostile and even abusive to American POWs he was in charge of interrogating. Ichioka challenged an unquestioned categorization of Uno as a "disloyal Nisei" when he was raised in an American society that "refused to accept the Nisei as Americans." Ichioka then called for a Japanese American history "inclusive" of complex cases like Uno's.[41] One of Kazumaro Buddy Uno's brothers was none other than Edison Uno, a widely respected leader of the redress movement in the 1980s. Ichioka, himself a redress activist, feared that his article might create a backlash against public support for redress legislation and delayed its publication until 1997, after redress recipients were paid by the U.S. government.[42]

It is no coincidence that most English-language works on the history of the Nisei transnational experience have been memoirs and autobiographies written by individual Nisei in the mid-1990s, after the U.S. government issued an official apology and paid reparations for the wartime incarceration of Japanese Americans.[43] These accounts reveal remarkable complexities in Kibei experiences that complicate not only the history of the Japanese American community but also the history of immigration and Asians in diaspora. Stories of these individuals in various corners of the Pacific also challenge the meaning of loyalty in nation-centered immigrant narratives. In one of the earliest autobiographies published by an academic press, labor activist Karl Yoneda detailed his patriotic movement in the internment camps during World War II. The Glendale, California, native spent his formative years in a poverty-stricken rural town in Hiroshima Prefecture, where he developed his social consciousness through the literary works of Marxist and anarchist thinkers on the wretched conditions of the Japanese countryside. Yoneda also traveled through the Japanese colonial world in Korea and Manchuria in 1922 to study under Russian anarchist Vasily Eroshenko in China and participated in labor strikes in major Japanese cities in the mid-1920s. In 1926, twenty-year-old Yoneda left Japan to avoid conscription into the Japanese military. He returned to California as a seasoned labor organizer and staunch critic of Japanese militarism.[44]

Yoneda and other Japanese American activists like him that had spent their youth in Japan hardly fit V. S. McClatchy's description of Kibei as fanatical emperor worshipers or sneaky Japanese agents. During the Pacific War, Yoneda and other Kibei members of the U.S. Communist Party actively supported the U.S. war effort against Japan based on their internationalist consciousness and cooperated with the U.S. government's internment policies. Yoneda enthusiastically advocated Japanese American support for the U.S. war against what he described as the "fascist militarists" in Japan.[45]

Yoneda's zeal to prove his support of the U.S. government even led him to turn against some of his fellow Japanese American prisoners at Manzanar, as he served as an informer for the FBI to report on any sign of subversive behaviors in the internment camp. He did not hesitate to report on the activities of other Kibei in the camp that did not share his commitment to wartime loyalty and cooperation. Ironically, many Kibei at Manzanar considered Yoneda their worst enemy and even attempted to attack his family for his treatment of fellow Kibei internees. The war had turned Yoneda's internationalist idealism into radical patriotism, which earned him the nickname *inu* (literally, "dog"), or a traitor of his own people.[46]

Another California-born Kibei, Iwao Peter Sano, wrote a memoir entitled *One Thousand Days in Siberia: The Odyssey of a Japanese American POW,* depicting a drastically different wartime experience. Unlike Yoneda, Sano was a young student in wartime Japan and was conscripted into the Japanese army on the China front during the final days of the Pacific War in 1945 and lost his U.S. citizenship as a result of his service to the emperor. Sano survived three years of hard labor in a Soviet POW camp in Siberia after the conclusion of World War II. Upon his repatriation to Japan, Sano worked for the Allied occupation forces in Tokyo and returned to the United States in 1952 as a Japanese immigrant. Having lost his U.S. citizenship, Sano had to apply for naturalization to regain his U.S. citizenship, going through the citizenship test, interviews, and pledge of allegiance as part of the procedure designed to assess foreign-born immigrants' loyalty and Americanization. Trained as a suicide bomber during the Pacific War, he became a passionate antiwar activist during the Vietnam War and a fierce critic of Japan's militarist past.[47] An architect, he refused to work on any project related to the military and continues to this day to talk publicly about his dedication to pacifism and his wartime experiences as a cautionary tale against military indoctrination.[48]

Stories of Japanese Americans like Toshiko Inaba, Kazumaro Buddy Uno, Karl Yoneda, Iwao Peter Sano, and other diverse Kibei reveal the theoretical limits prevalent in the examination of second-generation experiences in both U.S. immigration history and diaspora studies. In recent years, migration scholars have attempted to place second-generation experiences in multiple sociopolitical, cultural, and legal settings encompassing several nations. They position the U.S.-born children of immigrants in similar transnational "social fields" that have affected their parents' experiences, such as anti-Asian sentiments in the United States, international war, and developments in diplomatic relations involving both "sending" and "host" nations. These theorists also add that second-generation communities may find ways to respond to these social and political realities that they constantly experience because of the circulation of people, ideas, and cultural values within and between countries.[49]

However, these studies tend to focus exclusively on second-generation communities within U.S. borders. An example of this type of second-generation transnationalism could be found in the Japanese American community in the 1930s when the long existing anti-Japanese sentiment on the U.S. West Coast increased because of Japan's military aggression in China. As noted by David Yoo, when the mainstream press in the United

States relentlessly criticized Japan's actions in Asia, many Nisei found themselves and their first-generation parents facing intensified racial hostility. Nisei writers in the United States responded to this situation by using English-language articles in community newspapers to convince the general public that the hostility against Japan in the international arena was fueling unwarranted anti-Japanese sentiment in the United States.[50]

A theoretical debate has emerged questioning how salient this representation of second-generation transnational engagement really was for the rest of the ethnic community. Some scholars argue that like the Nisei writers in the above example, the actions and choices of the second generation operated fundamentally in a transnational world. Others disagree, noting that by virtue of being geographically and culturally rooted in the United States, many among the second generation could not have experienced the truly bilingual and bicultural experiences of their immigrant parents.[51] This argument emphasizes the localization of immigrant communities and their offspring who, in Shu-mei Shih's words, may "choose to end their state of diaspora by the second or third generation."[52] In both arguments, however, the second generation remained essentially a U.S.-based group whose contact with transnational developments occurred primarily in terms of the social relations defined by their specific "ethnic" affiliation within U.S. society.

In contrast, individuals like Inaba, Uno, Yoneda, and Sano, who experienced trans-Pacific migrations and spent various amounts of time in the Japanese colonial world, exemplify transnational individuals whose experiences transcend the limits and premises presented by both sides of the debate. Their experiences were shaped by their physical presence on both sides of the Pacific. Their identities were both socially constructed and self-defined through their interactions with Issei and Nisei within the Japanese American community as well as with people of multiple generations in Japan. Therefore, tracing their movements and experiences offers a unique analytical lens that can help explore the embeddedness of Nisei lives in multiple transnational sociopolitical fields as they engaged complex legal, political, and social transformations in the United States and Japan that shaped their lives as migrants.

The issue of Nisei loyalty and nationalism has had a lasting impact on the public narrative of Japanese American history in the United States. Postwar scholars have grappled with the need to challenge and complicate the meanings and implications of history centered on Nisei Americanism in the context of Japanese American internment. However, the volatile international relations in the 1920s and 1930s that culminated in the Pacific War also forced the Nisei in the Japanese colonial world to negotiate ways to deal with their national allegiance and citizenship. Moreover, as Peter Sano's case demonstrates, these transnational individuals' experiences had lasting legacies that shaped the intersected histories of the U.S. occupation in Japan, post–World War II immigration to the United States, and the Asian American social movement. Peter Sano's emergence as an American peace activist after the war was a culmination of his exile as an American migrant and a Japanese prisoner of war; and his struggle to navigate the postwar American system of immigration and citizenship to reclaim his place in Asian American history through his diasporic identity.

The Japanese American diaspora is a sum of these moments of change when Asian history and Asian American history have converged. Recent scholars such as Eiichiro Azuma have started to bridge the divide between ethnic studies and area studies and shed light on the history of Japanese Americans in the context of larger U.S.–Japan relations. As Azuma notes, however, immigration history and the history of Japanese colonialism still tend to operate in separate academic domains despite recognition of the critical need for examining "intersections."[53] These intersections exist even beyond the connection between Japanese overseas emigration history and the history of Japanese colonial expansion before World War II. The history of American-born Nisei who emigrated from the United States can reveal complex and unexpected implications of the legal, political, and diplomatic developments in the United States and Japan that have been largely overlooked in scholarship and classrooms alike. The varied experiences of the Japanese American transnational generation offer an intricate, yet meaningful, intersection of the histories of migration, transnational families and communities, and diplomatic policies on both sides of the Pacific. These experiences remind us of the critical need to rethink the spatial, temporal, and conceptual boundaries of Asian and Asian American studies.

MICHAEL JIN is an assistant professor of global Asian studies and history at the University of Illinois at Chicago. His current manuscript project, *Citizens, Immigrants, and the Stateless: Migration and Transnationalism of Japanese Americans in the Pacific,* includes extended life histories of U.S.-born Japanese Americans in the Cold War Pacific.

NOTES

1. U.S. Department of Labor Immigration Service Board of Special Inquiry, "In the Matter of Inaba, Toshiko and Inaba, Ikiba, Natives," September 1928, Records of the Immigration and Naturalization Service, RG 85 Box 8375, National Archives and Records Administration, Washington, D.C. (hereafter cited as NARA); "Honpo ni oite kon'in shitaru nikkei shimin no shiminken soshitsu ni yoru sokan ni kansuru ken," May 1, 1930, Nikkei Gaijin Kankei Zakken Vol. 1, K.1.1.0.9.1, Diplomatic Record Office, Ministry of Foreign Affairs of Japan (hereafter cited as Nikkei Gaijin Kankei Zakken).

2. U.S. Department of Labor Immigration Service Board of Special Inquiry, "In the Matter of Inaba," NARA; "Honpo ni oite kon'in shitaru nikkei shimin no shiminken soshitsu ni yoru sokan ni kansuru ken," Nikkei Gaijin Kankei Zakken.

3. U.S. Department of Labor Immigration Service Board of Special Inquiry, "In the Matter of Inaba," NARA; "Honpo ni oite kon'in shitaru nikkei shimin no shiminken soshitsu ni yoru sokan ni kansuru ken," Nikkei Gaijin Kankei Zakken.

4. Mae M. Ngai, "The Architecture of Race in American Immigration Law: A Reexamination of the Immigration Act of 1924," *Journal of American History* 86, no. 1 (June 1999): 70–71.

5. Paul R. Spickard, *Japanese Americans: The Formation and Transformations of an Ethnic Group* (New York: Twayne, 1996), 89, 167. See also Robert Lee's introduction to Mary Kimoto Tomita, *Dear Miye: Letters Home from Japan, 1939–1946,* ed. Robert Lee (Stanford: Stanford University Press, 1995), 18–19; Yuji Ichioka, introduction to *Ganbatte: Sixty-Year Struggle of a Kibei Worker,* by Karl G. Yoneda (Los Angeles: Asian American Studies Center, University of California, Los Angeles, 1983), xii. *Zaibei Nihonjinshi* [History of Japanese in America] in 1940 reported that 10,000 Nisei returned to the United States from Japan, which left the number of Nisei remaining in Japan to be 20,000: *Zaibei Nihonjinshi* (San Francisco: Zaibei Nihonjinkai, 1940), 1117–18. Brian Hayashi notes that figures suggested by contemporary estimations were probably too low: see Brian Masaru Hayashi, *Democratizing the Enemy: The Japanese American Internment* (Princeton: Princeton University Press, 2004), 44–45, 238n11.

6. For critiques of the postwar scholarship's emphasis on Japanese American loyalty, see Yuji Ichioka, "The Meaning of Loyalty: The Case of Kazumaro Buddy Uno," *Amerasia Journal* 23, no. 2 (Winter 1997–1998): 45–71; Naoko Shibusawa, "The Artist Belongs to the People: The Odyssey of Taro Yashima," *Journal of Asian American Studies* 9, no. 3 (October 2005): 257–75. For a detailed study on the multiple representations of the history of the Japanese American internment, see Alice Yang Murray, *Historical Memories of the Japanese American Internment and the Struggle for Redress* (Stanford: Stanford University Press, 2008).

7. Eiichiro Azuma, *Between Two Empires: Race, History, and Transnationalism in Japanese America* (New York: Oxford University Press, 2005); Azuma Eiichiro, "Nisei no nihon ryugaku no hikari to kage: Nikkei amerikajin no ekkyo kyoiku no rinen to mujun," in *Amerika nihonjin imin no ekkyo kyoikushi,* ed. Yoshida Akira (Tokyo: Nihon Tosho Center, 2005); Eiichiro Azuma, "'Pioneers of Overseas Japanese

Development': Japanese American History and the Making of Expansionist Ortho-doxy in Imperial Japan," *Journal of Asian Studies* 67, no. 4 (November 2008): 1187–226.

8. See diasporic approaches to Chinese migrations in Madeline Y. Hsu, *Dream of Gold, Dream of Home: Transnationalism and Migration between the United States and South China, 1882–1943* (Stanford: Stanford University Press, 2000); Adam McKeown, *Chinese Migrant Networks and Cultural Change: Peru, Chicago, Hawaii, 1900–1936* (Chicago: University of Chicago Press, 2001). Japanese Americanists' diasporic approach has largely focused on migrations and settlements in the Ameri-cas: Lane Ryo Hirabayashi, Akemi Kikumura-Yano, and James H. Hirabayashi, eds., *New World, New Lives: Globalization and People of Japanese Descent in the Americas and from Latin America in Japan* (Stanford: Stanford University Press, 2002).

9. Shelly Chan, "The Case for Diaspora: A Temporal Approach to the Chinese Experience," *Journal of Asian Studies* 74, no. 1 (February 2015): 107–10.

10. "In the Matter of Inaba, Toshiko and Inaba, Ikiba, Natives"; "Honpo ni oite kon'in shitaru nikkei shimin no shiminken soshitsu ni yoru sokan ni kansuru ken."

11. Act of September 22, 1922, 42 Stat. 1021.

12. *Ozawa v. United States,* 260 U.S. 178 (1922).

13. *Toshiko Inaba v. John D. Nagle, Commissioner of Immigration* (N.D.Cal. 1929), petition for writ of habeas corpus, No. 19919 L.

14. Ibid.

15. See Ngai, "The Architecture of Race."

16. *Toshiko Inaba v. John D. Nagle, Commissioner of Immigration* (N.D.Cal. 1929), petition for writ of habeas corpus, No. 19919 L.

17. Toshiko Inaba v. John D. Nagle, Commissioner of Immigration, San Fran-cisco, Calif. (9th. Cir. 1929).

18. "Nihon ni kikoku seru mono no beikoku shiminken ni kan suru ken," March 1927, Nikkei Gaijin Kankei Zakken.

19. Vice Consul of Japan in Los Angeles to Ray E. Nimmo, December 9, 1926, Nikkei Gaijin Kankei Zakken.

20. Ray E. Nimmo to Vice Consul of Japan in Los Angeles, December 30, 1926, Nikkei Gaijin Kankei Zakken.

21. Consul General of Japan in Los Angeles to the Minister of Foreign Affairs of Japan, February 15, 1927, Nikkei Gaijin Kankei Zakken.

22. Yuji Ichioka, "Dai Nisei Mondai: Changing Japanese Immigrant Concep-tions of the Second-Generation Problem, 1902–1941," in *Before Internment: Essays in Prewar Japanese American History,* ed. Gordon H. Chang and Eiichiro Azuma (Stanford: Stanford University Press, 2005), 19.

23. See accounts of former Japanese American servicemen in the Japanese armed forces: Jim Yoshida, *The Two Words of Jim Yoshida* (New York: William Mor-row, 1972); Yoshida Mitsuru, "Sokoku to tekikoku no aida," in *Chinkon senkan Yam-ato* (Tokyo: Kodansha, 1974); Tachibana Yuzuru, *Teikoku kaigun shikan ni natta nikkei nisei* (Tokyo: Tsukiji Shokan, 1994); Iwao Peter Sano, *One Thousand Days in Siberia: The Odyssey of a Japanese-American POW* (Lincoln: University of Nebraska Press, 1997).

24. "Nihonjin to kon'in ni yori soshitsu shitaru fujin beikoku shiminken no rikon go kaifuku shinsei ni taisuru kyōka hanketsu no ken," March 1927, Nikkei Gaijin Kankei Zakken.

25. Rinjiro Sodei, *Watashitachi wa teki datta noka* (Tokyo: Iwanami Shoten, 1995), 12.

26. "Honpo ni kyojuseru bei, ka shussei nikkeijin sūchō no ken," 1932, Nikkei Gaijin Kankei Zakken.

27. Interim Consul General of Japan in San Francisco to Minister of Foreign Affairs, July 25, 1936, Nikkei Gaijin Kankei Zakken.

28. "Honpo ni oite kon'in shitaru nikkei shimin no shiminken soshitsu ni yoru sokan ni kansuru ken, Nikkei Gaijin Kankei Zakken."

29. V.S. McClatchy, "The Story of Japanese Immigration: Japan Demands What May Not Be Conceded," California Joint Immigration Committee Document 507, September 1937, William Randolph Hearst Papers, Box 5, Folder 19, BANC MSS 77/121C, Bancroft Library, University of California, Berkeley.

30. V.S. McClatchy to William Randolph Hearst, January 10, 1938, William Randolph Hearst Papers, Box 5, Folder 19, BANC MSS 77/121C, Bancroft Library, University of California, Berkeley.

31. "Nikkei shimin kibei kinshi un'un no fusetsu ni kansuru ken, June 29, 1937, Nikkei Gaijin Kankei Zakken.

32. President of Hiroshima Overseas Association to Director, America Division, Ministry of Foreign Affairs, July 25, 1937, Nikkei Gaijin Kankei Zakken.

33. Governor of Wakayama Prefecture to Director, America Division, Ministry of Foreign Affairs, June 28, 1937, Nikkei Gaijin Kankei Zakken; "Dai nisei beikoku ni kiraharu," Osaka Mainichi Shimbun, *Wakayama Edition*, June 11, 1937.

34. "Keisho," May 1937, Nikkei Gaijin Kankei Zakken.

35. "Nikkei shimin kibei kinshi un'un no fusetsu ni kansuru ken, Nikkei Gaijin Kankei Zakken."

36. "Nichibei seinen renmei no koenkai kaisai ni kansuru ken," February 2, 1939, Nikkei Gaijin Kankei Zakken.

37. Ibid.

38. Naoko Shibusawa, "The Artist Belongs to the People: The Odyssey of Taro Yashima," *Journal of Asian American Studies* 8, no. 3 (October 2005): 259.

39. In the 1970s and 1980s, "revisionist" scholars like Gary Y. Okihiro, Arthur A. Hansen, David A. Hacker, and Roger Daniels made efforts to dispel the popular myth of Kibei resistance as a sign of disloyalty. Their works still employed an interpretive framework that considers the question of loyalty within the realm of "Americanism." See Gary Y. Okihiro, "Resistance in America's Concentration Camps: A Re-evaluation," *Amerasia Journal* 2 (Fall 1973): 20–34; Gary Y. Okihiro, "Tule Lake under Martial Law: A Study in Japanese Resistance," *Journal of Ethnic Studies* 5, no. 3 (Fall 1977): 71–85; Arthur A. Hansen and David A. Hacker, "The Manzanar Riot: An Ethnic Perspective," *Amerasia Journal* 2 (Fall 1974): 112–57; Roger Daniels, *Concentration Camps, North America: Japanese in the United States and Canada during World War II*, rev. ed. (Malabar, Fl.: Robert E. Krieger, 1981), 106–7.

40. Alice Yang Murray, *Historical Memories of the Japanese American Internment and the Struggle for Redress* (Stanford: Stanford University Press, 2008), 342.

41. Ichioka, "The Meaning of Loyalty."

42. Murray, *Historical Memories*, 342.

43. Examples include Karl G. Yoneda, *Ganbatte: Sixty-Year Struggle of a Kibei Worker* (Los Angeles: Asian American Studies Center, University of California, Los Angeles, 1983); Mary Kimoto Tomita, *Dear Miye: Letters Home from Japan, 1939–1946*, ed. Robert Lee (Stanford: Stanford University Press, 1995); Minoru Kiyota, *Beyond Loyalty: The Story of a Kibei*, trans. Linda Klepinger Keenan (Honolulu: University of Hawai'i Press, 1997); Sano, *One Thousand Days*.

44. Yoneda, *Ganbatte*, xi–17.

45. Yoneda, *Ganbatte*; Karl Yoneda, *Manzanar kyosei shuyojo nikki* (Tokyo: PMC Shuppan, 1988), 163–64.

46. Ibid.

47. Sano, *One Thousand Days*.

48. Peter Sano, interview with the author, Palo Alto, Calif., July 12, 2007; Peter Sano, "World War II Memories in the United States and Japan" (guest lecture, University of California, Santa Cruz, February 15, 2013); Peter Sano, "Fighting for the Emperor: Nisei Soldiers in the Imperial Armed Forces" (guest lecture, Japanese American Museum of San Jose, San Jose, Calif., February 7, 2015).

49. Peggy Levitt and Mary C. Waters, eds., *The Changing Face of Home: The Transnational Lives of the Second Generation* (New York: Russell Sage Foundation, 2002), 3–17.

50. David Y. Yoo, *Growing Up Nisei: Race, Generation, and Culture among Japanese Americans in California, 1924–49* (Urbana: University of Illinois Press, 2000), 87–90.

51. Levitt and Waters, *The Changing Face*, 4.

52. Shu-mei Shi, "Against Diaspora: The Sinophone as Places of Cultural Production," in *Global Chinese Literature: Critical Essays*, ed. David Dewei Wang and Jing Tsu (Leiden: Brill, 2010), 45.

53. Azuma, "'Pioneers,'" 1189.

Ronald Reagan, the College Movie

Political Demonology, Academic Freedom, and the University of California

CURTIS MAREZ

M y title is a reference to an essay by the late Berkeley professor Michael Rogin entitled, "Ronald Reagan, the Movie," in which he argues that the forms of political demonology President Reagan directed at leftists, women, unions, and people of color were profoundly informed by his prior career in Hollywood. It was while working in the film industry, according to Rogin, that the future U.S. president first learned how to objectify himself as an image on the screen, removed from the world of everyday reality and safely enclosed within the universe of Hollywood films. The actor's talent for self-reification, as it were, would come in handy when he became president, imaginatively clothing his self-image in the quasi-religious raiment of U.S. nationalism while distancing himself from responsibility for the destructive consequences of his administration's policies. Rogin's claims were influential well beyond academia, generating a number of high-profile media events. When he delivered an early version of "Ronald Reagan, the Movie" at the American Political Studies Association in 1985, it was reported on in the *New York Times*, complete with photos of Reagan playing Notre Dame football star George Gipp, as well as pictures of Sylvester Stallone as Rambo and Clint Eastwood as Dirty Harry, two other actors whose film lines Reagan had famously borrowed. When Rogin published the essay as part of a University of California Press book entitled *Ronald Reagan the Movie, and Other Episodes in Political Demonology* (1987), the *Times* gave it a detailed, positive review, primarily focused on the chapter about Reagan. Rogin's research even inspired a segment on *60 Minutes,* also called "Ronald Reagan, the Movie," in which he was interviewed by reporter Morley Shafer.[1] Building on Rogin's work, in this essay I turn to Ronald Reagan's college films, arguing that they presage contemporary models of academic freedom

that emerge from a matrix of white supremacy, settler colonialism, and heteropatriarchy.

My thinking about academic freedom is inspired by the response to the
American Studies Association's passage of a resolution calling for a boycott
of Israeli academic institutions in 2013, when I was ASA president. Afterward,
according to Jodi Melamed, the ASA "would become the target of a hegemonic bloc of university presidents and regents, politicians and watchdog
institutions connected through their condemnations of the ASA resolution
to boycott Israeli academic institutions." Answering a call from Palestinian
civil society, the ASA national council endorsed a resolution calling for an
academic boycott not of individual scholars but of Israeli academic institutions complicit in the occupation of Palestine and the violation of Palestinian human rights and academic freedom. In response, almost 250 university
presidents publically denounced the ASA in the name of academic freedom.
In "Dangerous Associations"—a response to my presidential address—
Melamed presents a compelling reading of the statements by university
presidents, concluding that they represented a version of academic freedom
that supported repressive police power while encouraging individuals and
institutions to willfully ignore violence and exploitation. As she and many
others have argued, the statements by the university presidents refused to
acknowledge the routine violation of the academic freedom of Palestinian
scholars. Such constructions of academic freedom exercise "a kind of epistemological violence" that radically limits knowledge about the contradictions between, on the one hand, abstract articulations of the university as
a place of dialogue and diversity, and on the other hand, the university as a
"key institution within racialized and gendered capitalism," "[a] locus for
the social reproduction of racial, class, and gender inequalities and normative morality," and "[a] center and transit for the ongoing neoliberal debt
economy, controlling dissent, and perpetuating old and new forms of settler
colonialism."

In my ASA presidential address, "Seeing in the Red: Looking at Student
Debt," I presented an intersectional analysis of university regimes of debt as
modes of race, class, gender, and settler exploitation in ways that connected
the Palestinian question to the crisis in contemporary universities. I argued
that both the Israeli occupation and student debt undermine a right to education, while the "student-led BDS movement on college campuses could
thus also be described as part of a broader effort to take some control over the
student debt financing of settler colonial violence." The various statements by
university presidents denouncing the ASA thus depended on disconnecting

precisely what I had attempted to connect—academic freedom, occupation, and exploitation. At the same time, the university presidents promoted global universities and knowledge production as capital accumulation. Among other things, the ASA boycott laid bare the ways in which dominant models of academic freedom have turned universities into the educational equivalent of free-trade zones.[2] The forms of political demonology that the university presidents and others aimed at the ASA have compelled me to write "Ronald Reagan, the College Movie" as part of a genealogy of campus militarization in tandem with the neoliberal redefinition of academic freedom. The comparison of militarization and the forms of academic freedom mobilized by contemporary university administrators is revealing since they function in similar ways, combining both repression of students and faculty and the production of market-driven forms of pedagogy and research.

Ronald Reagan's five college films—three playing a student and two a professor—anticipate in multiple ways his subsequent political demonization of the University of California system. Reagan became California governor partly by vilifying the system, especially Berkeley, as sites of radical anticapitalist, antiwar, and anti-heteronormative politics. As Christopher Newfield has argued, such attacks were part of a larger effort to discredit the ideals of social equality that had, however imperfectly, guided the University of California since its inception.[3] When Reagan was elected governor, he raised fees at state colleges and universities, repeatedly slashed construction budgets for state campuses, and engineered the firing of University of California (henceforth UC) president Clark Kerr and the firing of Angela Davis from UCLA. According to Gary Clabaugh, as governor and subsequently as president, Reagan "demagogically fanned discontent with public education, then made political hay of it" and "bashed educators and slashed education spending while professing to value it."[4] At the same time, Governor Reagan initiated a new militarization of college campuses, deploying the National Guard against students and faculty in ways that anticipate our contemporary education-scape of baton-swinging, pepper-spraying, tank-driving campus cops.

Recently, a number of scholars have produced important work at the intersection of critical ethnic studies and critical university studies. Melamed, in her cultural history *Represent and Destroy: Rationalizing Violence in the New Racial Capitalism,* analyzes how university and other official antiracisms and models of multiculturalism sustain and extend capitalist investments in racial inequality. In *The Reorder of Things: The University and Its Pedagogies of Minority Difference,* Roderick Ferguson demonstrates how contemporary universities became leading laboratories for the management of difference, containing the radical demands of students and the challenges of the interdisciplines (notably ethnic studies) with forms of symbolic inclusion that reproduce material inequalities. In her study of diversity work in British and Australian higher education, *On Being Included: Racism and Diversity in Institutional Life,* Sara Ahmed argues that critical diversity talk is often co-opted by administrative discourse, while the formulation of written policy is substituted for action. Meanwhile, in *The Undercommons: Fugitive Planning and Black Study,* Stefano Harney and Fred Moten argue that universities often aim to police, expel, or effectively deport from campus all forms of what they call "study," a practice of collective thought and social action antagonistic to market logics. Finally, the contributors to the volume *The Imperial University: Academic Repression and Scholarly Dissent,* edited by Piya Chatterjee and Sunaina Maira, analyze the multiple ways in which contemporary universities are ideological and material agents of imperialism. Essays focus, for example, on CIA and FBI efforts to recruit Black and Latino college students, the complicity between neoliberal universities and the prison-industrial complex, administrative clamp downs on BDS campus activism and scholarship critical of Israel, and the policing of research and activism about immigrant rights.[5] All of these authors study universities as spaces of containment that suggest comparison with and are often in fact connected to other carceral spaces, such as reservations, prisons, and detention centers.

Immensely valuable, such critical ethnic studies work on higher education—like research in critical university studies more broadly—focuses on the post–World War II university. A CES account of the longer history of the university and its conditions of possibility thus remains to be written. Craig Steven Wilder has made an important contribution to that project with his book *Ebony and Ivy: Race, Slavery, and the Troubled History of America's Universities,* which begins in the 1600s and extends to the mid-nineteenth century. Wilder argues that the establishment and growth of the Ivy League depended on settler colonialism and slavery. Colonial-era colleges often functioned as military forts protecting white settlers, while administrators, teachers, students, and alumni served as missionaries and soldiers in anti-Indian campaigns. The growth of colleges was made possible by the expropriation of Indian land and investments in Southern and Caribbean plantations. Boards of trustees were filled with plantation owners, slavers, and the merchants who profited from slavery, who were also the most important donors in the early history of American universities. In addition, the schools themselves were constructed by Indian and African slaves while many college presidents, faculty, and students owned slaves. Finally, early universities helped to produce "knowledge" about white superiority and Black and Indian inferiority.[6] My contribution to constructing this longer history requires turning to the early twentieth-century social and cultural formation that produced Reagan and his higher education policies. First as a college student and subsequently as a Hollywood actor, Reagan inherited an early twentieth-century understanding of universities as centers of white settler-colonial containment articulated in terms Christianity, white respectability ("good character"), and team sport spectacles. Ultimately, it was as an actor that Reagan learned how to effectively mediate that vision, becoming one of its most powerful representatives. In terms of contemporary political demonology, Reagan casts a long shadow, and his performance of the white settler university continues to inform the neoliberal institutions of higher learning CES scholars and students struggle within and against.

Reagan's own experiences as a college student were central to his political identity. Looking back on his college years while governor, he concluded, "Everything good in my life . . . began at Eureka." Between 1947 and 1980, he served a total of eighteen years on the college's board of trustees. Starting in 1941, Reagan returned to campus eleven times for official events, including (while governor) the dedication of a new PE facility named in his honor. The overlap between college sports and politics is suggested by the fact that he spoke at a Eureka pep rally during his 1980 presidential campaign. Reagan also spoke at commencement three times (1957, 1982, 1992).[7] In his 1982 commencement address, now known as "The Eureka Speech," he presented a major foreign policy statement about the Strategic Arms Reduction Treaty (START) negotiations with the Soviets, and returned in 1984 to give another major speech on nuclear arms control, suggesting the extent to which for Reagan the idealized image of college life incorporated students into forms of Cold War military authority.

Raised in a relatively poor family, in 1928, Reagan was admitted to Eureka College near Normal, Illinois, as a financial aid student. In contrast with a large, public university like Berkeley, Eureka was a small, private, Christian, liberal arts college.[8] The first two decades of the twentieth century witnessed the emergence of large new secular research universities that were self-consciously distinguished from colleges like Reagan's, which were often invested primarily in moral subjects. For their part, many of the older colleges responded to the new universities by reasserting their distinctive commitments to a conservative pedagogy. Which is not to say that universities were liberatory institutions—far from it. But colleges in the 1910s and 1920s were often distinctly reactionary, answering the university and the perceived moral permissiveness of the larger culture by reasserting a mission to maintain the authority of Western canons of knowledge and hand them down to students. According to historian Frederick Rudolph, "By the 1920s, the temper of American higher education was really counterrevolutionary as far as the university movement was concerned" and bent on a "return to aristocratic ideals."[9] Such colleges thus tended to be paternalistic, devoted to "guiding" students morally, inculcating discipline, and encouraging submission to authority. In their commitment to an American agrarian ideal, colleges also tended to be located in rural settings so as to shield students from the dangers of racially diverse cities.[10] Finally, while colleges were sometimes co-ed, most of their students were male, and the curricular focus on character building aimed to turn bright white boys into good white men.

As he explained in his autobiography, *An American Life,* Reagan found his small rural college idyllic:

> There were five Georgian-style brick buildings arranged around a semicircle with windows framed in white. The buildings were covered in ivy and surrounded by acres of rolling green lawn studded with trees still lush with their summer foliage. . . . Eureka was everything I had dreamed it would be and more. In later life, I visited some of the most famous universities in the world. As Governor of California, I presided over a university system regarded as one of the best. But if I had to do it over again, I'd go back to Eureka or another small college like it in a second.[11]

Reagan here recalls the historical tension between the two models of higher education, asserting his preference for a college over a university in ways that help frame his attack on the University of California while governor. During the 1910s and 1920s, while there was a small but significant increase in coeducational universities and colleges, as well as access for Black students at Black colleges (although many such schools were dramatically under resourced), women were underrepresented and the number of Black college graduates remained tiny. In the first decades of the twentieth century when at least 5 percent of white people in the United States between the ages of 18 and 21 were attending college, the figure for Black people was less than one-third of 1 percent.[12] Many colleges and universities, especially in the South, expressly barred Black students, while many more did so unofficially. Higher education as a whole remained racially segregated, and even schools that admitted Black students consigned them to segregated dorms and dining halls.[13] Reagan's ideal campus was hence a largely white and male world.

Such segregation was further reproduced in U.S. mass media. "It was standard practice to exclude the black colleges from the national media, whether major newspapers or other publications about college life," writes historian John R. Thelin. For example, he continues, "the anthologies of college songbooks published between 1900 and 1920 claimed to be all-inclusive, but the black colleges were not among the hundreds of institutions from all over the country."[14] Similarly in 1929, when Reagan was a college sophomore, one of the most popular films was *Horse Feathers,* a Marx Brothers comedy set at a fictional college where the entire faculty and student body are white and the only Black character is a maid.[15] As a result, terms like "university" and "college student" became ideological terms for heteropatriarchal whiteness. The title of Daniel A. Clark's history could be usefully revised as *Creating the (White) College Man: American Mass Magazines and Middle-Class Manhood, 1890–1915*, since, as he argues, the dominant image of the college student in the early twentieth century was a WASP young man, who partly came to eclipse the heroic self-made (white) businessman in period mass media.[16]

Reagan graduated from Eureka in 1932 with a degree in Economics and Sociology, although fifty years later he confessed to the graduating class at his alma mater that he was a C student who spent more time playing football than studying.[17] In addition to football and drama, Reagan's college life centered on his fraternity, Tau Kappa Epsilon. Which is to say that as a college student he was incorporated into white male institutions of homosocial power and schooled in the often-violent heteropatriarchal competition over women and territory. College football, in particular, continued to frame Reagan's appeals to voters while governor and ultimately president, when he was often photographed throwing a football or wearing a Eureka football jersey, and so it is worth considering sporting spectacles in some detail.[18] Historically, college football—with its largely all-white, male teams; hierarchical military organization; staged battles over territory; Indian mascots; and often-literal occupation of indigenous land—has constituted a settler-colonial entertainment spectacle rivaled only by Hollywood Westerns. To further complicate Clark's title, we could describe the role of football in

"Creating the (White Settler)Man." Middle-class magazines directed at white audiences, Clark argues, celebrated college football as part of the "muscular Christianity" and social Darwinist reform movements to renew the vitality of white masculinities threatened by "over-civilization." With the so-called closing of the frontier, athletic contexts emerged as a substitute means of forging "martial virtues as well as Christian character through competition and physical exertion," which partly explains why imperialists like Teddy Roosevelt were also football fans.[19] As Rudolph reminds us, the "rise of college football was contemporaneous with the development of a martial spirit which manifested itself in two forms: in those warlike developments that led to such victories as those of the Standard Oil Company, and in that series of imperial adventure and bellicose adventures that planted the American flag in the Caribbean and the Pacific and paraded the American navy around the world."[20] Whereas people of color and Indian "savages" possessed the "primitive urges vital for successful competition," they lacked the "higher governing ideals of civilization." Social Darwinists claimed that only WASPs could "harness both primitive impulses and civilized traits," while boosters represented the college football player as "the perfect manly embodiment of disciplined physical strength *and* virtuous character, the man to carry the race forward."[21] Just as white settlers claim indigenous land as their own and just as white settler colleges often incorporate Indian mascots, the college football player was praised for seemingly incorporating and sublating Indian "savagery." In this context it is striking that the mascot for Reagan's alma mater—the "Red Devil"—is named for an anti-Indian slur.

Reagan often remembered college football as an exercise in character building, in which good coaches impart the values of hard work, sportsmanship, and competition to student athletes. "As a coach," Reagan told graduating students at Notre Dame in 1981, Rockne "did more than teach young men how to play a game. He believed truly that the noblest work of man was building the character of man."[22] Invocations of nobility notwithstanding, in the 1910s and 1920s college football was big business. It was during those years that many universities built massive football "coliseums" and earned millions of dollars in ticket sales and other revenue.[23] Despite their distinct mission, the colleges that could afford it attempted to emulate universities in terms of football. College and university football games thus became mass spectacles, avidly followed by large newspaper, radio, and film audiences. Given the relatively small percentage of students who attended college in the United States, football served as the most significant representation of higher education for the vast majority of people and the most important vehicle of university public relations.[24] As a result, many people in the early twentieth century began to act "as if *the* purpose of an American college or university were to field a football team."[25] The kinds of lessons imparted in these years by the big business of college football can be further gleaned from a scathing 1929 report by the Carnegie Foundation. College football, the report documented, had led to large revenues and inflated salaries for coaches that skewed a school's mission away from education and toward commerce. Football also created an opening for wealthy alumni and other donors to influence and control colleges and universities. College football became an ideological spectacle that effectively disappeared the violence of capitalist exploitation by celebrating the seeming dissolution of class differences as farmer's sons supposedly played ball members of the elite and the middle class. Football further promoted the virtues and excitements of free-market competition and the ethics of team loyalty that reconciled an older individualism and a new corporate mentality.[26]

While we are accustomed to thinking about the corporate university as a contemporary phenomenon, I would argue for historicizing it in terms of the kinds of patriarchal racial capitalism represented by college football. As Thorstein Veblen argued in *The Higher Learning in America* (1918), the prominence of college football was symptomatic of "the corrupting influence of the business ethos."[27] The game generated capital for white institutions and linked capital to whiteness in the figure of successful coaches and players. College football represented a struggle for white power, to preserve white power over capital at the expense of people of color. College football teams were overwhelmingly white. Southern teams were all white and when they played northern teams with a Black player or two they were forced to sit out the game. College football powerhouses did play the Carlisle Indian teams but did not themselves include Native American players. Even when allowed to compete, Black athletes experienced racist violence and segregation on campus. At Rutgers in 1915, where he was the only Black student, Paul Robeson was beaten and nearly lynched by his white football teammates.[28] Two decades later, despite his phenomenal success on the field, Black track star Jesse Owens was excluded from campus dorms and forced to live off campus at Ohio State University.[29]

By contrast, in Reagan's reconstruction of his own collegiate history, football symbolically transcends anti-Black racism. In 1986 remarks to students and faculty at Martin Luther King Jr. Elementary School, for example, he spoke nostalgically about his Black teammate Franklin "Burgie" Burghardt:

He's departed this world now—but he's probably the closest friend I ever had. . . . You see, just one individual with principles like that, like Dr. King and like Franklin Burghardt. . . . The world is so different today. And those of us who were a part of that revolution that Martin Luther King performed in, all of us, we are so happy for what has happened and so happy to see all of you here together in this different kind of America.[30]

Here King's death is collapsed with Reagan's dead Black classmate so as to suggest that racism is confined to the past. At the same time, he suggests that the Reagan "revolution" was part of a long civil rights movement that originated with college football. In death, then, the two Black men are subsumed by a nationalist ideal represented by Reagan.

Reagan's most famous film role as a college student tells a similar story of white leaders incorporating and transcending racial difference. In *Knute Rockne All American* (1940), a film biography of the Notre Dame coach, he plays star fullback George Gipp. As Rogin reminds us, Reagan brought the idea for the film to Warner Brothers because he desperately wanted the part. It was his favorite role and he invoked it over and over while president.[31] In his 1981 Notre Dame commencement speech, for example, Reagan claimed that *Knute Rockne All American* was a quintessential story of American exceptionalism:

Growing up in Illinois, I was influenced by a sports legend so national in scope, it was almost mystical. . . . Knute Rockne as a boy came to America with his parents from Norway. And in the few years it took him to grow up to college age, he became so American that here at Notre Dame, he became an All American in a game that is still, to this day, uniquely American.[32]

One of the few Black characters in the film is a child quarterback against whom a young Rockne plays football. Rockne repeatedly sacks him in the first few minutes of the film, and after that, with the exception of a Black train porter and a cameo by a Native American athlete (see below), the world of college football in *Knute Rockne All American* is all white. Moreover, Reagan's character is introduced to that world as the fulfillment of a white wish. As Rockne muses to his team, "What I would give my right arm for is a halfback who can carry the mail, a fast boy who can run, pass and kick, somebody on the order of Jim Thorpe. . . . That sort of fellow comes along maybe once or twice in a coach's lifetime. But I'm still hoping. And if I ever do find a boy like that . . ."As Rockne trails off and looks dreamily into the distance, the scene dissolves into a new one on the field where the coach's dream comes true in the form of Reagan as Gipp the football prodigy. In settler-colonial fashion, Reagan's character becomes the great white hope of college football, displacing while symbolically incorporating the great Sac and Fox athlete Jim Thorpe, the dominant fullback and star of college football before Gipp. The displacement and subordinate incorporation of indigeneity is further suggested by the film's credits, where Reagan is a star and Thorpe, who has a cameo in the film, remains uncredited.

The settler-colonial reading of *Knute Rockne All American* is in keeping with Reagan's preference for Westerns. As Rogin explains, "While fighting communists off screen, he fought Indians in front of the camera," as in *Last Outpost* (1951), where the Indian threat "makes allies out of Union and Confederate soldiers," and *Cattle Queen of Montana* (1954), where "Reagan saves Barbara Stanwyck from Indians."[33]

At the center of *Knute Rockne All American,* after having symbolically displaced and incorporated Blackness and indigeneity, Reagan as Gipp dies in the flesh but is reborn in spirit. On his deathbed Reagan/Gipp tells Rockne his coach and father figure to urge the team to "win just one for the Gipper,"

Figure 1. Sac and Fox athlete Jim Thorpe makes an uncredited cameo opposite Ronald Reagan in *Knute Rockne All American* (Warner Brothers, 1940).

a line Reagan would refunction throughout his political career. In his death scene, Reagan lies in a hospital bed with his hands arranged across his chest like a living corpse in a coffin. Dressed in a white gown and covered in a white blanket decorated with stars, his face is illuminated by the kind of high-key lighting Richard Dyer argues Hollywood has historically used to visually fetishize whiteness.[34]

In a subsequent halftime speech, Rockne does indeed tell his team to "win one for the Gipper," but, like his star player, the coach is also marked for death and ultimately dies in a plane crash. The film thus "doubles the theme of regenerative sacrifice by having Rockne catch Gipp's martyrdom."[35] As a celebratory retrospective biography, the film presupposes not only the pathos of death and loss but also spiritual redemption. The death of both college student and teacher are sublated into larger mythical ideals of heteropatriarchy, whiteness, and nation. Later when President Reagan would repeat the words of a dead college student as ventriloquized by a dead college coach—"win one for the Gipper"—he "spoke as if, playing the Gipper, he was witness to his own death and ascension."[36] Via images of "redemptive suffering," Reagan the actor and ultimately politician thus articulated his image to "victimhood" and distanced it from violence and aggression.

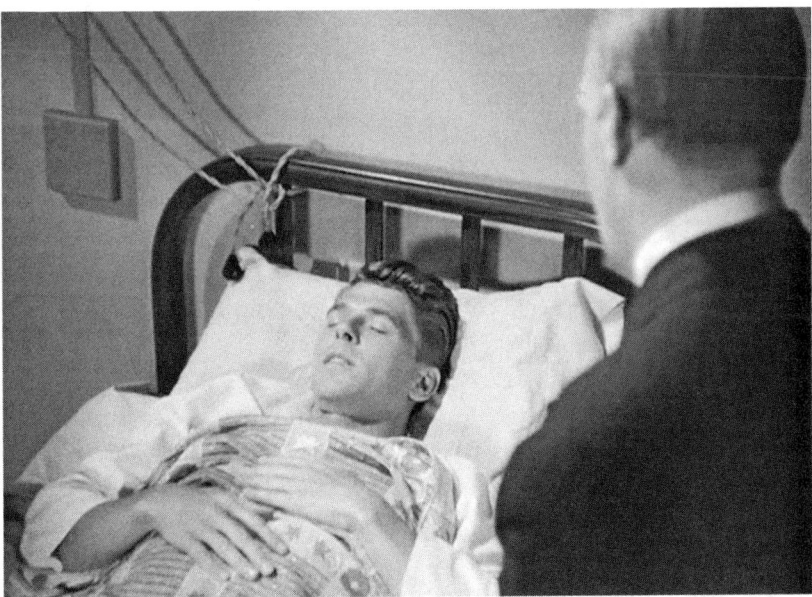

Figure 2. George Gipp (Ronald Reagan) on his death bed in *Knute Rockne All American* (Warner Brothers, 1940).

In Reagan's two other film roles as a college student, sports are supplemented with military drills. In *Brother Rat* (1938), a romantic comedy in which three college roommates at the Virginia Military Institute compete with one another over co-eds from a nearby women's college, Reagan plays Dan Crawford, a star on the baseball team (in publicity photos he is pictured in a VMI sweatshirt). Filmed on location at VMI, *Brother Rat* begins with a military review to the sound of the song "VMI Spirit." As the college fight song morphs into the song "Dixie," the camera focuses on a bronze statue of Stonewall Jackson with saber and field glasses, looking at the parade grounds. On the strength of his military successes during the U.S.–Mexico War, Jackson was appointed chair of Natural and Experimental Philosophy at VMI, where he also trained students in the use of artillery. The statue depicts him as he surveyed his army just before the Battle of Chancellorsville, where he was fatally wounded.[37] Near the end of the film, the three college roommates, including Reagan as Crawford, meet at the foot of the statue to plan their futures, where they resolve to "fight" on like Jackson. The film thus implicitly invokes redemptive suffering in nostalgic narratives of a defeated South that would rise again.

Reagan's final role as a college student is also set at a military academy and also framed by racialized intimations of tragic military losses redeemed into higher ideals of masculinity, whiteness, and nation. In *The Santa Fe Trail* (1940), he plays a young George Custer in his senior year at West Point. In an early dorm scene, a fellow student (Van Heflin) reads aloud a pamphlet by radical abolitionist John Brown, and Reagan as Custer responds by joining his friend, future Confederate general Jeb Stuart (played by Errol Flynn), in beating their abolitionist classmate, who is then expelled for his subversive views. After a graduation ceremony in which Jefferson Davis delivers the commencement address and Robert E. Lee hands out the diplomas, Stuart and Custer begin competing with one another for the affections of Kit Carson Holliday (Olivia De Havilland).

While Stuart ultimately gets the girl and captures the villainous John Brown, it is Reagan as Custer who heroically helps lead the cavalry against the radical abolitionist in what the trailer for the film calls "Custer's First Stand."[38] As Cedric J. Robinson argues, *The Santa Fe Trail* is "indebted to Griffith cinematically and ideologically," and indeed Custer's cavalry charge recalls scenes of D.W. Griffith's *The Battle of Elderbush Gulch* (Biography, 1913) in which the cavalry rides to the rescue of white settlers besieged by Indians, as well as scenes from *The Birth of a Nation* (David W. Griffith Corp., 1915) in which the Ku Klux Klan saves a white family from rapacious

Figure 3. George Custer (Ronald Reagan) and Jeb Stuart (Errol Flynn) at their graduation from West Point, *The Santa Fe Trail* (Warner Brothers, 1940).

Figure 4. Custer (Reagan) watches the execution of radical abolitionist John Brown, *The Santa Fe Trail* (Warner Brothers, 1940).

former slaves.[39] Recalling *Knute Rockne All American,* in *The Santa Fe Trail* Reagan plays the college student as tragic figure since, unlike his character, the audience knows Custer will die at Little Big Horn. Here Reagan once again assumes the role of college student as militarized agent of settler colonialism and antiblackness whose ultimate sacrifice redeems the spirit of heteropatriarchal white nationalism.

Rogin argues that Reagan's film roles in effect enabled him to become a neoliberal ideologue who cut state spending while ramping up police and military power. "For Reagan to gain presidential stature, he had to acquire a falsely vulnerable objectified self," reconnecting "through his film roles to the dependence in his personal history in order, finally, to find a substitute for that dependence and play at freedom." As an actor, Reagan played vulnerable characters whose violent sacrifice produced forms of transcendence or "happy endings" based in punishing others. As President, Reagan channeled his film career and embodied "national fears of helplessness and dependence in order to overcome them by punishing the enemies responsible for American weakness."[40] Reagan's projection of a falsely vulnerable objectified self simultaneously motivated forms of political demonology while de-realizing state violence and imaginatively insulating Reagan from the consequences of his policies.

While Rogin's essay was focused on Reagan's presidency, it also provides an illuminating framework for thinking about his tenure as California governor. In the film *Juke Girl* (1942), for instance, Reagan plays at vulnerability and powerlessness in his role as Steve Talbot, a migrant farmworker who, in the words of *New York Times* critic Bosley Crowther, "starts on a one-man crusade against the local big-shot packer, who is a crook."[41]

Set in the tomato fields of Florida but filmed in California's San Joaquin Valley, *Juke Girl* is derivative of *The Grapes of Wrath,* whose Okie farmworkers were themselves partly based on Mexican farmworkers. The film positions Reagan's performance as a kind of symbolic brown face, in which a white man falls to the lowly level reserved for workers of color.[42] A 1980 reviewer referenced this trope by writing that Reagan played a "Cesar Chavez type."[43] Ultimately, however, Talbot escapes a lynch mob; finds love with Lola, the titular "juke girl" (who is thereby "saved" from a sordid life of taxidancing); and receives the gift of a parcel of land to farm. Reagan's farmworker vulnerability and degradation pay off with a happy ending, serving as an implicit judgment against farmworkers of color who do not similarly rise. By comparison, as California governor, Reagan used his office to undermine and attack the United Farm Workers. He actively solicited the support of California agribusiness interests, redbaited the UFW, and famously ate grapes for the cameras to express his opposition to the grape boycott. Having previously played at being a farmworker but then rising above it, Reagan claimed to protect the people of California from the threat represented by actual farmworkers.

Similarly, as governor and later president, Reagan learned how to scapegoat college students and professors for their seeming dependence on the state. Such a structure of feeling, for example, informed Governor Reagan's efforts to discipline and punish University of California students with fees and militarized violence. Just as Reagan played college students whose deaths contributed to some greater good, as governor he insisted that students had to pay.

In response to campus unrest, Reagan wrapped his calls for discipline and violence in the symbols of settler colonialism. Along with a group of conservative politicians, businessmen, and Hollywood stars and executives, Reagan helped to build modern California's successful Republican Party, and settler symbolism was key to his efforts. During the 1962 presidential race he joined John Wayne and a host of other stars of western film and television to fundraise and campaign for another politician associated with the West,

Figure 5. Ronald Reagan as migrant farmworker Steve Talbot in *Juke Girl* (Warner Brothers, 1942).

Arizona's Barry Goldwater. While running for governor in 1966, Reagan mobilized support from stars of western films and television shows including Dale Evans, Roy Rogers, Randolph Scott, John Ford, Joel McCrea, Walter Brenan, Buddy Ebsen, and John Wayne.[44] Reagan also campaigned from on horseback, riding in a parade while wearing a cowboy hat, bolo tie, boots, and a red, white, and blue western shirt.[45] At his largest campaign event, called "The Reagan Roundup" and staged at San Francisco's Cow Palace, Reagan's speech attacking bureaucracy, taxes, welfare recipients, and "The Morality Gap at Berkeley" was packaged with a western theme including country and western bands, actors dressed as cowboys and Indians, chuck wagons dispensing box lunches, and actor Chuck Connors, star of the TV Western *The Rifleman,* serving as master of ceremonies. In keeping with his self-representation as a settler colonial icon, Reagan also helped pioneer militarized reactions to student dissent and struggles over state-occupied territory.[46] When activists occupied a parcel of university land in Berkeley and named it "People's Park," Governor Reagan called in the National Guard and authorized them to use shotguns against protestors in order to reassert the university's property rights. As a result, one person was killed, one was blinded, and hundreds were injured. He also authorized the aerial teargasing of the entire city of Berkeley. Afterward, Reagan defended the police response by saying, "If it takes a bloodbath, let's get it over with. No more appeasement." Similarly, when told by a reporter for the Berkeley student paper that he had blood on his hands, Reagan recalled the U.S. Boraxo Company, sponsor of his western-themed TV show *Death Valley Days* (1964–65), saying, "I'll wash it off with boraxo."[47]

In terms of the political symbolism of settler colonialism, it is illuminating to consider the relationship between the twentieth-century's two most famous Western icons, Reagan and John Wayne. Like Reagan, Wayne was a fraternity member and college football player at USC in the 1920s and he is remembered as the school's most famous alum.[48] Also like Reagan, although even more famously, Wayne was a star of Hollywood Westerns, including *Fort Apache* (1948), where he played a character based on Custer. In his eulogy for Wayne, Reagan remembered him as "one of the few stars with the courage to expose the determined bid by a band of communists to take control of the film industry."[49] In the 1960s, Wayne threw his considerable public and private influence behind a number of conservative political candidates, campaigning and fundraising for George Murphy, Barry Goldwater, Richard Nixon, and ultimately his good friend Reagan. In 1964, for example, Wayne tapped his former USC fraternity brothers to pay for the

TV broadcast of Reagan's famous speech supporting Goldwater for president, "A Time to Chose."[50] And like Reagan, Wayne was particularly incensed by protests on college campuses. In 1966 Wayne returned to USC to speak at a fundraising event, and when he was heckled by antiwar protestors he went off script and proceeded to harangue the students in the audience: "A university should be a quiet place where you go to learn, not to destroy property belonging to someone else. Getting an education is a privilege, not a right. Your professors and administrators should be treated with courtesy and respect. While you're here you ought to be learning a sense of responsibility. We aren't going to sit by and let you destroy our schools and system." Wayne's outburst echoed the sentiments of Reagan, who had been elected governor that fall.

Near the end of Reagan's first term as California governor, Wayne gave a defiantly anti-Indian, anti-Black interview to *Playboy Magazine* that also made explicit the structure of feeling animating conservative attacks on the University of California. Wayne argues that communist professors such as Angela Davis "pervert the natural loyalties and ideals of our kids." In response to the interviewer's claim that Davis has been subject to racial discrimination, Wayne answers:

> I believe in white supremacy until the blacks are educated to a point of responsibility. I don't believe in giving authority and positions of leadership and judgment to irresponsible people. But some blacks have tried to force the issue and enter college when they haven't passed the tests and don't have the requisite background. I think any black who can compete with a white today can get a better break than a white man. I wish they'd tell me where in the world they have it better than right here in America. I've directed two pictures and I gave the blacks their proper position. I had a black slave in *The Alamo*.

In a related vein, when the interviewer asks Wayne about the important though subordinate role of Native Americans in his films, he responds, "I don't feel we did wrong in taking this great country away from them, if that's what you're asking. Our so-called stealing of this country from them was just a matter of survival. There were great numbers of people who needed new land, and the Indians were selfishly trying to keep it for themselves." Moreover, Wayne rejects indigenous demands for university access as a form of reparations, arguing that "what happened between their forefathers and our forefathers is so far back—right, wrong or indifferent—that I don't see why we owe them anything. I don't know why the government should give them something that it wouldn't give me." For Wayne, students were like women and children around whom men circle the wagons to protect them from Black and indigenous people. Like other conservatives, the greatest icon of western expansion and U.S. militarism viewed universities through the lens of settler colonialism and antiblackness.

To return to Reagan, however, his investments in settler colonialism were not only symbolic but also material. In 1951, while still a Hollywood actor, Reagan bought a 290-acre ranch in Malibu he named Yearling Row. It had previously belonged to the Chumash Indians before being appropriated as private property, and when Reagan purchased the land it was surrounded by the Century Ranch, where Fox Studios filmed Westerns and other projects. Ultimately, Reagan made his personal fortune when, shortly after being elected governor, he sold the ranch he purchased for $85,000 to Fox Studios for $1.9 million. Government and journalistic investigators have raised questions about this remarkable windfall, suggesting that it was part of a scheme by Fox to secure tax breaks for the film industry or by Reagan's wealthy backers to help pave the way for a future presidential campaign.[51] But while the details of the transaction remain shadowy, one thing is clear—Reagan became a rugged, frontier individual via speculation in indigenous lands. As governor, Reagan's indigenous land speculation extended to the UC system and his efforts to acquire land for the building of UC Irvine. Reagan's personal lawyer, closest advisor, and UC Regents appointee William French Smith was also the lawyer for the Irvine Company, which in the mid-1960s owned 130 square miles of ranch land in Orange County. When the company donated 1,000 acres to the state for a university it secured a substantial tax break that became the seed money for the settlement of the city of Irvine. By 1970 the Irvine Company decided to expand the city but needed approval from the regents to do so. Despite opposition, Reagan and his six appointees pushed the proposal through. Similarly, Reagan's State Lands Commission agreed to give 2.5 miles of prime state-owned shoreline to the Irvine Company in exchange for what one state official called "450 acres of useless swampland." By contrast, the previous administration's Land Commission had rejected such a trade, calling it the theft of state resources.[52] As governor, then, Reagan was in the forefront of a particular form of neoliberalism we might call settler-colonial privatization.

In his approach to higher education, Reagan thus combined symbolic and material attacks, imagining the UC system on the model of a white settler colonial family and his role as governor as one of paternal protector and disciplinarian. When discussing tuition and budget cuts, he compared state spending to a home economy and argued that, like members of a family on a budget, students and professors would have to do without. He also argued that, like children in the home, students needed to be protected from subversive ideas, sexual deviancy, and immoral and disgusting speech. As Rogin and John L. Shover argue in *Political Change in California: Critical Elections and Social Movements, 1890–1966*, Reagan represented a Southern California right-wing tradition based in ideas about race and family. Such a tradition injected white family values into the public arena where they served as models for public institutions including universities. The goal of right-wing family ideology was to produce "an unnatural family unity, in which mastery and striving aim at . . . total security. . . . Indeed, in the fury against children who will not be mastered and incorporated, the southern California family enters politics with a vengeance. That ideal, applied to student rebels, hippies, and drugs, helped elect Ronald Reagan."[53]

Reagan further rode a wave of "white backlash" into office, stoking white fear and anger over Black rioters in Watts, the enactment of the Rumford Fair Housing Act outlawing racial discrimination in housing, and the passage of the Civil Rights Act of 1964.[54] Or as Rogin and Shover argue, Reagan became governor by "running on an openly anti-university, anti-obscenity, anti-welfare, and anti-fair housing platform" and thus by successfully appealing to a Southern California political tradition of right-wing antiblackness.[55] As governor and regent of the University of California, Reagan became an expert in the forms of racial coding that Michael Omi and Howard Winant have argued characterized his presidency.[56] When vilifying Berkeley, for example, Reagan often spoke of a dangerous "minority" that took academic freedom too far and disrespected police authority. In a 1967 letter to San Francisco State Chancellor Glenn Dumke, however, Governor Reagan almost makes explicit the racialized scenarios he imaginatively brought to bear on California higher education:

> How far do we go in tolerating these people & this trash under the excuse of academic freedom & freedom of expression? . . . We wouldn't let a LeRoi Jones in our living room and we wouldn't tolerate this kind of language in front of our families. Hasn't the time come to take on those neurotics in our faculty group and lay down some rules of conduct for the students comparable to what we'd expect in our own families?[57]

Here, in reference to Jones's appointment as an inaugural Black studies professor at San Francisco State, Reagan imagines kicking such "trash" out of the university—just as he would from his home—in order to protect white family values.

According to Rogin and Shover, in the Southern California right-wing tradition represented by Reagan, the hallucinatory Black threat to white families was transferred to other groups as well.

> The need to cure or eliminate is extended to cover Communists, the young, drugs, pornography—targets that seem to express relations of sensuality, rebellion, and acknowledged dependence not permitted in the southern (California) world. Thus the students who want to leave home threaten family unity. . . . The Negro threat to property values, the students' rejection of property, and the Communists' desire to take it away—all metaphorically threaten ownership and control of the self, that is, self-government, self-mastery, and protection against the world of significant objects. . . . The Southwest was always the home of unassimilable minorities—Mexicans, Indians, Orientals—rather than the melting pot immigrants of European stock. Not believing in assimilation, the right-wing (Southern Californian) turns to elimination.[58]

"Elimination" is, of course, a primary ideology and technique of settler colonialism, which partly explains why Reagan was so invested in the genre of film westerns and the heroic symbols of Indian wars. As a "robot, a sleep-walker, an image on a screen, whose acts are dissociated from his being," Governor Reagan plays the cowboy hero in a "twentieth-century reenactment of the nineteenth-century drama."[59]

Reagan's racialized familial model for the university recalls his most famous role as a college professor. In *Bedtime for Bonzo* (1951), he plays Sheridan College psychology professor Peter Boyd. Boyd is engaged to his dean's daughter, but the dean becomes suspicious when he is visited by Knucksy Breckenridge, the former prison cellmate of Boyd's late father, a brilliant con man nicknamed "The Professor." When Knucksy encounters Boyd's photo on the cover of his book *Slum Crime* he sees the resemblance and shows a mug shot of "The Professor" to the dean, who then presses Boyd to resign and break off the engagement to his daughter.

In order to "prove (as if he were the chimp), that environment can triumph over heredity," Professor Boyd hires a nanny named Jane Linden to pretend to be his wife and help simulate a home for a chimp named Bonzo and teach him right from wrong.[60] To hide his experiments, he tells the dean

Figure 6. Psychology professor Peter Boyd (Ronald Reagan) leads class in *Bedtime for Bonzo* (Universal International Pictures, 1951).

Figure 7. Mug shot for "The Professor" (Ronald Reagan), Professor Boyd's con-man father in *Bedtime for Bonzo* (Universal International Pictures, 1951).

that Bonzo is an exchange student from Africa, and, in the privacy of his home, Boyd and Linden pretend to be Bonzo's "mama" and "papa." In this way the pair ultimately succeed in teaching Bonzo to respect private property and the police such that the chimp voluntarily returns a diamond necklace he had previously stolen. In the end, Dr. Boyd and Miss Linden marry and the dean beams over the new prestige brought to the university by "Operation Bonzo."

Bedtime for Bonzo's happy ending is secured by the substitution of a good professor for a bad one. Anticipating Governor Reagan's efforts to reform the UC system and discipline wayward professors, Reagan's character in the film can only emerge as its hero by displacing and transcending his father, the criminal "Professor." Hence as governor, Reagan recalled Professor Boyd, since he seemed to bring to the University of California system a vision of teaching and research focused on promoting moral character in the form of family values, respect for private property and the police, and the promotion of private initiative over state welfare provisions. In 1967, just two years after the Moynihan Report pathologized Black families led by women for the expansion of welfare, Governor Reagan called on university researchers at USC to help eliminate dependence on welfare in ways that anticipate his use of the racially coded term "welfare queen" while president. More broadly, he charged professors with teaching national morality. In his 1967 inaugural address, Governor Reagan asserted, "It does not constitute political interference with intellectual freedom for the taxpaying citizens—who support the college and university systems—to ask that, in addition to teaching, they build character on accepted moral and ethical standards."[61] Shortly afterward, in a speech installing a new president at Chico State College, Reagan went further, arguing that academic freedom required universities to teach nationalism.

> But I think there is a third element in academic freedom. In addition to the rights of the students to learn, and the teachers to teach, there is the right of society to insist the educational system it supports will further the goals and the aspirations and the moral principles and precepts of that society. There is no question that the publically-supported colleges and universities contributed to the emerging greatness not only of California but also of our nation, and that is good; but we have a right to insure that they do not, in some far-out interpretation of "freedom," weaken the social structure essential to the nation's strength and to the perpetuation of these very educational institutions.[62]

In this way, Reagan imagined resolving the contradictions of an emergent neoliberalism and its neoconservative variants that combined attacks on state power while promoting military and police violence, since the governor represents universities as the place where students learn submission to the status quo—at the end of a club, if necessary.

At first viewing, Reagan's final college film, the musical comedy *She's Working Her Way through College* (1952), may seem like the dialectical negation of his others. Here Reagan plays drama professor John Palmer at the fictional Midwestern College, where President Fred Copeland favors the football team over the arts. Copeland disrespects Palmer and underfunds the drama department, leaving the professor and his wife, Helen, on a tight budget that requires them to take in lodgers. Professor Palmer is further at odds with Shep Slade, a wealthy businessman and influential alum who returns to Midwestern near the start of the film and proceeds to make a play for Helen, his college flame. Meanwhile, Palmer mentors a working-class student named Angela Gardner, telling her "college is the inalienable right of every American," and agrees to help her stage a "modern" musical she wrote and will star in. But when the school paper and ultimately the national press report rumors of Gardner's sexual improprieties, President Copeland

Figure 8. Professor John Palmer (Reagan), *She's Working Her Way through College* (Warner Brothers, 1952).

threatens to expel her and forces Palmer to read a speech before the student body canceling the play. Defying the administration, Reagan as Professor Palmer delivers an impassioned speech against discrimination and for the universal right to an education. As a result he becomes a hero among the students, inspires Helen's admiration and saves his marriage, and even earns the grudging respect of his rival Slade. Finally, President Copeland promotes Palmer to the rank of full professor and the play opens as scheduled.

And yet *She's Working Her Way through College* presents an image of higher education that significantly downgrades the stakes of its source, which is focused on a politically volatile question of academic freedom. Reagan's film is loosely based on *The Male Animal* (1942), a movie starring Henry Fonda as Midwestern College English professor Tommy Turner. When an undergraduate writes an editorial calling the trustees fascist while praising Turner's commitments to free speech and announcing that in his next class the professor plans to read aloud a letter written by executed anarchist Bartolomeo Vanzetti, a trustee expels the student and warns Professor Turner he will be fired if he exposes students to "un-American" views. Nonetheless, Turner's dean defends him, and the professor gives a stirring public address about the values of free speech before proceeding to read the anarchist's letter.

As *New York Times* reviewer Bosley Crowther wrote, *She's Working Her Way through College* "watered down the plot of the original." Whereas *The Male Animal* is "pointedly concerned with the fate of a college professor on the verge of losing his wife and his job," *She's Working Her Way through College* "has blithely shifted attention to the college career of an ex-burlesque queen." As Professor Palmer in *She's Working Her Way through College,* Reagan defends a student, Angela Gardner, who worked as a stripper to pay for college. He ultimately refuses to expel her, decries discrimination against people in "show business," and defends the academic freedom of students to stage a musical review. However, rather than take up the kinds of critical, challenging ideas usually conveyed by concepts of academic freedom, the resulting show is a didactic lesson about the gendered virtues of the market. Its central musical number delivers this historical lesson:

> Education is not what its cracked up to be.
> For instance take the famous women through the ages.
> They got to where they got by turning heads, not pages.

Meanwhile, costumed as the courtesan Madame Du Barry, Gardner performs the song "Love is Not For Free," while in the finale she and the rest of the chorus girls wear mortarboards and miniskirts for gowns. In this way the film turns academic freedom into a spectacle celebrating the free market and the traffic in women.

In a radical departure from recent history, California governor Reagan helped redefine academic freedom as synonymous with market freedoms. According to Christopher Newfield, "As the fundamental condition of creating and disseminating valid and useful knowledge," academic freedom was "the hallmark of the postwar university."

> One result was the sort of intellectual liberty that challenged the status quo, not just now and then but all the time. Another result of the university's expanded intellectual scope was the cultural capability that enables individuals to see themselves as agents in complicated systems where they must work with (and against) people and groups quite different from them.[63]

This postwar model of academic freedom, Newfield contends, presupposed an interpretive understanding of knowledge, "since the truth is not given in advance of systematic encounters with the beliefs of others."[64] This understanding of academic freedom "was so important to the discovery of truth," he concludes, "because it allowed for freedom of interpretation, revision, and reinterpretation."[65] Finally, a model of academic freedom based in encounters with otherness further presupposed the necessity of public education on a mass scale, as represented by the University of California Master Plan.

In stark contrast, throughout his career Reagan argued that public universities threatened academic freedom, which in his view could only be sustained at private schools. For example, in 1957, just five years after starring in *She's Working Her Way through College,* Reagan delivered a commencement address at his alma mater in which he praised Eureka and other private schools as the wellsprings of academic freedom:

> Today we enjoy academic freedom in America as it is enjoyed nowhere else in the world. But this pattern was established by the independent secular and church colleges of our land, schools like Eureka. Down through the years these colleges and universities have maintained intellectual freedom because they were beholden to no political group, for when politics control the purse strings, they also control the policy. No one advocates the elimination of our tax-supported universities, but we should never forget that their academic freedom is assured only so long as we have the leavening influence of hundreds of privately endowed colleges and universities throughout the land.[66]

Here Reagan redefines "private" to mean "independent," as in private institutions free from state interference. Less than a decade later, in a rhetorical move that can only be understood as what Rogin called "political demonology"—a kind of "that's what you are, but what am I?" logic whereby political leaders adopt the vilified tactics they project onto their enemies—Governor Reagan would attempt to impose conservative politics onto students and faculty in the UC system, partly by controlling "the purse strings" but also through the use of state police power. So while to the Eureka graduates he denies a desire to eliminate "our tax-supported universities," as governor he sought to dramatically and sometimes violently impose on the University of California a privatizing vision of academic freedom wed to white supremacy and heteropatriarchal family values.

Governor Reagan further honed his heteropatriarchal white settler model of academic freedom in dialectical opposition to faculty and especially student demands for a new, decolonizing pedagogy. As Jorge Mariscal and Roderick Ferguson have demonstrated, in the late 1960s Chicano and Black students, including Angela Davis, demanded the establishment of a largely student-controlled college at UCSD, to be named Lumumba-Zapata College, after the two great Congolese and Mexican anticolonial revolutionaries.[67] The proposed curriculum of L-Z College would focus on Black and Chicana/o history, histories of Western imperialism and anticolonial struggle, and a particular problem-solving "Third World" perspective on science and engineering, including opposition to military research. Such demands, according to Ferguson, challenged "(Western) man's self-representation as the universal basis of life, labor, and language. Indeed, the various units of the curriculum point to investigations of how Western man achieved a terrible specificity through the violent suppression of racialized and economically disfranchised communities."[68] L-Z College proponents in effect rearticulated the conservative college ideal represented by Reagan for radical ends. Students and faculty saw these and related protest movements on campus as aimed against Reagan's politics of racist backlash. With his racist appeals to voters, editorials in the student paper, the *Triton Times,* compared Reagan to racist populist George Wallace, while students attended—no doubt with ironic distance—screenings of his western *Cattle Queen of Montana* (1954).[69] The student paper also published remarks by Herbert Marcuse from a campus rally protesting the Reagan regents in which the Frankfurt School intellectual and UCSD lecturer connected UCSD to the larger world student movement.[70] Similarly, the *Triton Times* reprinted an editorial from the UC Berkeley student paper that included this assessment: "They are shooting students in Mexico. They are shooting black people in America. And they are on the verge of shooting students. The Governor seems eager to send the national guard onto the campus."[71] On October 11, 1968, UCSD students invited to campus radical Black scholar Harry Edwards. Edwards, who was completing his PhD in sociology at Cornell, had recently organized the Olympic Project For Human Rights, which, several days after his UCSD speech, inspired the Black power fist protest by Black collegiate track medalists Tommie Smith and John Carlos at the 1968 Mexico City Olympics.[72] In his visit to UCSD, then, Edwards represented the antithesis of Reagan's view of college sports.

Students and faculty at UCSD were particularly motivated to protest by Reagan's attacks on academic freedom. Under his leadership, the UC Regents revoked credit for an experimental class at UC Berkeley taught by Black Panther Eldridge Cleaver and prevented the renewal of Marcuse's UCSD lectureship. In both cases, Reagan and the regents argued that despite faculty approval of the two instructors, they were unqualified to teach. Reagan also threatened to strip the faculty of final control over the curriculum and appointments, which he claimed should instead rest with the regents (this proposal was ultimately forestalled, however, by faculty and student resistance). In these ways Governor Reagan's white settler vision of the limits of academic freedom anticipated more recent events at the University of Illinois at Urbana-Champaign, where university trustees, with the support of the governor of Illinois, violated the autonomy and academic freedom of the American Indian Studies Program by firing a professor they had recommended hiring, Steven Salaita, over his Tweets critical of Israel.

Reagan's market-driven redefinition of academic freedom while California governor not only continued to frame his approach to higher education while president but also helped pave the way for the broader attacks on state power that have come to be called "neoliberalism." In 1981, at the start of his first presidential term, Reagan returned to Notre Dame to deliver a commencement address that echoed his earlier Eureka address:

You are graduating from a great private, or, if you will, independent university. Not too many years ago, such schools were relatively free from government interference. In recent years, government has spawned regulations covering virtually every facet of our lives. The independent and church-supported colleges and universities have found themselves enmeshed in that network of regulations and the costly blizzard of paperwork that government is demanding. . . . I hope when you leave this campus that you will do so with a feeling of obligation to your alma mater. She will need your help and support in the years to come. Almost every aspect of campus life is now regulated—hiring, firing, promotions, physical plant, construction, recordkeeping, fundraising and, to some extent, curriculum and educational programs. . . . If ever the great independent colleges and universities like Notre Dame give way to and are replaced by tax-supported institutions, the struggle to preserve academic freedom will have been lost.[73]

Given its reputation as the most famous Catholic university in the United States, it is striking that Reagan would champion it as a center of academic freedom, suggesting that his version of freedom presupposes obedience to religious orthodoxies and conversely, that his free-market rhetoric burns with religious fervor.

Joining Reagan on the Notre Dame commencement stage was Pat O'Brien, the actor who played Knute Rockne opposite Reagan as Gipp, and it was in this address that the president referred to the mystical national legend represented by Rockne and Notre Dame football. In my reading, Rockne, Gipp, and their ghosts combine to form the holy trinity of white supremacy, settler colonialism, and heteropatriarchy. Analyzing Reagan's educational politics in light of his early college films thus suggests a different way of thinking about neoliberalism. As indicated by David Harvey's influential book titled *A Brief History of Neoliberalism*, Reagan has long been considered a central figure in the history of neoliberalism.[74] Indeed, the cover of Harvey's book is decorated with headshots of Reagan, Deng Xiaoping, Augusto Pinochet, and Margaret Thatcher, forming a sort of "Mount Rushmore" of neoliberal icons. My reference to the famous nationalist monument sculpted on the granite face of a mountain the Lakota referred to as "Six Grandfathers" is meant to recall the matrix of white supremacy, settler colonialism, and heteropatriarchy out of which neoliberalism emerged and where it continues to reside. And finally, this "Mount Rushmore effect" suggests that neoliberal forms of "academic freedom"—from Reagan to the university presidents who condemned the ASA—can be understood as products of that same matrix of domination.

CURTIS MAREZ is professor and chair of the ethnic studies department at the University of California, San Diego. He is the author of *Drug Wars: The Political Economy of Narcotics* (Minnesota, 2004) and *Farm Worker Futurism: Speculative Technologies of Resistance* (Minnesota, 2016).

NOTES

This essay is dedicated to the memory of Michael Paul Rogin. An earlier version of this essay was delivered as part of the Unsettling the University: Confronting Capitalism and the Crisis in Higher Education conference at UC Riverside, April 3, 2015. I am grateful to audience members for their feedback. I also want to thank the editors of *Critical Ethnic Studies*, Junaid Rana and John David Márquez, and the anonymous external reviewer for their helpful feedback. I am also grateful to the journal's managing editor, Kelly Chung, for all her assistance. Finally, I want to thank Shelley Streetby.

1. Andrew Hacker, "He Found It at the Movies: 'Ronald Reagan,' the Movie," *New York Times*, April 19, 1987. Previously, the *New York Times* had reported on an early version of the argument Rogin delivered at the American Political Science Association convention. See Martin Tolchin, "How Reagan Always Gets the Best Lines," *New York Times*, September 9, 1985. The *60 Minutes* segment "Ronald Reagan, the Movie" aired on CBS on December 15, 1985. http://www.paleycenter.org/collection/item/?q=ronald+reagan&p=3&item=T86:1625.

2. Building on Michael Rogin's work, in my 2013 American Studies Association Presidential Address, "Seeing in the Red: Looking at Student Debt" (*American Quarterly* 66, no. 2 [June 2014]), I had initially planned a section in which I examined Reagan's films. While space limitations prevented me from pursuing that topic, it was nonetheless one inspiration for my address.

3. Christopher Newfield, *The Unmaking of the Public University: The Forty-Year Assault on the Middle Class* (Cambridge, Mass.: Harvard University Press, 2008), 51–54.

4. Gary K. Clabaugh, "The Educational Legacy of Ronald Reagan," *Educational Horizons* 82, no. 4 (Summer 2004): 256, 259.

5. Jodi Melamed, *Represent and Destroy: Rationalizing Violence in the New Racial Capitalism* (Minneapolis: University of Minnesota Press, 2011); Roderick Ferguson, *The Reorder of Things: The University and Its Pedagogies of Minority Difference* (Minneapolis: University of Minnesota Press, 2012); Sara Ahmed, *On Being Included: Racism and Diversity in Institutional Life* (Durham: Duke University Press, 2012); Stefano Harney and Fred Moten, *The Undercommons: Fugitive Planning and Black Study* (New York: Minor Compositions, 2013); Piya Chaterjee and Sunaina Maira, eds., *The Imperial University: Academic Repression and Scholarly Dissent* (Minneapolis: University of Minnesota Press, 2014).

6. Craig Steven Wilder, *Ebony and Ivy: Race, Slavery, and the Troubled History of America's Universities* (New York: Bloomsbury, 2013).

7. "Reagan Timeline: Timeline of Participation in Events at Eureka College, 1941–2007," https://www.eureka.edu/reagan/timeline/.

8. Unlike the Ivy League schools analyzed by Wilder, Eureka was founded by Christian abolitionists; but, as we shall see, that did not prevent it from being a conservative institution.

9. Frederick Rudolph, *The American College and University: A History* (New York: Alfred A. Knopf, 1990), 449, 453.

10. Rudolph, *The American College*, 87–88, 95.

11. Ronald Reagan, *An American Life* (New York: Simon and Schuster, 1990), 45–46.

12. Christopher J. Lucas, *American Higher Education: A History* (New York: St. Martin's Press, 1994), 207.

13. Ibid., 209.

14. John R. Thelin, *A History of American Higher Education* (Baltimore: Johns Hopkins University Press, 2004), 186.

15. Ibid., 215–16.

16. Daniel A. Clark, *Creating the College Man: American Mass Magazines and Middle-Class Manhood, 1890–1915* (Madison: University of Wisconsin Press, 2010).

17. Ronald Reagan, Address at Commencement Exercises at Eureka College, May 9, 1982, http://www.reagan.utexas.edu/archives/speeches/1982/50982a.htm.

18. A search of Getty Images for the key terms "Ronald Reagan" and "football" yields numerous photos of Reagan from throughout his career. See, for example, a publicity still of Reagan throwing a football while posing for a sculpture (1939), 3205546; Reagan catching a football during his gubernatorial campaign (1966), 541018555; and Reagan in a Eureka jersey during his presidential campaign (1980), 124131580. http://www.gettyimages.com.

19. Clark, *Creating the College Man*, 85.

20. Rudolph, *The American College*, 379–80.

21. Clark, *Creating the College Man*, 86.

22. Ronald Reagan, Address at Commencement Exercises at the University of Notre Dame, May 17, 1981, http://www.reagan.utexas.edu/archives/speeches/1981/51781a.htm.

23. On the building of campus coliseums, as well as the magnitude of the college football audience and the revenues generated, see Rudolph, *The American College*, 388–89; Thelin, *A History*, 202–7, 208.

24. Rudolph, *The American College*, 384.

25. Ibid., 387.

26. Clark, *Creating the College Man*, 88, 90; Rudolph, *The American College*, 374–93. See also Thelin, *A History*, 177–80.

27. Lucas, *American Higher Education*, 192.

28. Paul Robeson, *Here I Stand* (New York: Beacon Press, 1998), xii.

29. Thelin, *A History*, 253.

30. Despite the claim that Burghardt was his best friend, Reagan reportedly confused him with George Wilson, a black teammate from Reagan's high school team (*Jet*, September 3, 1981, 2).

31. Rogin, "Ronald Reagan, the Movie," in *Ronald Reagan, the Movie and Other Episodes in Political Demonology* (Berkeley: University of California Press, 1987), 15.

32. Ronald Reagan, Address at Commencement Exercises at the University of Notre Dame, May 17, 1981, http://www.reagan.utexas.edu/archives/speeches/1981/51781a.htm.

33. Rogin, "Ronald Reagan, the Movie," 38.

34. Richard Dyer, *White: Essays on Race and Culture* (London: Routledge Press, 1997).

35. Rogin, "Ronald Reagan, the Movie," 16.

36. Ibid., 15.

37. "Stonewall Jackson and VMI," http://www.vmi.edu/content.aspx?id=13243.

38. Original trailer, *Santa Fe Trail,* http://www.tcm.com/tcmdb/title/3623/Santa-Fe-Trail/videos.html.

39. Cedric J. Robinson, *Forgeries of Memory and Meaning: Blacks and the Regimes of Race in American Theater and Film Before World War II* (Chapel Hill: University of North Carolina Press, 2007), 99, Robinson goes on to argue that *The Santa Fe Trail* is part of the "plantation genre" initiated by Griffith in which "prominent white abolitionists" are represented as "megalomaniacal fanatics" or Judases" (123).

40. Rogin, "Ronald Reagan, the Movie," 35.

41. Bosley Crowther, "Juke Girl (1942)," *New York Times,* June 20, 1942, http://www.nytimes.com/movie/review?res=9405E7DE173EE13BBC4851DFB0668389659EDE.

42. This is a common trope in U.S. films and literature about farm workers. See Curtis Marez, *Speculative Technologies: Farmworkers and the Hidden Histories of New Media* (Minneapolis: University of Minnesota Press, 2016).

43. See http://www.tcm.com/this-month/article/221743%7C0/Juke-Girl.html.

44. Donald T. Critchlow, *When Hollywood Was Right: How Movie Stars, Studio Moguls, and Big Business Remade American Politics* (London: Cambridge University Press, 2013), 191–92.

45. Reagan on the campaign trail on horseback, in western costume (1966), http://www.gettyimages.com, 53379300.

46. Seth Rosenfield, *Subversives: The FBI's War on Student Radicals and Reagan's Rise to Power* (New York: Picador, 2013), 321–22.

47. Quoted in Michael Rogin and John L. Shover, *Political Change in California: Critical Elections and Social Movements, 1890–1966* (Westport, Conn.: Greenwood, 1970), 111n, 212n.

48. Rick Jewell, "John Wayne, an American Icon," *Trojan Family Magazine,* August 1, 2008, http://www.usc.edu/uscnews/stories/15465.html.

49. Ronald Reagan, "The Unforgettable John Wayne," *Reader's Digest,* October 1979; reprinted in *Duke, We're Glad We Knew You: John Wayne's Friends and Colleagues Remember His Remarkable Life,* ed. Herb Fagen (New York: Citadel Press, 1979), xxiii.

50. Donald T. Critchlow and Emilie Raymond, *Hollywood and Politics: A Sourcebook* (London: Routledge Press, 2009), 9.

51. Howard Kohn and Lowell Bergman, "Ronald Reagan's Millions," *Rolling Stone Magazine,* August 26, 1976, http://www.rollingstone.com/politics/news/reagans-millions-19760826.

52. Ibid.

53. Rogin and Shover, *Political Change in California,*198.

54. Rosenfield, *Subversives,* 359.

55. Rogin and Shover, *Political Change in California,* 177.

56. Michael Omi and Howard Winant, *Racial Formations in the United States*, 3rd. ed. (New York: Routledge Press, 2014), 221–22.

57. See http://www.gilderlehrman.org/history-by-era/sixties/resources/ronald-rea gan-unrest-college-campuses-1967.

58. Rogin and Shover, *Political Change in California*, 200.

59. Ibid., 201.

60. Rogin, "Ronald Reagan, the Movie," 25.

61. See http://www.reagan.utexas.edu/archives/speeches/govspeech/01051967a .htm.

62. See http://www.reagan.utexas.edu/archives/speeches/govspeech/05201967a .htm.

63. Newfield, *Unmaking of the Public University*, 257.

64. Ibid.

65. Ibid., 258.

66. http://www.pbs.org/wgbh/americanexperience/features/primary-resources /reagan-eureka/.

67. Jorge Mariscal, "To Demand That the University Work for Our People," *Brown-Eyed Children of the Sun: Lessons from the Chicano Movement, 1965–1975* (Albuquerque: University of New Mexico Press, 2005), 210–46; Roderick Ferguson, "The Proliferation of Minority Difference," in *The Reorder of Things*, 41–75.

68. Ferguson, *The Reorder of Things*, 53.

69. "Editorial: Cleaver Frozen, Ronnie and Co. Do it Again," *Triton Times*, October 4, 1968, 2, and December 6, 1968, 8. The IMDB synopsis for *Cattle Queen of Montana* is instructive, since it imagines college education in support of settler colonialism: "The Jones family, about to prove claim to prime Montana land, is raided by renegade Indians in league with villainous neighbor McCord, who gets most of the stolen cattle. Two survivors are helped by the college-educated chief's son Colorados. Now Sierra Nevada Jones must fight for her land against legal technicalities and assorted villains. Can she gain the help of McCord's hired gun, Farrell (Reagan)?" (http://www.imdb.com/title/tt0046839/).

70. Marcuse Speaks," *Triton Times*, November 26, 1968.

71. "Editorial: Let Us Sing Together," *Triton times*, October 11, 1968.

72. "Edwards Calls for New Black Identity," *Triton Times*, October 11, 1968.

73. See http://www.reagan.utexas.edu/archives/speeches/1981/51781a.htm.

74. David Harvey, *A Brief History of Neoliberalism* (New York: Oxford University Press, 2007).